100 SMART Board™ LESSONS

TERMS AND CONDITIONS

IMPORTANT - PERMITTED USE AND WARNINGS - READ CAREFULLY BEFORE USING

Copyright in the Control software contained on this CD-ROM and in its accompanying material belongs to Scholastic Ltd. All rights reserved. © 2007, Scholastic Ltd.

Notebook™, including the Notebook™ artwork (contained within the Gallery), incorporated on this CD-ROM is the exclusive property of SMART Technologies Inc. Copyright © 2007 SMART Technologies Inc. All rights reserved. SMART Board is a registered trademark of SMART Technologies Inc in the UK.

The material contained on this CD-ROM may only be used in the context for which it was intended in *100 SMART Board™ Lessons*. Scholastic Ltd accepts no liability for any adaptation of Scholastic or SMART copyrighted material. School site use is permitted only within the school of the purchaser of the book and CD-ROM. Any further use of the material contravenes Scholastic Ltd's copyright and that of other rights holders.

Save for these purposes, or as expressly authorised in the accompanying materials, the software including artwork or images may not be copied, reproduced, used, sold, licensed, transferred, exchanged, hired, or exported in whole or in part or in any manner or form without the prior written consent of Scholastic Ltd. Any such unauthorised use or activities are prohibited and may give rise to civil liabilities and criminal prosecutions.

This CD-ROM has been tested for viruses at all stages of its production. However, we recommend that you run virus-checking software on your computer systems at all times. Scholastic Ltd cannot accept any responsibility for any loss, disruption or damage to your data or your computer system that may occur as a result of using either the CD-ROM, software, website links or the data held on it.

Due to the nature of the web, the publisher cannot guarantee the content or links of any websites referred to. It is the responsibility of the user to assess the suitability of websites.

IF YOU ACCEPT THE ABOVE CONDITIONS YOU MAY PROCEED TO USE THIS CD-ROM.

Minimum specification:
- PC/Mac with a CD-ROM drive and at least 128 MB RAM
- Microsoft Office 2000 or higher
- Adobe® Reader®
- Interactive whiteboard
- Notebook™ software
- Facilities for printing and sound (optional)

PC:
- Pentium II 450 MHz processor
- Microsoft Windows 2000 SP4 or higher

Mac:
- 700 MHz processor (1 GHz or faster recommended)
- Mac OS X.4 or higher

For all technical support queries, please phone Scholastic Customer Services on 0845 6039091.

YEAR R

Scottish Primary 1

CREDITS

Authors
Rachel Ager (CLL), Julia Rutherford-Bate (CLL), Ann Montague-Smith (PSRN), Susanna Shukla (KUW), Liz Cambray (CD), Jenny Mitchell (PSED lessons 1-6), Kate Cooper (PD and PSED lessons 7-12)

Development Editor
Niamh O'Carroll

Editor
Nicola Morgan

Assistant Editors
Margaret Eaton and Kim Vernon

Illustrators
Jim Peacock (Notebook file illustrations), Jenny Tulip (book and additional Notebook file illustrations), Theresa Tibbetts (additional Notebook file illustrations)

Series Designer
Joy Monkhouse

Designers
Shelley Best, Rebecca Male, Allison Parry, Andrea Lewis, Melissa Leeke and Anna Oliwa

CD-ROM developed in association with
Q & D Multimedia

ACKNOWLEDGEMENTS

SMART Board™ and Notebook™ are registered trademarks of SMART Technologies Inc.

Microsoft Office, Word and Excel are either registered trademarks or trademarks of Microsoft Corporation in the United States and/or other countries.

With grateful thanks for advice, help and expertise to Angus McGarry (Trainer) and Fiona Ford (Education Development Consultant) at Steljes Ltd.

All Flash activities designed and developed by Q & D Multimedia.

The publishers gratefully acknowledge:
The Peters, Fraser and Dunlop Group for the use of an extract from *We're going on a bear hunt* by Michael Rosen © 1993, Michael Rosen (1993, Walker Books).
The Children's Audio Company for the use of 'Ten in a Bed', traditional, arranged by R Bruce. Recording © CYP Limited, published by CYP Music.
The Royal Mint for the use of images of coins © Crown copyright

Thank you to all the people of Leamington Spa and Warwick who allowed us to use images of their premises.

Every effort has been made to trace copyright holders for the works reproduced in this book, and the publishers apologise for any inadvertent omissions.

Designed using Adobe InDesign.

Made with Macromedia is a trademark of Macromedia, Inc. Director ®
Copyright © 1984-2000 Macromedia, Inc.

Published by Scholastic Ltd
Villiers House
Clarendon Avenue
Leamington Spa
Warwickshire CV32 5PR

www.scholastic.co.uk

Printed by Bell and Bain Ltd, Glasgow

123456789   7890123456

Text © 2007 Rachel Ager (CLL), Julia Rutherford-Bate (CLL), Ann Montague-Smith (PSRN), Susanna Shukla (KUW), Liz Cambray (CD), Jenny Mitchell (PSED lessons 1-6), Kate Cooper (PD and PSED lessons 7-12)

© 2007 Scholastic Ltd

British Library Cataloguing-in-Publication Data
A catalogue record for this book is available from the British Library.

ISBN 978-0439-94536-3

The rights of the authors of this work have been asserted by them in accordance with the Copyright, Designs and Patents Act 1988.

Extracts from the DfES document *The Early Years Foundation Stage: Every Child Matters* © 2006 Crown copyright. Reproduced under the terms of HMSO Guidance Note 8.

All rights reserved. This book is sold subject to the condition that it shall not, by way of trade or otherwise, be lent, hired out or otherwise circulated without the publisher's prior consent in any form of binding or cover other than that in which it is published and without a similar condition, including this condition, being imposed upon the subsequent purchaser.

No part of this publication may be reproduced, stored in a retrieval system, or transmitted, in any form or by any means, electronic, mechanical, photocopying, recording or otherwise, other than for the purposes described in the lessons in this book, without the prior permission of the publisher. This book remains copyright, although permission is granted to copy pages where indicated for classroom distribution and use only in the school which has purchased the book, or by the teacher who has purchased the book, and in accordance with the CLA licensing agreement. Photocopying permission is given only for purchasers and not for borrowers of books from any lending service.

Due to the nature of the web, the publisher cannot guarantee the content or links of any of the websites referred to in this book. It is the responsibility of the reader to assess the suitability of websites. Ensure you read and abide by the terms and conditions of websites when you use material from website links.

CONTENTS

4 INTRODUCTION
6 HOW TO USE THE CD-ROM

CHAPTER 1: COMMUNICATION, LANGUAGE AND LITERACY

8 OVERVIEW GRID
11 LESSONS
41 PHOTOCOPIABLES

CHAPTER 2: PROBLEM SOLVING, REASONING AND NUMERACY

55 OVERVIEW GRID
58 LESSONS
88 PHOTOCOPIABLES

CHAPTER 3: KNOWLEDGE AND UNDERSTANDING OF THE WORLD

103 OVERVIEW GRID
106 LESSONS
126 PHOTOCOPIABLES

CHAPTER 4: OTHER AREAS OF LEARNING

136 OVERVIEW GRID
139 LESSONS
139 Personal, social and emotional development
148 Physical development
151 Creative development
159 PHOTOCOPIABLES

170 GENERAL PHOTOCOPIABLES
172 USING YOUR SMART BOARD™
174 USING NOTEBOOK™ SOFTWARE
175 TOOLS GLOSSARY

Introduction

100 SMART BOARD™ LESSONS

Interactive whiteboards are fast becoming the must-have resource in today's classroom as they allow teachers to facilitate children's learning in ways that were inconceivable a few years ago. The appropriate use of interactive whiteboards, whether used daily in the classroom or once a week in the ICT suite, will encourage active participation in sessions and should increase learners' determination to succeed. Interactive whiteboards make it easier for teachers to bring the areas of learning to life in new and exciting ways.

'There is a whiteboard revolution in UK schools.'
(Primary National Strategy)

What can an interactive whiteboard offer?

For the **practitioner**, an interactive whiteboard offers the same facilities as an ordinary whiteboard, such as drawing, writing and erasing. However, the interactive whiteboard also offers many other possibilities to:
- save any work created during a session
- prepare as many pages as necessary
- display any page within the Notebook™ file to review teaching and learning
- add scanned examples of the children's work to a Notebook file
- change colours of objects and backgrounds instantly
- use simple templates and grids
- link Notebook file to websites and presentations.

Using an interactive whiteboard in the simple ways outlined above can enrich teaching and learning in a classroom, but that is only the beginning of the whiteboard's potential to educate and inspire.

For the **learner**, the interactive whiteboard provides the opportunity to share learning experiences as sessions can be enhanced with sound, still and moving images, and websites. Interactive whiteboards can be used to cater for the needs of all learning styles:
- kinaesthetic learners benefit from being able to physically manipulate images
- visual learners benefit from being able to watch videos, look at photographs and see images being manipulated
- auditory learners benefit from being able to access audio resources such as voice recordings and sound effects.

With a little preparation all of these resource types could be integrated in one session, a feat that would have been almost impossible before the advent of the interactive whiteboard!

Access to an interactive whiteboard

In schools where learners have limited access to an interactive whiteboard the teacher must carefully plan lessons in which the children will derive most benefit from using it. As teachers become familiar with the whiteboard they will learn when to use it and, importantly, when not to use it!

Where permanent access to an interactive whiteboard is available, it is important that the teacher plans the use of the board effectively. It should be used only in ways that will enhance or extend teaching and learning. Children still need to gain practical first-hand experience of many things. Some experiences cannot be recreated on an interactive whiteboard but others cannot be had without it. *100 SMART Board™ Lessons* offers both teachers and learners the most accessible and creative uses of this most valuable resource.

About the series

100 SMART Board™ Lessons is designed to reflect best practice in using interactive whiteboards. It is also designed to support all teachers and practitioners in using this valuable tool by providing resources that can be used on a whiteboard with little or no preparation. These inspirational lessons cover all areas of learning. They are perfect for all levels of experience and are an essential for any SMART Board users.

Safety note: Avoid looking directly at the projector beam as it is potentially damaging to eyes, and never leave the children unsupervised when using the interactive whiteboard.

Introduction

About the book
This book is divided into four chapters. Each chapter contains lessons and photocopiable activity sheets covering:
- Communication, language and literacy (CLL)
- Problem solving, reasoning and numeracy (PSRN), previously called mathematical development
- Knowledge and understanding of the world (KUW)
- Other areas of learning: including personal, social and emotional development (PSED); physical development (PD); creative development (CD).

At the beginning of each chapter a **planning grid** identifies the title, the objectives covered and any relevant cross-curricular links in each lesson. Objectives are taken from the *Early Years Foundation Stage: Every Child Matters* (2007). All of the lessons should therefore fit into your existing medium-term plans. The planning grids have been provided in Microsoft Word format on the CD-ROM for this purpose.

The *Early Years Foundation Stage: Every Child Matters*, which came into force in 2007, supports practitioners in tracking children's progress across the six Areas of Learning and Development. These should *support and enable practitioners to provide opportunities for children to play, learn and succeed in an atmosphere of care and feeling valued* (EYFS, 2007). *100 SMART Board™ Lessons* reflects the 'Development matters' by offering appropriate objectives matched to the new guidelines.

Lesson plans
The 'lessons' have a consistent structure and can be used across one or more sessions. They each include a starter activity, activities for whole class, group and planned independent work and a plenary to round up the teaching and learning and identify any assessment opportunities. A number of lessons also include opportunities for child-initiated activities. Crucially, each lesson plan identifies resources required (including photocopiable activity sheets P and Notebook files that are provided on the CD-ROM). Also highlighted are the whiteboard tools that could be used in the lesson.

Photocopiable activity sheets at the end of each chapter support the lessons. These sheets provide opportunities for group or individual work to be completed away from the board, but link to the context of the whiteboard lesson. They also provide opportunities for whole-class plenary sessions in which children discuss and present their work.

Two general record sheets are provided on pages 170 and 171. These are intended to support the teacher in recording ways in which the interactive whiteboard is used, and where and how interactive resources can be integrated into a lesson.

What's on the CD-ROM?
The accompanying CD-ROM provides an extensive bank of Notebook files. These support, and are supported by, the lessons in this book. As well as texts and images, a selection of Notebook files also include specially commissioned interactive files.

Printable PDF versions of the photocopiable activity and record sheets, as well as the answers to the PSRN activities, are also provided on the CD-ROM.

A 'Build your own' file is also supplied on the CD-ROM. This contains a blank Notebook page with a bank of selected images and interactive tools from the Gallery, as well as specially commissioned images. It is supported by lesson plans in the book to help you to build your own Notebook files.

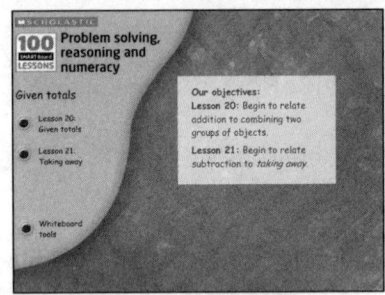

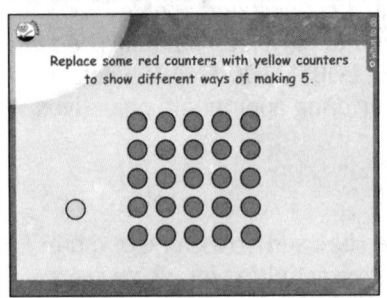

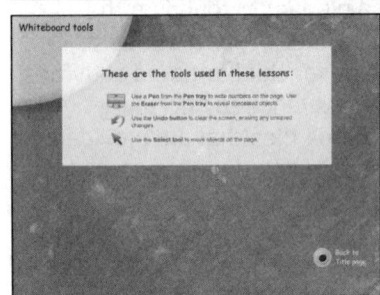

Introduction

The Notebook files
All of the Notebook files have a consistent structure as follows:

Title and objectives page
Use this page to highlight the focus of the lesson. You might also wish to refer to this page at certain times throughout the session or at the end of the session to assess whether the learning objective was achieved.

Introduction activity
This sets the context to the lesson and usually provides some key questions or learning points that will be addressed through the main activities.

Main activities
These activities support whole-class, independent and collaborative group work. The activities draw on the full scope of Notebook software and the associated tools, as well as the SMART Board tools.

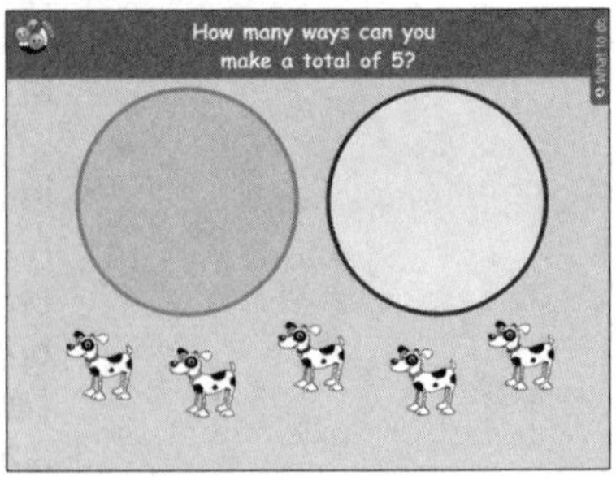

What to do boxes are also included in many of the prepared Notebook files. These appear as tabs in the top right-hand corner of the screen. To access these notes, simply pull out the tabs to reveal planning information, additional support and key learning points.

Plenary
A whole-class activity or summary page is designed to review work done both at the board and away from the board. In many lessons, children are encouraged to present their work.

Whiteboard tools page
The whiteboard tools page gives a reminder of the tools used in the lesson and provides instructions on how they are used.

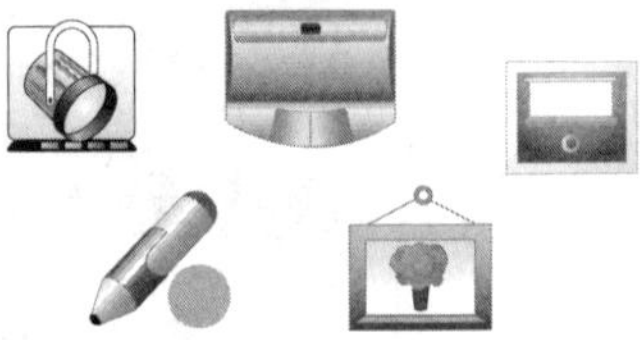

HOW TO USE THE CD-ROM

Setting up your screen for optimal use
It is best to view the Notebook files at a screen display setting of 1280 × 1024 pixels. To alter the screen display, select Settings, then Control Panel from the Start menu. Next, double-click on the Display icon and then click on the Settings tab. Finally, adjust the Screen area scroll bar to 1280 × 1024 pixels. Click on OK.

If you prefer to use a screen display setting of 800 × 600 pixels, ensure that your Notebook view is set to 'Page Width'. To alter the view, launch Notebook and click on View. Go to Zoom and select the 'Page Width' setting. If you use a screen display setting of 800 × 600 pixels, text in the prepared Notebook files may appear larger when you edit it on screen.

Viewing the printable resources
Adobe® Reader® is required to view the printable resources. All the printable resources are PDF files.

Visit the Adobe® website at **www.adobe.com** to download the latest version of Adobe® Reader®.

Introduction

Getting started
The program should run automatically when you insert the CD-ROM into your CD drive. If it does not, use My Computer to browse to the contents of the CD-ROM and click on the *100 SMART Board™ Lessons* icon.

When the program starts, you are invited to register the product either online or using a PDF registration form. You also have the option to register later. If you select this option, you will be taken, via the Credits screen, to the Main menu.

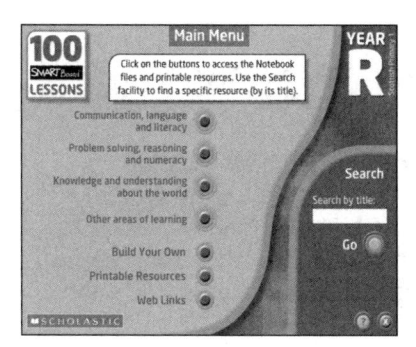

Main menu
The Main menu divides the Notebook by subject: CLL, PSRN, KUW and Other Areas of Learning. Clicking on the appropriate blue button for any of these options will take you to a separate Subject menu (see below for further information). The activity sheets are provided in separate menus. To access these resources, click on Printable resources.

Individual Notebook files or pages can be located using the search facility by keying in words (or part words) from the resource titles in the Search box. Press Go to begin the search. This will bring up a list of the titles that match your search.

The Web Links button takes you to a list of useful web addresses. A help button is included on all menu screens. The Help notes on the CD-ROM provide a range of general background information and technical support for all users.

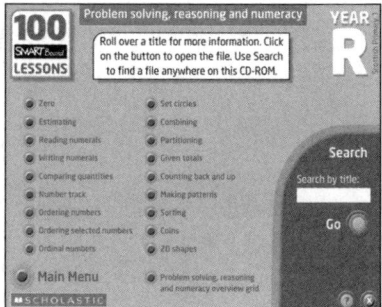

Subject menu
Each Subject menu provides all of the prepared Notebook files or each chapter of the book. Roll over each Notebook title to reveal a brief description of the contents in a text box at the top of the menu screen; clicking on the blue button will open the Notebook. Click on Main menu to return to the Main menu screen.

'Build your own' file
Click on this button to open a blank Notebook page and a collection of Gallery objects, which will be saved automatically into the My Content folder in the Gallery. You only need to click on this button the first time you wish to access the 'Build your own' file, as the Gallery objects will remain in the My Content folder on the computer on which the file was opened. To use the facility again, simply open a blank Notebook page and access the images and interactive resources from the same folder under My Content. If you are using the CD-ROM on a different computer you will need to click on the 'Build your own' button again.

Printable resources
The printable PDF activity sheets are also divided by chapter. Click on the subject to find all the activity sheets related to that subject/chapter. The answers to Chapter 2, Problem solving, reasoning and numeracy (PSRN), are also provided.

To alternate between the menus on the CD-ROM and other open applications, hold down the Alt key and press the Tab key to switch to the desired application.

CLL Chapter 1

Communication, language and literacy

This chapter provides 30 inspiring and interactive activities based on objectives taken from the Primary National Strategy framework and linked to the Early Learning Goals in the Curriculum Guidance for the Foundation Stage.

Some of the lessons in this chapter are double lessons, designed to be spread over two separate sessions. In each case, the start of the second session is indicated in the lesson plan.

The interactive software is used by the adult for demonstration purposes and the children are also given many opportunities to use and explore the range of software tools and devices. This interactive approach enables the children to be active learners and allows them to make choices and decisions, providing further opportunities to explore words, texts and their meaning.

Lesson title	Objectives	Cross-curricular links
Lesson 1: Print around the classroom	**Development matters (Language for Thinking)** Use talk to connect ideas. **ELG** Use talk to organise, sequence and clarify thinking. **ELG** Know that print carries meaning.	**KUW** Use information and communication technology to support their learning.
Lesson 2: Print all around us	**Development matters (Writing)** Ascribe meanings to marks that they see in different places. **ELG** Write their own names and other things such as labels and captions.	**KUW** Use information and communication technology and programmable toys to support their learning.
Lessons 3 and 4: The alphabet	**Development matters (Linking Sounds and Letters)** Hear and say the initial sound in words and know which letters represent some of the sounds. **ELG** Link sounds to letters, naming and sounding the letters of the alphabet.	**CD** Explore colour, texture, shape, form and space in two or three dimensions.
Lesson 5: Rhyming sounds	**Development matters (Linking Sounds and Letters)** Listen to and enjoy rhythmic patterns in rhymes and stories; continue a rhyming string and hear and say the initial sound in words. **ELG** Hear and say sounds in words in the order in which they occur. **ELG** Explore and experiment with sounds, words and text.	**CD** Match movements to music.
Lesson 6: Listening to recounts	**Development matters (Language for Communication)** Initiate conversation, attend to and take account of what others say. **ELG** Interact with others, negotiating plans and activities and taking turns in conversation.	**KUW** Find out about past and present events in their own lives, and in those of their families and other people they know.

CLL Chapter 1

Lesson title	Objectives	Cross-curricular links
Lesson 7: Writing recounts	**Development matters (Linking Sounds and Letters)** Distinguish one sound from another. **ELG** Use their phonic knowledge to write simple regular words and make phonetically plausible attempts at more complex words.	**CD** Explore colour, texture, shape, form and space in two or three dimensions.
Lessons 8 and 9: Bear hunt	**Development matters (Reading)** Have some favourite stories, rhymes, songs, poems or jingles; begin to be aware of the way stories are structured; know that information can be retrieved from books and computers. **ELG** Explore and experiment with sounds, words and texts.	**CD** Recognise and explore how sounds can be changed, sing simple songs from memory, recognise repeated sounds and sound patterns and match movements to music. **PSRN** Use everyday words to describe position.
Lessons 10 and 11: Writing captions	**Development matters (Writing)** Use writing as a means of recording and communicating. **ELG** Attempt writing for different purposes **ELG** Write things such as labels and captions.	**KUW** Find out about their environment, and talk about those features they like and dislike.
Lesson 12: Greeting cards	**Development matters (Reading)** Know that information can be relayed in the form of print. **ELG** Know that print carries meaning.	**PSED** Understand that people have different needs, views, cultures and beliefs that need to be treated with respect.
Lessons 13 and 14: Writing greeting cards	**Development matters (Writing)** Ascribe meanings to marks; use writing as a means of recording and communicating. **ELG** Write their own names and other things such as labels and captions.	**PSED** Have a developing respect for their own cultures and beliefs and those of other people.
Lesson 15: Memory game	**Development matters (Linking Sounds and Letters)** Hear and say the initial sound in words and know which letters represent some of the sounds. **ELG** Interact with others, negotiating plans and activities and taking turns in conversation. **ELG** Hear and say sounds in words in the order in which they occur.	**PSED** Form good relationships with adults and peers.
Lessons 16 and 17: Sequences	**Development matters (Language for Communication)** Use vocabulary and forms of speech that are increasingly influenced by experience of books; link statements and stick to a main theme or intention. **ELG** Extend their vocabulary, exploring the meanings and sounds of new words.	**KUW** Observe, find out about and identify features in the place they live and the natural world.

CLL Chapter 1

Lesson title	Objectives	Cross-curricular links
Lessons 18 and 19: Instructions	**Development matters (Language for Communication)** Link statements and stick to a main theme or intention. **ELG** Speak clearly and audibly with confidence and control and show awareness of the listener.	**KUW** Observe, find out about and identify features in the place they live and the natural world.
Lessons 20 and 21: Three Little Pigs	**Development matters (Reading)** Begin to be aware of the way stories are structured. **ELG** Retell narratives in the correct sequence, drawing on language patterns of stories.	**CD** Use their imagination in art and design, music, dance, imaginative and role play and stories.
Lesson 22: Goldilocks	**ELG** Retell narratives in the correct sequence, drawing on language patterns of stories. **ELG** Read a range of familiar and common words and simple sentences independently. **ELG** Show an understanding of the elements of stories, such as main character, sequence of events, and openings.	**CD** Use their imagination in art and design, music, dance, imaginative and role-play and stories.
Lessons 23 and 24: Circle game	**ELG** Hear and say sounds in words in the order in which they occur. **ELG** Link sounds to letters, naming and sounding the letters of the alphabet.	**PSED** Work as part of a group or class, taking turns and sharing fairly.
Lessons 25 and 26: Kim's game	**Development matters (Linking Sounds and Letters)** Continue a rhyming string. **ELG** Use their phonic knowledge to write simple regular words.	**PSRN** Use everyday words to describe position.
Lesson 27: Making words	**ELG** Hear and say sounds in words in the order in which they occur.	**CD** Use their imagination in art and design.
Lessons 28 and 29: Shopping lists	**Development matters (Writing)** Use writing as a means of recording and communicating. **ELG** Know that print carries meaning. **ELG** Attempt writing for different purposes, using features of different forms such as lists.	**PD** Use a range of small and large equipment.
Lesson 30: Robotic words	**ELG** Read a range of familiar and common words independently.	**KUW** Build and construct with a wide range of objects, selecting appropriate resources, and adapting their work where necessary.

CLL Lesson 1

Print around the classroom

Learning objectives
- Development matters (Language for Thinking): Use talk to connect ideas.
- ELG: Use talk to organise, sequence and clarify thinking.
- ELG: Know that print carries meaning.

Resources
'Print around us' Notebook file; photocopiable page 41 'Classroom labels (1)'; digital cameras.

Links to other ELGs
KUW
Use information and communication technology to support their learning.
- Help the children to take several photographs of others doing things in the identified areas of the classroom. Scan these digital photographs onto the whiteboard and match the photographs to the classroom labels (or add some new labels).

Whiteboard tools
Use the Lines tool to draw arrows to match signs to pictures. If a microphone is available, use Windows® Sound Recorder (accessed through Start>Programs>Accessories>Entertainment) to record the instructions for some labels. Then open your Notebook file and attach the sound files by selecting Insert, then Sound, and browsing to where you have saved the sound files.

- Pen tray
- Highlighter pen
- Lines tool
- Select tool

Introduction
Discuss with the children what they do in different areas of the classroom. Ask: *What do we do in this area? Where do we hang up our coats? Where can we get a drink?*

Highlight the labels on page 2 of the Notebook file and link them to those that already exist around the classroom. Ask: *What are these? What do you think this label says? What else could it say? Who or what are the labels for?*

Adult-focused whole-class activity
- Display page 3 of the Notebook file. Read the label aloud and then demonstrate that you can press on the label to listen to the words being read.
- Ask: *Which picture do you think the label belongs to? Why have you chosen that picture? Could the label work with any other pictures?*
- Allow the children plenty of time to talk to their friends and think about their answers. Encourage them to explain their answers. Ask: *Why? Why not?*
- Use the Lines tool to draw an arrow on page 3 to identify which picture the children think matches best with the label. They can check if their answer is right by pressing on the relevant picture to hear the label read aloud.
- Leave the remaining pictures on the page and discuss why the label might not match them.
- Repeat the activity using pages 4 to 6.

Adult-focused group activity
- Write your own labels or use the labels on photocopiable page 41 'Classroom labels (1)'.
- Cut out the labels and give one to each pair of children. Invite them to take a digital photograph to go with each label. Alternatively, ask the children to choose an area in the classroom where the label might be displayed.

Planned independent activity
- Show the children how to press on the label to listen to the words being read on pages 7 and 8 of the Notebook file.
- Direct the children to talk about which picture works best with the label. Reduce the size of the picture and let a volunteer move the picture up to the label to indicate the children's choice.
- If time is available, show the children how to use Windows® Sound Recorder to record labels for the other pictures on pages 7 and 8.

Plenary
- Refer back to the labels around the room that the children looked at earlier. Can they think of any places in the room that need a label?
- Ask: *What labels can we think of to put around the room?* If time is available, make some labels on the whiteboard, print them and attach them in the places suggested by the children.

CLL Lesson 2

Print all around us

Learning objectives
- Development matters (Writing): Ascribe meanings to marks that they see in different places.
- ELG: Write their own names and other things such as labels and captions.

Resources
'Print around us' Notebook file; photocopiable page 42 'Classroom labels (2)'; collection of photographs or pictures from magazines; pens, pencils, blank labels.

Links to other ELGs
KUW
Use information and communication technology to support their learning.
- Use this opportunity to show the children how to effectively use the sound recorder on the interactive whiteboard and the digital camera to take pictures for use on the computer.

Whiteboard tools
Use a Pen from the Pen tray or the On-screen Keyboard, accessed through the Pen tray or the SMART Board tools menu, to make a note of the children's ideas for labels. If a microphone is available, use Windows® Sound Recorder (accessed through Start> Programs>Accessories> Entertainment) so that the children can record their label suggestions.

- Pen tray
- On-screen Keyboard
- Select tool

Introduction
Revise Lesson 1 and ask the children to point out labels that exist around the classroom. Ask: *What are the labels for? What do they say? Which other labels do you know?*

Compare the pictorial and textual labels that the children might see. Display the labels on page 9 of the Notebook file. Ask: *What does the picture mean? What does the writing mean?* Encourage the children to think about the purpose of the labels: *Who are they for? What are they trying to say?*

Adult-focused whole-class activity
- Go to page 10 of the Notebook file. Invite the children to tell you what they can see. Ask: *What kind of label do you think we could put near the door?*
- Give the children time to talk in pairs and decide on an idea for a label.
- Ask them to share their ideas and discuss them. Ask: *Why would that be a good label? Who do you think would like to read that label?*
- As a class, decide on the label. Then use a Pen from the Pen tray or the On-screen Keyboard to write the label into the empty box. Read the label aloud together.
- Repeat the activity on page 11.

Planned independent activity
- Take your own photographs or use photocopiable page 42 'Classroom labels (2)'. Cut out the pictures and give each child a picture (or collection of pictures).
- Set up a mark-making area with pens, pencils and blank labels for the children to write on. Ask them to write labels to go with the pictures you have given them.

Adult-focused group activity
- Allow the children to use Notebook pages 12 to 16 with appropriate levels of support. Encourage them to try to write into the label space provided.
- Show the children how to use Windows® Sound Recorder. Direct them to talk about an appropriate label for each picture and then record themselves saying the instruction: for example, *Do not disturb*.

Plenary
- Invite the children to read out their labels without telling the other children what their purpose might be. The other children should then try to guess where the label might be placed.
- Play the children's recordings of labels from the Notebook file. Can they explain why they decided on particular labels? Ask: *Why did you choose that label? Who is your label for?*
- Use page 17 of the Notebook file to write up the children's comments.

CLL Lessons 3 and 4

The alphabet

Learning objectives
- Development matters (Linking Sounds and Letters): Hear and say the initial sound in words and know which letters represent some of the sounds.
- ELG: Link sounds to letters, naming and sounding the letters of the alphabet.

Resources
'The alphabet' Notebook file; photocopiable page 43 'Alphabet'; a large bag containing small objects such as an apple, ball, pencil and toy; Voisec or dictaphone; paper; glue; scissors; pencils; crayons.

Links to other ELGs
CD
Explore colour, texture, shape, form and space in two or three dimensions.
- Encourage the children to add collage pictures, colours and a variety of materials to decorate and enhance their alphabet books.

Introduction
Prepare a bag with several small objects inside, such as an apple, a ball, a pencil and so on. Pull out each object in turn. Ask the children to make the initial sound of the name of each object: for example, pull out an apple and encourage the children to make the sound *a*. Use page 2 of the Notebook file to write the names of the objects as they are removed from the bag. Add images from the Gallery to go with each object if they are available.

Vary the game by giving the children clues as to the object before you show it. For example, say: *I begin with 'a'. I am red and round and tasty to eat. I am a fruit. What am I?* (An apple.)

Adult-focused whole-class activity
- Go to page 3 of the Notebook file. Ask the children to make the sound of the letter in the middle of the page (*s*).
- Press on the letter to hear the sound.
- Practise making the sound with the children. Ask them to draw the letter in the air with their finger. Trace the letter on the whiteboard with a Highlighter pen at the same time.
- Look at the pictures on page 3. Invite the children to think about the initial sound of each word.
- Ask: *Can you see any pictures that begin with 's'?* Draw lines to match the pictures with the letter *s*. Suggest that the other pictures should be deleted.
- Invite volunteers to come and delete the unwanted pictures. Ask them why they chose those particular pictures.
- Repeat with pages 4 to 8.

Adult-focused group activities
- For Lesson 4, open pages 9 to 14 of the Notebook file. These contain a greater, more complex collection of choices for the children to work with.
- For each page, ask the children to make the sound of the letter on the page. Press on the letter to hear the sound. Practise making the sound together and writing it in the air.
- Next, look at and discuss the pictures that are displayed on the page. Encourage the children to think about what sound they begin with. Ask: *Can you see any pictures that begin with the letter ___? Which pictures shall we put in the bin? Why?*
- Ask the children to give reasons why some pictures might stay. For example, they may wish to keep the cake on the *h* page as it might be a *Happy birthday* cake. Others may wish to keep the face on the *s* page because they see a smile!
- Use a Voisec (a small dictaphone that includes a small button for recording, storing and playing short, spoken messages) and record a letter sound. Invite the children to spend time collecting items that match the initial sound that they hear when they touch the sound button.
- Start a game and invite the children to join you. Say: *My mother went to the shops and bought a cake.* Explain that mother must buy things that begin with the same initial letter sound. Tell the children that for the first round of the game, they must think of objects beginning with *c*.
- Go to page 15 of the Notebook file. Invite the children to use this page to make a list of their items if they so wish.
- Show them how to use the Gallery to find any suitable pictures of the suggested items to add to the list.

CLL Lessons 3 and 4

Planned independent activity
- In the workshop or writing area, create opportunities for the children to make alphabet books. Provide home-made books with a letter on each page (in alphabetical order).
- Laminate copies of photocopiable page 43 for reference and to remind the children of all the letters of the alphabet.

Plenary
- Pick up your bag of objects again. Tell the children that you have something in your bag beginning with *b*, for example. Ask them to think of all the things that you might have beginning with *b*. Bring out your item to see if anyone has guessed correctly.
- Invite individuals to take turns to feel something inside the bag and then give clues to describe the object to the other children, including what letter it begins with.
- Review the children's work and make some alphabetical word lists on page 16 of the Notebook file.

Whiteboard tools
Use the Gallery to find images for the Introduction and the shopping list activity. Use a Highlighter pen to trace each letter in the whole-class activity.

- Pen tray
- Highlighter pen
- Delete button
- Select tool
- Gallery

CLL Lesson 5

Rhyming sounds

Learning objectives
- Development matters (Linking Sounds and Letters): Listen to and enjoy rhythmic patterns in rhymes and stories.
- Development matters (Linking Sounds and Letters): Continue a rhyming string and hear and say the initial sound in words.
- ELG: Hear and say sounds in words in the order in which they occur.
- ELG: Explore and experiment with sounds, words and text.

Resources
'Rhyming sounds' Notebook file; photocopiable page 44 'Rhyming sounds' (copy and cut out the cards for a play activity); tape recorder with nursery rhyme tapes (for the listening corner).

Links to other ELGs
CD
Match movements to music.
- Perform some action rhymes in the Plenary. Record the children singing the rhymes and play them back. Add some simple percussion and develop a repertoire of moves to go with the recorded rhymes.

Whiteboard tools
Use the Shapes and Fill Colour tools to replace words on the screen in the Introduction.

- Pen tray
- Highlighter pen
- Shapes tool
- Fill Colour tool
- Select tool

Introduction
Display page 2 of the Notebook file which shows the rhyme 'Hey Diddle, Diddle'. Tell the children that you would like them to supply some alternative words for the rhyme.

Begin the rhyme: *Hey diddle diddle, the cat and the fiddle, the cow jumped over the...* and then select a child to choose an alternative to the word *moon*. Use the Shapes tool and the Fill Colour tool to draw a rectangle over the word *moon* on the Notebook page, then use a Pen from the Pen tray to write in the alternative suggestion. Continue the rhyme, asking the children for an alternative to *spoon* in the final line. Repeat the process of covering the word and replacing it with a rhyming alternative.

Adult-focused whole-class activity
- Move to page 3 and ask: *What can we see in the middle of the top row of the page?* Practise saying the word *cat*. Ask: *What is the sound at the end of the word? Can you think of any words that rhyme with 'cat'? How do you know?* Press on the pictures to hear the words read aloud.
- Discuss the different rhyming sounds with the children. Highlight rhyming words. Encourage them to practise saying the words. Ask: *Can you think of any more words that rhyme with 'cat'?* Add these in the space provided at the foot of the page.
- Explore pages 4 to 6, which also include rhyming sounds (*dog/log, coat/goat, bed/shed* and so on). Again, press on the pictures to hear the words.

Adult-focused group activity
- Challenge older or more confident learners to identify the more difficult sounds on pages 7 to 10 (for example, *cat, car, coat, bat* and *rat*).
- Help the children to understand that *cat* and *car* have different final sounds and do not rhyme. Ask: *What can we see in the middle of the page?* Practise saying the word *cat*. *What is the sound at the end of the word? What other words are there?* Press on the pictures to hear the words read aloud. Ask: *What is the rhyming sound on this page?* Highlight the rhyming words.
- Discuss the different rhyming sounds with the children. Encourage them to practise saying the words. Can they think of any more words that rhyme with *cat*? What about the other pictures: can they think of words that rhyme with *car, coat* and so on? Add the other words to the page.

Planned independent activity
- Set up a listening corner. Provide a range of nursery rhyme tapes for the children to select from.
- Cut out and laminate the pictures on photocopiable page 44 to make cards. Make these available with the tapes, so that the children can match the pictures to the nursery rhymes.

Plenary
- Perform some action nursery rhymes together. Allow the children to lead the session and use the nursery rhyme cards from photocopiable page 44 or the pictures on pages 11 and 12 of the Notebook file as a stimulus.
- Encourage the children to fall down (Humpty Dumpty) or walk around and fall over (Jack and Jill) to participate in and enjoy singing the familiar rhymes.

CLL　Lesson 6

Listening to recounts

Learning objectives
- Development matters (Language for Communication): Initiate conversation, attend to and take account of what others say.
- ELG: Interact with others, negotiating plans and activities and taking turns in conversation.

Resources
'Recount' Notebook file; photographs from home.

Links to other ELGs
KUW
Find out about past and present events in their own lives, and in those of their families and other people they know.
- Invite the children to bring in a photograph that shows them doing something special, such as celebrating a birthday, or being a bridesmaid at a wedding. Encourage the children to talk about their pictures and invite the rest of the class to listen and ask appropriate questions.

Introduction
Stimulate a sharing session with the children. Ask: *What did you do at the weekend? Did anyone play games? Did anyone go to a party?*
　　Allow the children time to take turns to talk about what they have done. Support the talking session with appropriate questions and responses. Ask: *Why? Where? When?* Encourage the children to also ask questions. Write down their comments on page 2 of the Notebook file.

Adult-focused whole-class activity
- Look at the picture on page 3. *What do you think the girl is doing?* Press on the picture to hear the girl talk. Repeat the description if necessary.
- Ask questions such as: *What did the girl do? Why did she go to bed? Do we know when she went to bed? What do you think happened next?*
- Go on to look at the pictures on pages 4 and 5 and listen to the narrative. Discuss with the children what they know and what they don't know about what the child is doing. For example, on page 4: *What is the girl going to wear? What did she say?*
- Encourage the children to focus on what they have heard, rather than what they think they know.

Adult-focused group activities
- Move to page 6. Ask: *What is happening in the picture?*
- Show the children how to use Windows® Sound Recorder. Help them to record the narrative that might go with the picture. For example: *The boy is playing with his train set.* Suggest that they give some more information. For example: *The boy is playing with his train set because he likes trains.*
- Support the children as they work through pages 6 to 9, recording what they think the children might be doing in each picture.
- At another session, ask the children to bring in photographs from home. Invite them to talk about the pictures with a partner. Model some questions to support their recount of the experiences. Ask: *Where were you? When did this happen? Who were you with?*
- Encourage other children to listen and ask questions. Allow time for thinking and for the children to frame their ideas in words.

Plenary
- Go to page 10. Ask: *What is happening in the picture? What do you think the boy is doing?* Listen to the sound recording.
- Decide which picture the little girl is talking about. Ask: *Why do you think it is this one? What can you see in the picture? What did you hear?*
- Repeat the activity on page 11.

Whiteboard tools
If a microphone is available, use Windows® Sound Recorder (accessed through Start> Programs>Accessories> Entertainment) to record the children's responses during the group activity.

　Pen tray
　Select tool

CLL Lesson 7

Writing recounts

Learning objectives
- Development matters (Linking Sounds and Letters): Distinguish one sound from another.
- ELG: Use their phonic knowledge to write simple regular words and make phonetically plausible attempts at more complex words.

Resources
Photographs from home; pens, pencils and paper; digital cameras.

Links to other ELGs
CD
Explore colour, texture, shape, form and space in two or three dimensions.
- Make beautiful book covers using collage and painting materials. Add pages of the children's work containing photographs and recount writing.

Whiteboard tools
Let the children use a Pen from the Pen tray or the On-screen Keyboard, accessed through the Pen tray or the SMART Board tools menu, to write simple sentences about the photographs they have brought in. Use a Highlighter pen to highlight features of the display. Upload scanned images by selecting Insert, then Picture File, and browsing to where you have saved the images.

- Pen tray
- Select tool
- On-screen Keyboard
- Highlighter pen

Introduction
Ask the children to bring in photographs from their home. Scan one or two examples and display them on the whiteboard.

Make time for the children to talk about the pictures. Question them to support their recount of the experiences. Ask: *Where were you? When did this happen? Who were you with?* Encourage the other children to listen and ask questions. Allow time for thinking and for the children to frame their ideas into words. Ask individual children to write simple words or sentences about the pictures on the whiteboard.

Notice if the children make use of their phonic knowledge to write about their family and friends in the photographs.

Adult-focused group activity
- Set up a writing table with pens, pencils and paper. Encourage the children to write about their photographs. Support their writing by getting them to answer questions such as: *Where? When? Why? What? Who?*
- Use the emergent writing and photographs to set up a display.
- Work closely with younger or less confident learners. Talk to them about the photographs they have brought in. Act as a scribe for these children. Encourage them to speak at a slow pace so that you can write down each word. Say each word as you write and read back each sentence when it is finished. Support the children's thoughts by encouraging them to answer questions: *Where? When? Why? What? Who?*

Planned independent activity
- Give the children, in pairs, a digital camera and ask them to take pictures of each other doing a range of activities in the classroom and outside.
- When they have done this, help them to download their pictures onto the computer.
- Import the pictures onto a Notebook page, leaving space under each picture for the children to write captions.
- Print out the finished Notebook pages to make a class display or book.

Plenary
- Open the Notebook pages with the children's photographs and writing.
- Read aloud some of the children's writing and ask them to point to the corresponding pictures. Use a Highlighter pen to draw their attention to any important features.

CLL Lessons 8 and 9

Learning objectives
- Development matters (Reading): Have some favourite stories, rhymes, songs, poems or jingles.
- Development matters (Reading): Begin to be aware of the way stories are structured.
- Development matters (Reading): Know that information can be retrieved from books and computers.
- ELG: Explore and experiment with sounds, words and texts.

Resources
Copies of *We're Going on a Bear Hunt* by Michael Rosen (Walker Books); 'Bear hunt' Notebook file; photocopiable page 45 'Bear hunt map'; props to help the children reproduce the sounds (such as a bucket of water); Plasticine or modelling clay; small-world figures and vehicles; digital camera.

Links to other ELGs
CD
Recognise and explore how sounds can be changed, sing simple songs from memory, recognise repeated sounds and sound patterns and match movements to music.
- Provide percussion instruments and explore the sounds that they make. Try to match the sounds of the instruments to the places on the bear hunt journey.

PSRN
Use everyday words to describe position.
- Play some games of hiding small-world people in the 3D maps that the children made. Model how to describe their position in order to find them again. Challenge the children to describe where the small-world people are.

Bear hunt

Introduction
Read the story *We're Going on a Bear Hunt* by Michael Rosen. Encourage the children to join in with suitable actions as the family in the book journeys through different places. Suggest that the children also make appropriate noises to represent the different settings: *swishy swashy* and so on.

Look at pages 2 to 8 of the Notebook file. Press on the words at the top of each page to hear them read aloud, and listen to the sounds by pressing on the sound words.

Adult-focused whole-class activity
- Display page 9 of the Notebook file. Look at the story map with all the different places that the family visited.
- Ask the children to point out the different areas. Press on the labels to hear them read out.
- Ask: *Can you remember where the family went first? Where did they go next?* Use the Lines tool to draw arrows to show the direction in which the family went.
- As you get to each area, ask the children if they can remember the sounds made, such as *swishy swashy* and so on.

Adult-focused group activity
- For the next session, go to page 10. Work with one group at a time.
- This time, ask the children to change the order of the story. Invite them to drag the images into positions of their choice on the map. Press on the labels to hear them read out. (To move the labels without activating the sound labels, simply press and drag them into position.)
- Explain to the children that they do not have to use all the images if they don't want to. Use the Delete button to delete these if necessary.
- Use the arrows provided on the page to link the images. Alternatively, you can draw your own arrows using a Pen from the Pen tray or the Lines tool.
- Once the children are happy with their map, show them how to use Windows® Sound Recorder to record the action sounds to go with their journey. Decide together on suitable props for making the sounds, such as a bucket of water to represent the river sound, *splash splosh*.
- Collect all the props together and practise making the sounds, then record them, one at a time, embedding them in the story map so that when the children press on the image it makes the corresponding sound.
- When the sound story map is complete, invite the children to retell the story with the actions and the sounds. Invite the other children to listen to this special retelling.

Planned independent activities
- Provide the children with copies of photocopiable page 45 'Bear hunt map' (enlarged to A3 size), and suggest that they use the map to retell the story.
- Encourage them to use props such as small-world people and objects to enhance their play and suggest that they make up noises and actions to accompany their storytelling.
- Provide modelling clay or Plasticine and ask the children to create different areas and characters for their own *bear hunt* story. Suggest that they use their imagination to think of different people and locations for the story.
- Use the sand pit or outside area for the children to create a 3D map of a bear hunt journey.

CLL Lessons 8 and 9

- Stimulate some role-play activities. Invite the children to go on their own bear hunt around the classroom or outside. Ask: *Where are you going to go? What noises will you make?*
- Give the children a digital camera so that they can collect images of the different places they visit.

Child-initiated activity
- Provide opportunities for the children to play freely with the 3D map they have made. Make available a selection of small-world vehicles and figures for them to use to enhance their play.
- Note whether the children use the materials for telling their own version of the bear hunt story, or if they develop their ideas in another way.

Plenary
- Invite the children who went on their own bear hunt around the classroom to share their journey with the rest of the class.
- Scan any digital pictures that the children took and display these on page 11 of the Notebook file. Encourage the children to use the photographs of their bear hunt as reminders of what they did on their journey.
- Support the children in their presentation of their bear hunt by asking questions such as: *Where did you go? What was the scariest part of your journey? Why was it scary?*
- Encourage the rest of the class to ask questions.

Whiteboard tools
Upload digital images of the children's bear hunts by selecting Insert, then Picture File, and browsing to where you have saved the images.

- Pen tray
- Select tool
- Lines tool
- Delete button

CLL Lessons 10 and 11

Writing captions

Learning objectives
- Development matters (Writing): Use writing as a means of recording and communicating.
- ELG: Attempt writing for different purposes.
- ELG: Write things such as labels and captions.

Resources
'Writing captions' Notebook file; photocopiable page 46 'Captions'; cardboard and other materials for the children to make models of buildings; small-world figures; large rectangular and square shapes; digital camera; paper; writing, drawing and colouring materials.

Links to other ELGs
KUW
Find out about their environment, and talk about those features they like and dislike.
- Go out to take some digital photographs of the local environment. Scan each picture into a new Notebook page on the whiteboard. Insert a rectangular-shaped box and encourage the children to add captions to go with the photographs. Ask them what they like or dislike about the local area.

Introduction
Open page 2 of the Notebook file. Tell the children that in this part of the lesson you are going to look at and talk about the photographs on the Notebook pages, then read the captions that go with them.

Look at the first photograph together. Ask: *What kind of building or shop do you think this is?* Invite the children to think of a caption that they would put with this photograph. Next, use the Delete button to remove the green box on the screen to reveal the prepared sentence underneath. Press on the text to hear the sentence read aloud. Is it similar to the children's idea? Ask: *Why is this a sentence?* (It has a full stop and capital letter.) Ask: *Why is this sentence helpful?* (It tells the readers what type of shop appears in the photograph.)

Repeat this activity for the photographs on pages 3 and 4.

Adult-focused whole-class activity
- Re-read the sentence on page 2. Tell the children that the sentence is too short and that they need to add some extra information. Invite them to consider what else can be added to make a longer caption for the picture. Ask: *What else can we tell people about the flower shop?*
- Give the children time to talk to a partner to think of some ideas for the photographs on pages 2 to 4.
- Listen to a range of suggestions and use page 5 to write down the children's ideas.
- Together, decide upon the best ideas and return to pages 2 to 4. Scribe the rest of each sentence (choose a different colour).
- Complete at least two captions for each photograph.

Adult-focused group activities
- Display page 6 of the Notebook file. Press on the text to hear the sentence read aloud. Say: *We need to write another sentence to tell people what this building is used for.* Show the children how to use Windows® Sound Recorder to record their ideas.
- Scribe the children's extra sentences for them on the Notebook page (in different colours). Complete at least one sentence for the photographs on pages 6 to 8.
- Give the children copies of photocopiable page 46. Ask them to talk in groups about the pictures displayed and to suggest captions for each picture. Ask another adult to support the groups by scribing these captions onto the sheet.
- Encourage older or more confident learners to try to write the sentences for the captions themselves.
- In subsequent sessions, provide the children with paper, pens and some square and rectangular shapes. Help them to draw round a square shape to make a box for a picture, and use a rectangular shape for a caption.
- Ask the children to use a digital camera to take a photograph and supply a caption to go with it.

Planned independent activity
- Set up a workshop area containing cardboard, reclaimed materials and other materials for the children to make buildings, with paper and pens available for the children to write labels or signs for the buildings. (If necessary, ask an adult to help the children write the labels.)
- Invite the children to talk about who works and lives in the different buildings they have made.

CLL Lessons 10 and 11

Child-initiated activity
- Leave out the models that the children have made so that they can play with them independently. Provide small-world people in the area so that they can add figures to the scene if they choose to.

Plenary
- Review the completed Notebook file and photocopiable pages.
- Ask the children to re-read the sentences they have written about the buildings. Point out that the captions now contain more than one sentence.
- Together, read out just the first sentence for one of the captions. Ask: *How will we know when to stop reading? How do we know it is the end of the sentence?* Remind the children that they have produced more than one sentence and that together these sentences form a caption.

Whiteboard tools

If a microphone is available, use Windows® Sound Recorder (accessed through Start>Programs>Accessories>Entertainment) for children to record more detail for the photographs and to record their ideas about the purposes of different buildings. Add the files to the Notebook page by selecting Insert, then Sound, and browsing to where you have saved the sound files. Use a Pen from the Pen tray or the On-screen Keyboard, accessed through the Pen tray or the SMART Board tools menu, to write the children's ideas for captions. Alternatively, select the Text tool and use your computer keyboard.

- Pen tray
- Delete button
- Select tool
- On-screen Keyboard
- Text tool

CLL Lesson 12

Greeting cards

Learning objectives
- Development matters (Reading): Know that information can be relayed in the form of print.
- ELG: Know that print carries meaning.

Resources
'Greeting cards' Notebook file; photocopiable page 47 'Greeting cards'; collection of greeting cards (or cards the children have brought in); tissue paper, glue, scissors, coloured pencils and crayons.

Links to other ELGs
PSED
Understand that people have different needs, views, cultures and beliefs that need to be treated with respect.
- Talk about when and why people send greetings cards to each other.

Introduction
Display a collection of greeting cards in the classroom. Invite the children to look at and talk about the cards. Then give each pair or small group one card to look at. Ask: *Who do you think might like a card like this? What do you think the card is for? When do you receive cards? When do you send cards?*

Encourage the children to explain their answers using the word *because*. For example: *I think this greeting card is for someone's birthday because there is a cake with candles on the front.*

Adult-focused whole-class activity
- Have a collection of greeting cards available for the children to look at.
- After the initial discussion, open up the greeting cards and ask the children to look at the caption text inside. Ask: *What words or letters do you recognise? Can you find the letter that your name begins with? What do you think this might say?*
- Collect and write a list of the captions or phrases from inside the cards on page 2 of the Notebook file (such as *Happy Birthday, Greetings* and *Get Well Soon*).

Adult-focused group activity
- Set up an activity table for the children to create their own greeting cards. Provide tissue paper, glue, scissors, coloured pencils and crayons and any other suitable equipment for the children to use.
- Show the children photocopiable page 47 'Greeting cards', and talk about the pictures on it. Look at the different characters and decide what sort of card you could send to them. Can the children tell you what captions might be suitable to go on their cards?

Plenary
- Choose some of the cards that the children have made. Invite the creators of these cards to stand up and show their cards to the rest of the class.
- Encourage the other children to explain what they like about each other's cards. Prompt them with questions, such as: *Who do you think this card is for? What does it say inside?*
- Explain that in the next lesson the children will be designing their own greeting cards on the whiteboard.
- Go to page 3 of the Notebook file, which displays three pictures and three greetings. Read the three greetings to the children. Ask them to consider which greeting would fit with each picture.
- Invite individual children to explain their answers. Show them how to press on the text and drag and drop each greeting to the matching card.

Whiteboard tools
Use a Pen from the Pen tray to scribe greetings.

- Pen tray
- Select tool

CLL Lessons 13 and 14

Writing greeting cards

Learning objectives
- Development matters (Writing): Ascribe meanings to marks.
- Development matters (Writing): Use writing as a means of recording and communicating.
- ELG: Write their own names and other things such as labels and captions.

Resources
'Greeting cards' Notebook file; tissue paper; glue; scissors; coloured pencils; crayons; old greeting cards; blank cards; collage materials (such as shiny paper, sequins, beads and so on).

Links to other ELGs
PSED
Have a developing respect for their own cultures and beliefs and those of other people.
- Find out about all the times that children remember receiving special cards.

Introduction
Display page 4 of the Notebook file. Explain to the children that you would like to send a card to Snow White. Press on each star button on the page to hear the different greetings read aloud.

After they have heard the different greetings, invite the children to decide what sort of greeting they would like to send to Snow White. Should it be a get well card or a happy birthday card, for example? Ask: *Which message do you think is best? Why don't you want to select this message?* Encourage the children to discuss the various options and to explain their choices.

When the children have chosen the message, press on the text to go to a page where they can choose an image for the card. Ask them what kind of picture they think Snow White would like.

Allow the children some opportunity to talk in pairs or small groups and decide on the most suitable picture for the greeting card that you are going to send her.

Ask questions such as: *Why do you think Snow White would like that picture? Why do you think that this picture would be good for someone who is feeling unwell? Which picture do you think that Snow White would not like?*

When the children have chosen an image, press on it, and you will be taken to a page that contains the final greeting card. *Is the greeting the right one?* (You can press on the box in the top right-hand corner of the page to go back to the start to select another greeting card if you wish.)

Adult-focused group activity
- Work with small groups one at a time and ask them to help you to write a personal note to Snow White on the card. Discuss what kind of note would be appropriate in this greeting card.
- Collate some useful words or phrases on a piece of paper, such as: *Dear, love from, best wishes* and so on. Support the children to write their message on the whiteboard, using the On-screen Keyboard.
- Show the children how to use Windows® Sound Recorder to record their own messages. Allow them some time to experiment.
- Print out the card and then use the Delete button to delete the text ready to work with the next group.

Planned independent activities
- For the next session, invite the children, in small groups, to repeat the previous activity. Ask them to decide who they would like to send a card to, and why. Show them how to select a new card and greeting and remind them how to use the sound recorder to record their messages.
- You could set a specific stimulus for the greeting card – for example, Baby Bear is going to be two years old! Print out the messages that the children create.
- Set up an activity table for the children to create their own greeting cards. Give them a specific focus for their cards, such as making a get well card for an absent member of staff, or a thank-you card for the dinner supervising staff. Once the children have created their cards, allow them some time to write a caption and a message, supporting them if necessary.
- Set up a writing area. Provide the children's names on cards. Encourage them to find their name cards and use them to practise writing their own names. Also provide old greeting cards and captions written onto card for the children to use when making their own cards.

CLL Lessons 13 and 14

- Encourage the children to use the resources freely, remembering to add greetings and their names to any cards they make.

Child-initiated activity
- Set up a class craft or treasure box and stock it full of greeting cards, blank cards, collage materials, shiny paper, sequins, beads and other treasures. Allow the children to choose to use the contents of the box freely.
- Make sure the children are aware of where to find all the other craft materials that they will need, such as card, mark-making materials, glue, tissue paper and so on.

Plenary
- Share some of the messages from the children's home-made greeting cards. Write a collection of words and phrases that have been used on page 33 of the Notebook file.
- Ask the children for suggestions of any other words that could be added to the list.

Whiteboard tools

Use the On-screen Keyboard, accessed through the Pen tray or the SMART Board tools menu, to add a message to the greeting card. If a microphone is available, use Windows® Sound Recorder (accessed through Start>Programs>Accessories>Entertainment) to record the children's messages. Then open the Notebook file and attach the sound files by selecting Insert, then Sound, and browsing to where you have saved the sound files.

- Pen tray
- Select tool
- Delete button
- On-screen Keyboard

CLL Lesson 15

Memory game

Learning objectives
- Development matters (Linking Sounds and Letters): Hear and say the initial sound in words and know which letters represent some of the sounds.
- ELG: Interact with others, negotiating plans and activities and taking turns in conversation.
- ELG: Hear and say sounds in words in the order in which they occur.

Resources
'Memory game' Notebook file.

Links to other ELGs
PSED
Form good relationships with adults and peers.
- Suggest that the children work together to make up or play another memory game. For example, they could use playing cards to play Pelmanism (or Pairs).

Whiteboard tools
Use the Screen Shade to hide and reveal the items. Use a Pen from the Pen tray to write down what the children remember. Add images to the page from the Gallery.

- Pen tray
- Select tool
- Screen Shade
- Gallery

Introduction
Open page 2 of the Notebook file. Ask the children to look carefully at all the items on the page. Tell them to try to remember everything they can see.

Enable the Screen Shade to hide the objects. Ask: *What can you remember seeing on the page?* Go to page 3 and write the names of the objects the children can remember. Sound out the words as you write them, encouraging the children to join in with any sounds that they can hear, especially the initial sounds.

Now go back to page 2. Reveal the items on the page slowly. Ask: *What is this? A coat? Who remembered there was a coat on the page?* Check the list you have written on page 3 to see if the word *coat* appears on it.

Adult-focused whole-class activity
- Go to page 4 of the Notebook file. Ask the children to look carefully at the objects on the page and try to remember everything.
- Use the Screen Shade to hide all the objects. Ask: *What can you remember seeing on the page?*
- As the children start to remember, use page 5 to write down the words.
- Sound out the words as you write them, asking questions such as: *What sound does 'egg' begin with?*
- Now return to page 4 and slowly reveal the items. Ask: *What is this? A banana? Who remembered there was a banana on the page?* Check your list on page 5 to see if the word *banana* appears on it.
- Repeat the activity on pages 6 to 9.

Adult-focused group activities
- Gather a collection of small objects, along with a tray and a cloth to cover the objects. Support the children to play the following memory game:
  - Let each child take a turn to decide which objects go on the tray. Suggest that they present the tray to the other children and allow them time to look at the objects.
  - The other children close their eyes while an item is removed by the first child. The tray is then presented for a short time while the children try to remember what is missing.
  - Suggest that older or more confident learners provide clues for the other children, such as: *You can wear this object on your head.*
- Go to page 10. Help the children to use the Gallery to build up their own page of items on the whiteboard to play a memory game. Subsequent groups of children can use blank Notebook pages to create their memory games.
- Differentiate this task by setting a particular challenge – perhaps by specifying that all the items should begin with the sound *m*, or that all the items should be blue. Show the children how to navigate through the images and how to drag the pictures onto the page. Demonstrate how to use the Screen Shade to hide and reveal the images. Ask questions such as: *Why have you chosen these pictures?*

Plenary
- Display page 10 showing one of the children's own Notebook files that they generated during the independent work. Support the children who made this page to lead the memory game with the class.
- Allow the children time to look at the page and then remove an item while they close their eyes. Ask them which object is missing. Invite volunteers to find it in the Gallery.

CLL Lessons 16 and 17

Sequences

Learning objectives
● Development matters (Language for Communication): Use vocabulary and forms of speech that are increasingly influenced by experience of books; link statements and stick to a main theme or intention.
● ELG: Extend their vocabulary, exploring the meanings and sounds of new words.

Resources
'Sequences and instructions' Notebook file; photocopiable page 48 'Sequences'; ingredients and equipment for making sandwiches; seeds, soil, empty plant pots, trowels and water; digital camera; paper; glue sticks; pretend food and kitchen equipment.

Links to other ELGs
KUW
Observe, find out about and identify features in the place they live and the natural world.
● Extend the sequencing activity in your work on growing things as well as how things are done in everyday activities such as cooking, going on a journey and so on.
● Ask children to use books and the internet to find population figures for Tudor times and compare these with modern data.

Introduction
Open the Notebook file and look at the images on page 2. Ask the children: *What is happening? What do you think the boy is doing?* Now look at the individual pictures of the boy on pages 3 to 6. Talk about each picture in more detail together. Explain that you would like the children to help you to write a caption to go with each picture that describes what the boy is doing.

As you go through the pages, ask the children to support you as you model the writing to go with each picture. Ask questions such as: *Who can help me remember how to write 'the'? What sound can we hear at the start of the word 'boy'?*

Occasionally make deliberate mistakes so that the children can help you. Invite individuals to come and point to the mistakes on the whiteboard.

Adult-focused whole-class activity
● Talk about the children's favourite types of sandwich together. Ask them to tell you the ingredients that they think they would need to make their favourite sandwich.
● Talk about the order in which they might make their sandwich. For example, should they add the filling before the butter? Should they put the 'lid' on the sandwich before they have added the filling?

Adult-focused group activities
● Provide some bread, butter and a choice of two or three popular fillings. (**Important note:** Check for any food allergies beforehand.) Help the children to make a simple sandwich to enjoy at snack time.
● As you make the sandwiches together, discuss the order in which they are being made. Encourage the use of sequencing vocabulary, such as *next, then* and *to begin with*.
● At the beginning of the next session, remind the children of the work you did together, making sandwiches. Invite a volunteer to describe the sequence they followed when making their sandwich.
● Show the children page 7 of the Notebook file. On this page there are some pictures of the boy making a sandwich.
● Invite the children to help you to put the pictures of the sandwich-making in order. Ask: *What should the boy do first?* Facilitate an open discussion: there are many ways to make a sandwich and although some things have to be done in order, there are many variations!
● Encourage the children to think about the sequence of the activity. Invite volunteers to come to the board and move the pictures into their preferred order. Ask them to describe and justify their sequence.
● As a class, agree on a sensible order. Discuss the sort of language and vocabulary used to describe the order of events. Encourage the children to use words such as *last, first, next, before* and *after*.
● Write a list of the useful words on page 8 of the Notebook file and read them together.
● Finish the activity with a singing session, using the opportunity to reinforce the sequencing vocabulary. Ask the children to spend a few minutes thinking about their bedtime routine. Ask: *What things do you do when you are getting ready for bed?* Invite volunteers to tell you one thing that they do.
● Write the children's ideas on page 9 and read them through together. Decide on an order for the song and move the words into the correct order on the page.
● Use a well-known tune such as 'Here we go round the mulberry bush' for

CLL Lessons 16 and 17

your song and sing it together. For example: *This is the way we brush our teeth; This is the way we put on our pyjamas; This is the way we read our story*, and so on.

Planned independent activities
- Set up an activity table outside with seeds, soil, empty plant pots, trowels and access to water. Before the children plant the seeds, ask them to explore the objects available and consider what they might do with them.
- Invite the children to describe to each other how to plant a seed. When they think they have the sequence correct they should come and tell an adult how they think it might be done. Once they have agreed on a sequence with an adult they may plant and water their seeds.
- Give the children a digital camera and ask them to record what they are doing, so that they can help the other children to do it later. Encourage them to use words such as *last, first, next, before* and *after*.
- Provide the children with copies of photocopiable page 48. Invite them to cut out the pictures and decide on the order in which they should go. Provide sheets of paper and glue sticks and suggest that the children stick the pictures onto the paper in their chosen sequence.
- Encourage them to talk about their ideas, justifying their sequences to a partner.

Child-initiated activity
- Provide pretend food and sandwich-making equipment (such as the type of items available from Early Learning Centre shops) in the role-play area.
- Allow the children to play freely with the equipment. Note whether they use any of the new or revised vocabulary as they are making things for each other in their play. Listen out for comments such as: *First I need some bread...*

Plenary
- Invite the children who took the pictures while planting their seeds to share their pictures with the rest of the class. You can help them to do this by scanning the images onto the whiteboard and displaying them.
- Encourage the other children to ask questions. For example: *What did you do first of all? After you had put soil into the pot, what did you do next?*
- Display page 10 of the Notebook file and discuss the pictures. Invite the children to help you to sort and put the pictures into the correct order.

Whiteboard tools
Use a Pen from the Pen tray to add writing to the page.

- Pen tray
- Select tool

CLL Lessons 18 and 19

Instructions

Learning objectives
- Development matters (Language for Communication): Link statements and stick to a main theme or intention.
- ELG: Speak clearly and audibly with confidence and control and show awareness of the listener.

Resources
'Sequences and instructions' Notebook file; photocopiable page 49 'Instructions'; paper and pens; glue sticks; scissors; shape templates; stapler; hole-punch; ribbons; colouring materials.

Links to other ELGs
KUW
Observe, find out about and identify features in the place they live and the natural world.
- Extend the sequencing activity in your work on growing things as well as how things are done in everyday activities such as cooking, going on a journey and so on.

Introduction
Open the Notebook file and look at the images on page 11. Ask: *What do you think is happening? Do you like eating toast? Have any of you helped to make your own toast before?*

Talk to the children about what happens when we put bread into the toaster. Ensure that they understand that they should always be with an adult when making toast. Explain that the toaster gets very hot and that the bread, when it comes out of the toaster, is also very hot.

Adult-focused whole-class activity
- Look more closely at the selection of images on page 11. What is happening? Does the little girl need to follow a special order to make the toast?
- Explain that you would like the children's help to write some instructions to go with each of the pictures.
- First, invite volunteers to come and help you to sort the pictures on page 11 into the correct order. At first, make some deliberate and obvious mistakes and encourage the children to explain and show you how to rectify your errors.
- Show the children how to add numbers to the pictures to show the order, using a Pen from the Pen tray.
- Now go to pages 12 to 16, looking at each picture in order. Discuss each picture in turn, asking the children for suggestions of an instruction to write for each page.
- Allow the children some time to decide what the first instruction might be. If you have a microphone, show them how to use Windows® Sound Recorder to record the instruction to embed into each page. Use a Pen from the Pen tray or the On-screen Keyboard, accessed through the Pen tray or the SMART Board tools menu, to write down the instructions to match each sound recording.

Adult-focused group activities
- Provide each child with a copy of photocopiable page 49.
- Invite the children to cut out the pictures from the photocopiable page and to think about the order that they might go in. Ask: *Is there more than one way that these pictures could be ordered?* Listen to the children's ideas.
- Provide paper and glue sticks and ask the children to stick down the pictures in their chosen order. Encourage them to explain their reasons and discuss the order of the pictures as a group. Make sure that they use appropriate sequencing vocabulary, such as *first, next, last of all, finally* and so on.
- Ask appropriate questions, such as: *Which picture might come first? After putting the bread into the toaster, what should the girl do next?*
- In preparation for the next session, set up a mark-making area with pens, pencils, paper, glue sticks, spare copies of photocopiable page 49, shape templates and so on.
- Invite the children to cut out the pictures from the photocopiable page. Ask them to stick each picture on a separate piece of paper with space underneath it.
- Help them to draw round a large rectangular shape to create a box under each picture in which they can add their own written instructions.
- Next, talk to them about how to order the pictures. Ask: *Which picture is first, which picture is next?* Arrange the pieces of paper in page order and

CLL Lessons 18 and 19

compile them into a book by stapling the pages, or by punching holes in the pages and tying them with a ribbon.
- Now discuss the instructions the children would like to add underneath their pictures.
- Support them to write their instructions either by scribing for them or giving the children the opportunity to make their own marks. Discuss the kind of words and phrases that are used to give instructions, such as *first, you need to, then, finally* and so on.

Planned independent activities
- Teach the children an instructional game called *First, next, and then*. Explain that they can play the game in the classroom, outside or in an activity area.
  - Tell the children that they must play that one child is in charge and must give instructions to the other children to follow.
  - In the instructions that they give, they must use the words: *First, next, and then*. For example: *First go to the toy box, next choose a toy and then bring it to me.*
  - Spend some time practising this order with the children *(first, next, and then)*. Then let the children continue to play in pairs or small groups.
- Let the children work in groups. Remind them of how to use Windows® Sound Recorder to add instructional labels to the pages in the Notebook file.
- Show the children how to save their Notebook file with a different file name so that you can review the work from each group.

Child-initiated activity
- Set up an exciting workshop area in your setting. Stock it full of materials suitable for making a range of types of books, such as shape, zigzag, peepo and pop-up books. Don't forget the ribbons, scissors, glue, paste, colouring materials and so on.
- Provide sets of instruction sheets that older or more confident readers can use to cut up and turn into their own home-made instruction books.
- Provide sequences of pictures for all the children to cut out and use during free-choice activity time.

Plenary
- Review some of the aural instructions that the children recorded to go with the Notebook file. Ask the children to explain their instructions and listen to see if the instructions make sense.
- Encourage the children to give positive and helpful feedback to each group as they listen to their instructions.
- Use page 17 of the Notebook file to write up the children's comments.

Whiteboard tools
Use a Pen from the Pen tray or the On-screen Keyboard, accessed through the Pen tray or the SMART Board tools menu, to add writing to the page. If a microphone is available, use Windows® Sound Recorder (accessed through Start>Programs> Accessories> Entertainment) to add aural instructions to the page.

- Pen tray
- On-screen Keyboard
- Select tool

CLL Lessons 20 and 21

Three Little Pigs

Learning objectives
- Development matters (Reading): Begin to be aware of the way stories are structured.
- ELG: Retell narratives in the correct sequence, drawing on language patterns of stories.

Resources
'Three Little Pigs' Notebook file; a storybook version of 'The Three Little Pigs'; finger puppets of the three little pigs and the wolf and a story sack (if available – see the group activities in the lesson plan for ideas on how you can create your own story sack); photocopiable page 50 'Three little pigs map', enlarged to A3 size; a range of materials and tools that can be used to make the three pigs' houses (straw, sticks, LEGO®, building bricks, small-world figures, boxes, cartons, PVA adhesive, spreaders and so on).

Links to other ELGs
CD
Use their imagination in art and design, music, dance, imaginative and role play and stories.
- Make some further story sacks linked to the children's favourite traditional tales. Leave them readily available in your story corner and allow the children to choose them freely to retell the stories.

Introduction
Share the story of 'The Three Little Pigs' with the children, encouraging them to join in with the refrains.

Retell the story, this time using the finger puppets as you tell it to the children (this will work better if you are able to retell the story without using a book). Invite individuals to come and take the parts of the three little pigs and the wolf as you narrate. Draw the children's attention to the dialogue between the characters.

Repeat the refrains together several times until the children know the phrases by heart.

Adult-focused whole-class activity
- Display page 2 of the Notebook file. Talk about the part of the story and picture it is showing (it introduces the three little pigs). Discuss what the characters might be saying to each other.
- Invite children to the board to move the characters and the speech bubbles into position. If necessary, explain what purpose the speech bubbles serve on the page. (They let us know that a character is speaking.)
- Demonstrate how to use Windows® Sound Recorder to record the children speaking the roles of each of the pigs. Attach these sound recordings to the speech bubbles and invite other children to come and play the recordings.
- Discuss what each character is saying and re-record if necessary until the whole class is happy with the results.

Adult-focused group activities
- For the next session, repeat the whole-class activity, this time using pages 3, 4 and 5 of the Notebook file. Explain to the children that you would like them to work in groups to add speech to the speech bubbles for one of the pages.
- Demonstrate again how to do this. Invite one of the children to choose one of the speech bubbles and record what might be said.
- Print pages 3 to 5 to allow other groups to work away from the whiteboard initially.
- Repeat the whiteboard activity with different groups, using a different page from the Notebook file with each group. Try to allow as many children as possible to record some speech.
- Support the activity by providing a story sack related to the story of 'The Three Little Pigs'. Use the objects in the story sack to act out the story, paying particular attention to what the characters say in the main parts of the story. You can make a simple story sack by adding the following items to a colourful soft bag:
  - finger puppets or soft toys of the three little pigs and the wolf
  - small bundles of straw and sticks
  - a small LEGO® house model (or similar).

Planned independent activities
- Provide some straw, sticks and building bricks. Ask the children to explore the different properties of the materials. Invite them to describe the weight and texture of each material. Which of the materials do they think is the strongest, and why?
- Provide an enlarged copy of photocopiable page 50 in your workshop area. Suggest that a small group of children colour and decorate the map, and

CLL Lessons 20 and 21

then make three-dimensional models to go onto it. Provide reclaimed materials such as boxes and cartons of different sizes and colouring; collage materials; bundles of straw and sticks; strong child-friendly glue such as PVA adhesive and spreaders. In addition, provide access to small construction pieces such as building bricks, LEGO® and other similar kits.
- Allow the children the freedom to experiment with the materials and create the houses for the three little pigs.
- Provide small-world animals (or similar) for the children to use with the map and models in order to retell the story in their own way.
- Invite the children to make their own story sacks that are related to the story. Encourage them to do this independently, deciding for themselves the sort of props that are needed to go in the sack to help them to retell the story.
- Once the children have had plenty of opportunities to explore the story in several ways, encourage them to act out the story themselves (rather than using small-world models or puppets). Ask for volunteers to play different roles. Encourage them to think about the kind of things their character said in the story. Then invite them to act out the story.
- Ask the children to search through the books in your story corner to find other traditional tales that feature animals.

Child-initiated activity
- Make the map, houses and small-world characters available to the children to use in their independent play.

Plenary
- Re-read the story of 'The Three Little Pigs' to the children.
- Review the children's completed recordings and remind them that this dialogue forms part of the text of the book. Find the pictures in the book that match the children's recordings.
- Ask the children to consider if they would change anything about the recordings that they made. Have they remembered the most important parts of the story?
- Show the children pages 6, 7 and 8 of the Notebook file. Discuss what is happening in each picture. On pages 6 and 7, if you press on the images of the houses and press the Delete button ⌧ (or select the Delete option from the dropdown menu), you can show the children what the wolf has done!
- Next, delete the clouds to reveal the text. Press on the star to hear the text read aloud. Invite the children to repeat the refrains several times.
- Look at the children's story sacks and ask them to act out parts of the story.
- As follow-up work (or for an alternative plenary session), consider alternative endings for the story. Use the characters on the Notebook page and other pictures from the Gallery 🗇 to help you with this.
- Ask: *Can you think of a version of the story that ended with the wolf becoming the hero of the story? How could the pigs become friends with the wolf?* Have fun making up some different variations of the story.
- Use page 9 of the Notebook file to write up the children's suggestions.

Whiteboard tools

If a microphone is available, use Windows® Sound Recorder (accessed through Start > Programs > Accessories > Entertainment) to record speech. To attach recorded sounds to the speech bubbles, first select a speech bubble, press Insert, then Sound, and browse to where you have saved the sound file. To remove objects from the page, select them and press the Delete button (or select the Delete option from the dropdown menu).

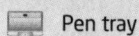

- Pen tray
- Select tool
- ⌧ Delete button
- 🗇 Gallery

CLL Lesson 22

Goldilocks

Learning objectives
- ELG: Retell narratives in the correct sequence, drawing on language patterns of stories.
- ELG: Read a range of familiar and common words and simple sentences independently.
- ELG: Show an understanding of the elements of stories, such as main character, sequence of events, and openings.

Resources
'Goldilocks' Notebook file; a role-play area and props for setting it up as the three bears' cottage; photocopiable page 51 'Goldilocks', enlarged to A3 size; a mark-making area stocked with paper, pencils, crayons, glue and scissors.

Links to other ELGs
CD
Use their imagination in art and design, music, dance, imaginative and role play and stories.
- Make a display of the class alternative to the Goldilocks story.

Whiteboard tools
To remove an object from the page, select it and then press the Delete button (or select the Delete option from the dropdown menu).

- Pen tray
- Select tool
- Delete button

Introduction
Ask the children what they know about the story of Goldilocks. Write their ideas on page 2 of the Notebook file. Ensure that they remember the key elements of the story. Discuss with them how they might set up a Goldilocks role-play area and allow them to play an active part in setting this up.

Adult-focused whole-class activity
- Read the story on pages 3 to 6. Discuss who the story is about, where she goes, what she eats, what she sits on and where she goes to sleep.
- Challenge the children to think of a different character and retell the story using the new character's name.
- Repeat this activity in a similar way, choosing another element to substitute, such as the location or the food tried and so on.
- Now explain to the children that you would like them to help you to create a new story that will be different but will follow the same pattern as the story of Goldilocks.
- Display page 7 of the Notebook file. Explain that the children will need to select one of the characters who will then replace Goldilocks in the story.
- When they have chosen which character to use, invite a volunteer to press on the relevant image on the Notebook page.
- Proceed through the story, reading out the text to the children. On each page, ask them to make their selection, deleting the unwanted pictures and text.
- When the story is complete, re-read it with the children, print it out and make this available for the children to access.

Adult-focused group activity
- Go to page 7. Explain to the group that they are going to create their own story together. Work through the story as in the whole-class activity.
- When the story is complete, save the Notebook file using another name so that it is available to another group.
- Print out the story and help the children to make it into a book, adding a cover and binding it in a way of their choice.

Planned independent activity
- Set up a mark-making area. Hand out copies of photocopiable page 51 and ask the children to cut out chosen pictures and stick them onto a larger sheet of paper to create a storyboard. Provide some extra sheets of paper with blank boxes for the children to use for their own ideas for a character, a house, some items and so on.
- Suggest that the children write captions for their storyboard using emergent writing. Support younger or less confident learners by scribing their ideas if necessary.

Child-initiated activity
- Allow the children regular access to the role-play area that they helped to set up in conjunction with the story. Note whether they go into role as the characters of the story or if they adapt their role play in other ways.

Plenary
- Use the Notebook file to remind the children of the story of Goldilocks.
- Encourage the different groups to share the Notebook files they have created with each other.

CLL Lessons 23 and 24

Circle game

Learning objectives
- ELG: Hear and say sounds in words in the order in which they occur.
- ELG: Link sounds to letters, naming and sounding the letters of the alphabet.

Resources
'Circle game' Notebook file; photocopiable page 52 'Circle game'.

Links to other ELGs
PSED
Work as part of a group or class, taking turns and sharing fairly.
- Monitor the children to check whether they are able to take turns fairly to use the whiteboard tools. Observe whether there are any particularly dominant or shy children.

Introduction
Open page 2 of the Notebook file. Ask the children to name and sound each letter. Demonstrate how the word *cat* can be made by using some of the letters at the bottom of the page. Press on the appropriate letters and drop them into the orange box. Use a Pen from the Pen tray or the On-screen Keyboard to write or type the word on the right-hand side of the page and then drag the letters in the orange box back to their original position at the bottom of the page.

Invite the children to think of another word they could make using some of the letters. Suggest that they share this with their partner. Allow sufficient time for them to discuss their ideas and to agree on one. Invite a pair to come to the board and make the word in the orange box. Before they drag the letters back (ready for the next pair to take a turn), remind them to write the word on the right-hand side so that the group can remember which words have been created. Repeat until all possible words have been created.

Adult-focused group activities
- Arrange the children into groups of six.
- Copy photocopiable page 52 onto card and cut out the individual letters.
- Display page 3 of the Notebook file and hand out the corresponding letters (one letter per child). Tell the children that the first word is *fat*. Point to the word and ask the children to check that the word is correct by saying the individual phonemes and then the whole word.
- Now challenge the children to make the word *pat* in their heads, by changing one of the letters in the word *fat*. Ask what letter they took away and which letter they added to change the word.
- Invite the children to look at the letter that they are holding. Is it the one that was needed to make the word *pat*? Ask the child holding the letter *p* to come to the whiteboard to change the word in the red box.
- Ask everyone to check that the word is correct by sounding out the word together. Ask the child at the board to write the new word under the word *fat* on the right-hand side of the page.
- Explain to the children that the challenge they are going to take part in is to keep making new words by only changing one phoneme at a time. They must try to think of all the words they can using the letters on the Notebook page, and get back to the word *fat* at the end.
- Repeat the process with the group, so that the children create the words in the sequence: *fat, pat, cat, can, pan, fan, fat*.
- Make sure that each child has the opportunity to use the tools on the whiteboard. Support younger or less confident learners by writing out the new words for them if necessary.
- Repeat the activity in the next session, using pages 4 to 11 as appropriate with your groups. The children will need to be told that *ck* and *ee* are single phonemes that can be replaced or added as though they are one letter. The following word lists can be created from the pages:
  - Page 4: *shop, ship, tip, tap, tack, back, bat, cat, cap, cop, shop*
  - Page 5: *song, sing, ring, rung, sung, sang, bang, back, sack, sick, sock, song*
  - Page 6: *slip, clip, flip, flap, slap, slack, black, flack, flick, slick, slip*
  - Page 7: *best, belt, bent, pent, pelt, melt, met, net, nest, best*
  - Page 8: *list, lift, gift, gilt, silt, silk, sink, rink, rick, lick, lip, lisp, list*
  - Page 9: *teen, tin, sin, seen, seep, steep, sleep, slip, tip, tin, teen*
  - Page 10: *born, corn, cord, ford, fort, port, pork, fork, cork, stork, storm, torn, born*

CLL Lessons 23 and 24

- Page 11: *mice, mine, line, life, wife, wine, wipe, wide, hide, hike, mike, mice.*
- Display an appropriate page for the children to work on. Help them to generate their own word list by changing one letter (or phoneme) at a time as you did together in the previous lesson.
- Explain that at the end of the session the children will be able to share their work with the rest of the class. Ensure that you save their work in a separate file.

Planned independent activities
- Provide the materials for the children to make small word-family books. For example, take the rime *-at* and create the *at* family, with each page of a mini book containing a picture of an object that ends in *-at* (such as a cat, a hat, a bat and a mat).
- Place rhyming objects in a feely bag. Show the children the first object and ask them to name it. Then provide clues for the subsequent objects, encouraging the children to guess what it might be. For example, show the children a soft toy cat and then describe a hat, a bat and a mat that are hidden in the feely bag.
- Concentrate on a different rhyme each week and encourage the children to play the game with a partner.
- Design a simple word search for older or more confident learners, hiding words from a group, such as words that rhyme with *ring* in a grid of letters. The children must highlight or circle the words when they find them.

Child-initiated activity
- Provide appropriate letter collections and have these available in your writing or mark-making area, so that the children can practise making words of their own.

Plenary
- Open pages that the children have worked on to create their own lists and celebrate their work.
- Read down the lists, discussing which letter they have changed to make each new word.
- Talk together about the difference between words that begin with the same letter and words that rhyme together. Ask: *Do words that rhyme have to start with the same letter sound? Which bit of the word needs to sound the same for it to rhyme with another?*
- Use page 12 of the Notebook file to record the children's comments.

Whiteboard tools
The On-screen Keyboard, accessed through the Pen tray or the SMART Board tools menu, can be used to input letters to type the new words on page 2 of the Notebook file.

- Pen tray
- Select tool
- On-screen Keyboard

CLL Lessons 25 and 26

Kim's game

Learning objectives
- Development matters (Linking Sounds and Letters): Continue a rhyming string.
- ELG: Use their phonic knowledge to write simple regular words.

Resources
'Kim's game' Notebook file; individual whiteboards and pens; a tray of objects.

Links to other ELGs
PSRN
Use everyday words to describe position.
- Encourage the children to talk about the position of the objects on the page or on the tray, as another device to help them to remember which object is missing.

Introduction
Display page 2 of the Notebook file and ask the children to say the sounds of the letters *(r, c, m, b, h)* as you point to them.

Next, say a sound and invite a child to come and point to it on the whiteboard page. Let that child say another sound, without pointing to it, and ask a further child to come up and point to that sound.

Now invite the children, in pairs, to blend the two letters *a* and *t* to find the rime. Invite one pair to tell you what it is. Ask the class to check this by sounding the individual letters and blending them.

Adult-focused whole-class activities
- Go to page 3. Ensure that the children are sure what each picture represents. Point to a picture at a time and invite the children to name the object *(rat, cat, bat, hat, mat)*.
- Demonstrate how you can move the individual letters and the *-at* rime together to create words. Choose one of the objects on the page and move it next to the rime. Select the appropriate letter (the onset) to make the word. Ask the children to say the word with you. Ask: *Is this the right word to match this picture?*
- Next, make a deliberate mistake and create a word that does not match the picture. Ask the children to tell you what you need to do to make the right word.
- Press the Undo button until the page is reset and invite a volunteer to have a go at making a word to match one of the pictures on the whiteboard. Say the word together and check that it matches the picture.
- Continue in this way until all the pictures have been named.
- Say all the words in a list as you point to each picture. What do the children notice about the words? (They rhyme and they use the same spelling pattern.) Listen to the children's explanations and ideas and jot down notes about any children who show particularly good understanding or who will need some extra help.
- Ask the children if they can think of any more words that belong to this family of words. Write down any further suggestions on the whiteboard page. Look carefully at the spelling patterns of the words that the children have suggested. Are they the same?
- Go to page 4 of the Notebook file. Explain to the children that you would like them to try to make some more words that rhyme with *at*. Invite them to tell you how they think they could do this. Show them an example, by dragging the rime *(-at)* and dropping it behind one of the letters (the onset). Ask: *What word have I made?*
- Provide the children with individual whiteboards and pens and ask them to have a go at making some words using the letters and rime displayed on the whiteboard.
- Share some of the children's ideas and invite individuals to come to the board to demonstrate how they made one of their words. Ensure that the children realise that *gat* isn't a real word.
- Go to page 5 to begin the second session. Remind the children of the words that rhyme with *at* that they have already made in the previous lesson. Invite a child to explain how he/she made those words.
- Explain that you would like the children to repeat the activity from the previous session, using their individual whiteboards to write down the words that they can make using the letters available.
- Repeat the activity using page 6 of the Notebook file. Explain that you would like the children to make as many *-at* words as possible.

CLL Lessons 25 and 26

Adult-focused group activities
- Display page 7 of the Notebook file. Read the words underneath each picture. Encourage the children to read them rhythmically with you: *hat, cat, mat, bat, rat*. Chant this with the children a few times.
- Explain to the children that you are now going to hide the objects with a blind. Tell them that when it goes up, one of the objects will be missing! They must think hard to try and work out which object is missing.
- Remind the children of the objects by repeating the chant.
- Go to page 8 and pull the Screen Shade up slowly from the bottom. Ask: *What object is missing?* Repeat the chant to help the children work out the answer.
- Go back to page 7, look at the objects, then go to page 9. Pull the screen up slowly to display the objects on the page. Again, use the chant to help the children work out which object is missing.
- Repeat the game on pages 10, 11 and 12.
- Suggest that pairs of older or more confident learners play the same game using pages 13 to 18 and 19 to 24 of the Notebook file.
- Finish with a fun session of playing a variation of Kim's game with real objects. If possible, find five objects that rhyme and place them on a tray. Talk with the children about the objects. Ask them to shut their eyes while you remove one object. Talk about the objects and see if they can work out which object is missing. Once they have worked it out, replace the object. Repeat, removing a different object each time.

Planned independent activity
- Leave the tray of objects available to play Kim's game. Encourage the children to gather their own group of five objects that they can use when they play the game.

Plenary
- Go to page 25. Remind the children how they can select an initial sound and a rime to make words. Repeat the activity that the children completed earlier in the lesson (making *-at* words), but this time they are going to make words with the rime *-an*.
- If appropriate, use page 26 (featuring the rime *-ed*) with the children. Be prepared to discuss the spellings of words such as *head* and *said* that rhyme, but are spelled differently.

Whiteboard tools
Use the Screen Shade to hide the objects on the screen in the group activity.

- Pen tray
- Select tool
- Screen Shade
- Undo button

CLL Lesson 27

Making words

Learning objective
- ELG: Hear and say sounds in words in the order in which they occur.

Resources
'Making words' Notebook file; photocopiable page 53 'Make words'.

Links to other ELGs
CD
Use their imagination in art and design.
- Encourage the children to draw pictures of common CVC words. Make letter cards to go underneath the picture and suggest that the children jumble up the letters and challenge a partner to put the letters in the order of the word that matches the object.

Whiteboard tools
- Pen tray
- Select tool

Introduction
Provide each child with a copy of photocopiable page 53. Help them to cut out the letter cards on the right-hand side of the page so that each child has a set of six letter cards.

Explain to the children that you would like them to put the letters in the phoneme frame to spell different words. Tell them that the first word is *cat*. Ask the children to talk to their partner and decide what is the initial sound needed to make the word *cat*. Invite one of the children to tell you what sound this is and then ask the class to agree whether this is correct. Once everyone is agreed on the letter, ask the children to place the correct letter card in the initial position on the phoneme frame on their photocopiable sheets.

Now ask the children to discuss with their partner the next sound in the word. Again, they should place this letter card in the correct position on the phoneme frame. Finally, ask them to discuss the final sound in the word and place the letter card in the final position on the phoneme frame.

Repeat with different words.

Adult-focused whole-class activity
- Display page 2 of the Notebook file. Explain to the children that they need to make the word *rat* using the letters available. Show them that by pressing on each letter they can listen to the sound it makes and by pressing on the picture they can listen to the word they are supposed to make.
- Encourage the children to talk to their partner and decide what is the initial sound needed to make the word *rat*. Invite a volunteer to tell you what sound this is and ask him/her to press on the letter to find the sound.
- Invite the child to press on the coloured strip at the foot of the letter and move it to the initial position in the phoneme frame.
- Repeat for the remaining letters.

Adult-focused group activity
- Practise this procedure to make other words, using pages 3 to 10 of the Notebook file.
- Go to page 11. Explain that the children need to make the word *sun* using the letters, but that this time there are too many letters. Help them to do this and continue to support them as they work through pages 11 to 16.

Plenary
- Go to page 17. Check that the word *dog* has been made correctly in the phoneme frame. Explain that the remaining letters may also be arranged to make a word.
- Ask the children to say each sound and invite them to help you to arrange the letters to make the word *dog*. Ask: *What word can we make with the remaining letters?*
- Move the remaining letters together in a row. Ask the children to discuss with their partner whether this makes a word.
- Select one of the pairs to tell the rest of the group their decision. Ask another child to re-arrange the letters to make a word. What does the word say? Say it together.
- Repeat this activity on pages 18 and 19.

CLL Lessons 28 and 29

Shopping lists

Learning objectives
- Development matters (Writing): Use writing as a means of recording and communicating.
- ELG: Know that print carries meaning.
- ELG: Attempt writing for different purposes, using features of different forms such as lists.

Resources
'Recipes' Notebook file; photocopiable page 54 'Recipes'; digital camera; selection of recipe books; pens, pencils and paper.

Links to other ELGs
PD
Use a range of small and large equipment.
- Encourage the children to explore a range of child-friendly cooking equipment during the making of the biscuits as well as in their role play.

Introduction
Ask the children to tell you about any cooking experiences they have had at home. Ask: *Did the grown-up who was helping you use a recipe to cook from? What do you think a recipe is?*

Read out a few pieces of writing, one of which is a recipe. Ask the children to tell you which piece of writing was the recipe. Ask: *How do you know it is a recipe?*

Have a number of recipe books available. Look at these and draw attention to the common format that most recipes have. Draw the children's attention to the list of ingredients. Ask them why they think it is important to read the list of ingredients before using the recipe. Explain that you need to know what is in the recipe so that you can ensure that you have all the ingredients, in case you need to go shopping to get any missing items.

Adult-focused whole-class activity
- Open page 2 of the Notebook file. Explain that this is the first part of a recipe for 'Face biscuits'.
- Point out the title and remind the children of the elements needed to write a recipe. Ask: *What do you need to check before you begin cooking?* (The ingredients, to make sure that you have everything you need.)
- Discuss the recipe that can be seen on page 3. Do the children think it contains all the elements needed in order to help someone make the biscuits?
- Next, go to page 4 of the Notebook file and read the ingredients. Point out that the ingredients are written in a list format.
- Go to page 5 and point out each ingredient that needs to be written on the shopping list.
- Invite a child to come to the board, double-press on the text and select the first item on the list (butter). This word can then be dragged into the blank space on the right-hand side of the page.
- Repeat this process with the remaining ingredients that need to be added to the shopping list. Check together that all the items have been included on the list.
- Save the Notebook page and print it out.

Adult-focused group activities
- Either arrange for an adult to take a group to a shop with the shopping list (page 5 of the Notebook file) to buy the ingredients or order the ingredients at one of the supermarket online shops.
- Use the bought ingredients to make the biscuits with the children. Refer to the recipe at each stage of the process. Which parts of the recipe did the children find particularly helpful during the process?
- Take a digital photograph of each stage of the process to use during the second session.
- Enjoy the finished biscuits at snack time. (**Important note:** Check for any food allergies beforehand.)

Planned independent group activities
- For the next session, upload the digital photographs from the biscuit-making exercise to the computer.
- Arrange the children into small groups. Look at each photograph with them and discuss what each one depicts.
- Read the first two instructions of the recipe at the top of page 6. Ask the children to discuss with their partner which photograph should illustrate

CLL Lessons 28 and 29

the page. Invite one of the children to move his/her chosen photograph to the page. Ask the rest of the group to discuss whether they think the photograph chosen is appropriate.
- Repeat the process for pages 7 to 12.
- Review pages 6 to 12. Ask the children to agree whether they are happy with the photographs.
- Print two copies of pages 6 to 12 and two copies of page 4. Bind one set of pages and make them available for the children to review.
- Laminate the second set of printed pages and have them available as separate laminated sheets. Invite the children to put the pages in the correct order so that someone could use the recipes. Ask them which page they think needs to come first, and why. (The list of ingredients.)

Planned independent activities
- Set up a grocery shop and a kitchen role-play area. Make copies of photocopiable page 54, cut to separate the different recipes and laminate. Put these in the kitchen area along with recipe books, pens, pencils and paper.
- Encourage the children to make a shopping list, using the laminated recipe sheets. Invite them to take the list to the shop role-play area, to 'buy' the ingredients and then take these to the kitchen area to 'bake' the food.

Plenary
- Go to page 13. Ask the children to think about their recipe. Ask: *How did you make it? What did you need to do?* Refer back to pages 2 to 5 if necessary, to remind the children of what they did with the 'Face biscuits' recipe and shopping list.
- Discuss how the children made the biscuits. Ask them to use the words from the recipe as they describe how they were made.

Whiteboard tools
Upload digital images by selecting Insert, then Picture File, and browsing to where you have saved the images.

- Pen tray
- Select tool

CLL Lesson 30

Robotic words

Learning objective
- ELG: Read a range of familiar and common words independently.

Resources
'Robotic words' Notebook file; tools and materials in the workshop area for children to make their own robots.

Links to other ELGs
KUW
Build and construct with a wide range of objects, selecting appropriate resources, and adapting their work where necessary.
- Help the children to select appropriate resources to make a model robot. Challenge more confident learners to make moving robots made from card with paper fasteners added to create jointed limbs.

Introduction
Gather a collection of objects/soft toys that fit into the CVC spelling pattern, such as a mug, a can, a mat, a jug, a dog and a cat. Show the objects to the children, one at a time, and ensure that the children know what they all are.

Display page 2 of the Notebook file. Ask the children what the picture shows. (A robot.) Invite a volunteer to speak how they think a robot might speak. Listen to various suggestions and then explain carefully how this robot speaks (by saying the sound of each letter individually). Demonstrate by pointing to one of the objects that you have just shown the children, saying each letter individually. For example: *j - u - g*.

Explain to the children that you are now going to write the name of one of the objects in the speech bubble. Do this using a Pen from the Pen tray and read it robotically. Ask the children to repeat this and then to blend the phonemes to make the word.

Use the Eraser from the Pen tray to erase the word in the speech bubble, then write the name of another object and repeat. Ask the children to sound out each letter and then to say the word with you.

Adult-focused group activity
- Display page 3 of the Notebook file. Press on the first word and listen to the robot speak.
- Remind the children of how the robot speaks and suggest that they can use the sounds that the robot makes to work out what each word is and then match it to the correct picture.
- Make sure that the children know what each picture represents and show them that if they are unsure of what a picture is they may press on it and hear the word.
- Support the children, as necessary, to move the words to match the pictures on page 3. Show them how to use the Lines tool to add arrows to link the words to the pictures.

Planned independent group activity
- Arrange the children in pairs or small groups. Allow them to take turns to work through pages 4 to 11 of the Notebook file.

Planned independent activity
- In the workshop area, provide a variety of tools and materials with which the children can make their own robots.
- Suggest that they make up a voice for their robot, where the robot says one letter at a time.
- Encourage the children to work with a partner and use real objects, sounding out each letter separately as they spell each word. Ask them to invite their partner to guess the word they have made.

Plenary
- Review the work that the children undertook, using the pages of the Notebook file.
- Make sure that everyone understands how to sound out the robot's phonemes and can match the words to the pictures accurately.

Whiteboard tools
Use a Pen from the Pen tray to write words in the speech bubble in the Introduction.

- Pen tray
- Select tool
- Lines tool

Classroom labels (1)

Wash your hands here.

Hang up your coats here.

Read your book here.

CLL LESSON 2

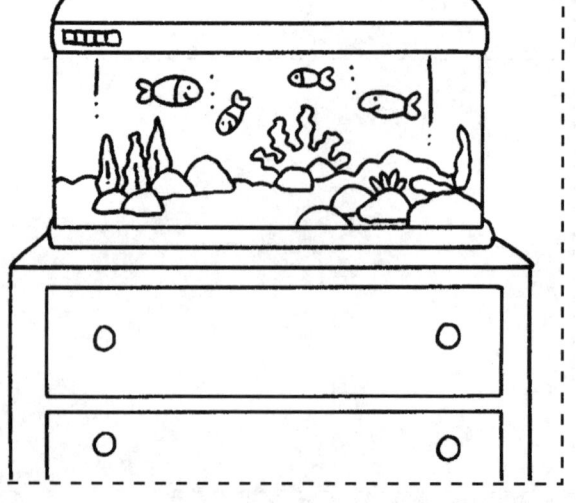

Classroom labels (2)

CLL LESSONS 3 & 4

Alphabet

a	b	c	d
e	f	g	h
i	j	k	l
m	n	o	p
q	r	s	t
u	v	w	x
	y	z	

CLL • LESSON 5

Rhyming sounds

What nursery rhyme am I from?

CLL LESSONS 8 & 9

Bear hunt map

CLL LESSONS 10 & 11   Name _____

Captions

- Write captions for the pictures in the boxes provided.

Greeting cards

What is happening in these pictures?

CLL LESSONS 16 & 17

Sequences

■ Put these pictures in order.

Instructions

- Cut out the pictures. Stick them on paper in the right order.
- Write instructions for each picture.

CLL LESSONS 20 & 21   Name _____

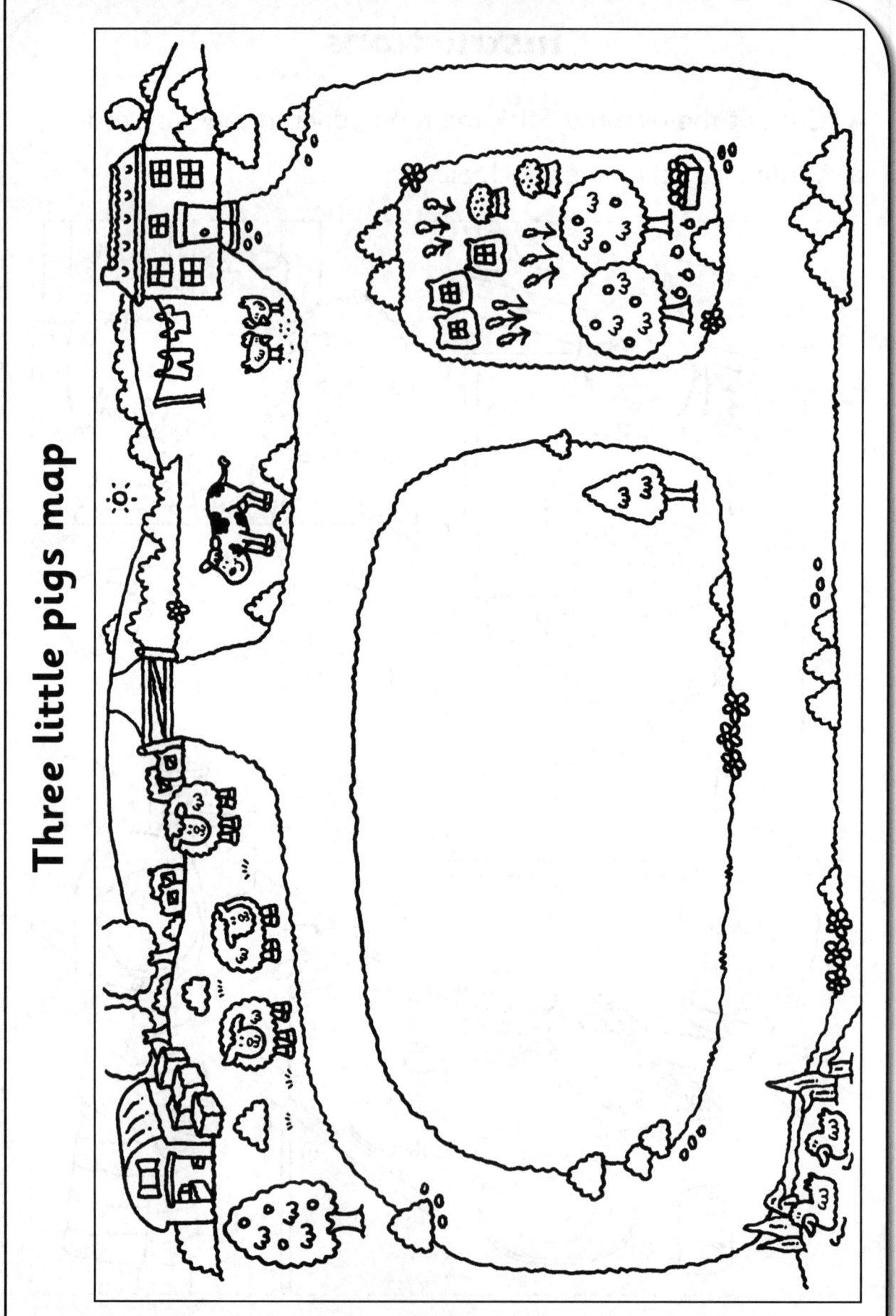

Three little pigs map

Goldilocks

■ Choose some pictures and cut them out.

CLL LESSONS 23 & 24

Circle game

Use these letters to make new words.

f	a
c	t
n	p

52 PHOTOCOPIABLE
100 SMART Board™ LESSONS • YEAR R

SCHOLASTIC
www.scholastic.co.uk

CLL LESSON 27   Name _____

c	a	t
m	r	n

Make words

- Cut out the letters. Put the letters in the frame to spell words.

Recipes

Tasty spuds

Ingredients:

4 large baking potatoes

butter

tin of tuna

small tin of sweetcorn

2–3 tablespoons mayonnaise

black pepper

What to do:

1. Ask an adult to pre-heat the oven to 200°C or Gas Mark 6.
2. Ask an adult to help you to prick the potatoes with a fork.
3. Ask an adult to place them directly onto the oven shelf. They need to cook for around one hour.
4. Mix together the tuna, sweetcorn, mayonnaise and a pinch of black pepper.
5. When the potatoes are cooked, ask an adult to cut a cross shape on them.
6. Fill with a little butter and some of the tuna mixture.
7. Enjoy!

Quick buns

Ingredients:

6oz self-raising flour

4oz soft butter

4oz soft brown sugar

2 eggs

To decorate:

Icing

Chocolate drops

What to do

1. Ask an adult to preheat the oven to 190°C/Gas Mark 5.
2. Sift the flour into a mixing bowl.
3. Add butter, sugar and eggs. Beat well until mixture is thick and glossy.
4. Add a little milk if required.
5. Put the mixture into paper cases in a bun tin.
6. Bake for 15 minutes, or until golden brown.
7. Ice and decorate.

PSRN Chapter 2

Problem solving, reasoning and numeracy

Introduction
This chapter provides 30 lessons based on objectives from the Early Learning Goals, taken from the *Early Years Foundation Stage*, for Problem solving, Reasoning and Numeracy.

The lessons show how the interactive whiteboard can be used to teach and model new mathematical concepts clearly for the whole class to see. There are also opportunities to reinforce and consolidate concepts and the Notebook files present the subject in a clear, lively and stimulating manner.

The lessons encourage the children to be actively involved in their learning by asking them to make choices by highlighting, writing and typing, and manipulating and moving objects around the screen.

Lesson title	Objectives	Cross-curricular links
Lesson 1: Counting small objects	**Development matters (Numbers as Labels and for Counting)** Show curiosity about numbers by offering comments or asking questions. **Development matters (Numbers as Labels and for Counting)** Use some number names accurately in play. **ELG** Count reliably up to ten everyday objects.	**KUW** Investigate objects and materials by using all of their senses as appropriate.
Lesson 2: Counting more	**Development matters (Numbers as Labels and for Counting)** Count an irregular arrangement of up to ten objects. **ELG** Count reliably up to ten everyday objects.	**KUW** Investigate objects and materials by using all of their senses as appropriate.
Lesson 3: Zero	**Development matters (Calculating)** Know that a group of things changes in quantity when something is added or taken away. **Development matters (Calculating)** Show an interest in number problems. **ELG** Begin to use the vocabulary involved in adding and subtracting.	**CLL** Listen with enjoyment, and respond to stories, songs and other music, rhymes and poems and make up their own songs, rhymes and poems.
Lesson 4: Estimating	**Development matters (Numbers as Labels and for Counting)** Estimate how many objects they can see and check by counting. **ELG** Count reliably up to ten everyday objects.	**KUW** Build and construct with a wide range of objects, selecting appropriate resources, and adapting their work where necessary.
Lesson 5: Reading numerals	**Development matters (Numbers as Labels and for Counting)** Recognise numerals 1 to 5. **ELG** Recognise numerals 1 to 9.	**KUW** Observe, find out about and identify features in the place they live and the natural world.
Lesson 6: Recording how many	**Development matters (Numbers as Labels and for Counting)** Begin to represent numbers using fingers, marks on paper or pictures. **ELG** Recognise numerals 1 to 9.	**CLL** Attempt writing for different purposes, using features of different forms such as lists, stories and instructions.
Lesson 7: Writing numerals	**Development matters (Numbers as Labels and for Counting)** Sometimes match number and quantity correctly. **Development matters (Numbers as Labels and for Counting)** Begin to represent numbers using fingers, marks on paper or pictures. **ELG** Recognise numerals 1 to 9.	**CLL** Attempt writing for different purposes, using features of different forms such as lists, stories and instructions.

PSRN Chapter 2

Lesson title	Objectives	Cross-curricular links
Lesson 8: Comparing quantities	**Development matters (Calculating)** Begin to make comparisons between quantities. **Development matters (Calculating)** Compare two groups of objects, saying when they have the same number. **ELG** Use language such as *more* or *less* to compare two numbers.	**CD** Use their imagination in art and design, music, dance, imaginative and role play and stories.
Lesson 9: What fits?	**Development matters (Numbers as Labels and for Counting)** Use some number language such as *more* and *a lot*. **ELG** Use language such as *more* or *less* to compare two numbers.	**CD** Use their imagination in art and design, music, dance, imaginative and role play and stories.
Lesson 10: Ordering numbers	**Development matters (Numbers as Labels and for Counting)** Count up to three or four objects by saying one number name for each item. **ELG** Say and use number names in order in familiar contexts.	**KUW** Find out about and identify the uses of everyday technology and use information and communication technology and programmable toys to support their learning.
Lesson 11: Ordering selected numbers	**Development matters (Numbers as Labels and for Counting)** Use some number names accurately in play. **Development matters (Numbers as Labels and for Counting)** Know that numbers identify how many objects are in a set. **ELG** Say and use number names in order in familiar contexts.	**KUW** Look closely at similarities, differences, patterns and change.
Lesson 12: Ordinal numbers	**Development matters (Numbers as Labels and for Counting)** Use ordinal numbers in different contexts. **ELG** Say and use number names in order in familiar contexts.	**CD** Recognise and explore how sounds can be changed, sing simple songs from memory, recognise repeated sounds and sound patterns and match movements to music.
Lesson 13: Word problems	**Development matters (Calculating)** Compare two groups of objects, saying when they have the same number. **Development matters (Calculating)** State the number that is one more than a given number. **ELG** Find one more or one less than a number from one to ten.	**PD** Move with confidence, imagination and in safety.
Lesson 14: Combining two groups	**Development matters (Calculating)** Know that a group of things changes in quantity when something is added or taken away. **Development matters (Calculating)** Find the total number of items in two groups by counting all of them. **ELG** Begin to relate addition to combining two groups of objects and subtraction to *taking away*.	**KUW** Look closely at similarities, differences, patterns and change.
Lesson 15: Combining three groups	**Development matters (Calculating)** Count repeated groups of the same size. **ELG** Begin to relate addition to combining two groups of objects and subtraction to *taking away*.	**PSED** Select and use activities and resources independently.
Lesson 16: Counting on	**Development matters (Calculating)** Know that a group of things changes in quantity when something is added or taken away. **ELG** Begin to use the vocabulary involved in adding and subtracting.	**PSED** Work as part of a group or class, taking turns and sharing fairly.
Lesson 17: Doubling	**Development matters (Calculating)** Find the total number of items in two groups by counting all of them. **Development matters (Calculating)** Count repeated groups of the same size. **ELG** Begin to relate addition to combining two groups of objects.	**PSED** Work as part of a group or class, taking turns and sharing fairly.
Lesson 18: Totals	**Development matters (Calculating)** Find the total number of items in two groups by counting all of them. **ELG** Begin to relate addition to combining two groups of objects.	**KUW** Investigate objects and materials by using all of their senses as appropriate.

PSRN Chapter 2

Lesson title	Objectives	Cross-curricular links
Lesson 19: Partitioning	**Development matters (Calculating)** Share objects into equal groups and count how many in each group. **ELG** Begin to use the vocabulary involved in adding and subtracting.	**KUW** Find out about their environment, and talk about those features they like and dislike.
Lesson 20: Given totals	**Development matters (Calculating)** Select two groups of objects to make a given total of objects. **ELG** Begin to relate addition to combining two groups of objects.	**CD** Recognise repeated sounds and sound patterns.
Lesson 21: Taking away	**Development matters (Calculating)** Show an interest in number problems. **Development matters (Calculating)** Know that a group of things changes in quantity when something is added or taken away. **ELG** Begin to relate subtraction to *taking away*.	**PSED** Work as part of a group or class, taking turns and sharing fairly.
Lesson 22: Counting back	**Development matters (Calculating)** Know that a group of things changes in quantity when something is added or taken away. **ELG** Begin to use the vocabulary involved in adding and subtracting.	**PSED** Work as part of a group or class, taking turns and sharing fairly.
Lesson 23: How many have gone?	**Development matters (Calculating)** Know that a group of things changes in quantity when something is added or taken away. **ELG** Begin to use the vocabulary involved in adding and subtracting.	**PD** Handle tools, objects, construction and malleable materials safely and with increasing control.
Lesson 24: How many more?	**Development matters (Calculating)** Show an interest in number problems. **ELG** Use language such as *more* or *less* to compare two numbers.	**CLL** Sustain attentive listening, responding to what they have heard with relevant comments, questions or actions.
Lesson 25: Making patterns	**Development matters (Shape, Space and Measures)** Show an interest in shape and space by making arrangements with objects. **ELG** Talk about, recognise and recreate simple patterns. **ELG** Use developing mathematical ideas and methods to solve practical problems.	**CD** Explore colour, texture, shape, form and space in two or three dimensions.
Lesson 26: Sorting	**Development matters (Shape, Space and Measures)** Sort objects, making choices and justifying decisions. **ELG** Use developing mathematical ideas and methods to solve practical problems.	**KUW** Look closely at similarities, differences, patterns and change.
Lesson 27: Coins	**Development matters (Calculating)** Show an interest in number problems. **ELG** Begin to use the vocabulary involved in adding and subtracting.	**CLL** Attempt writing for different purposes, using features of different forms such as lists.
Lesson 28: 3D shapes	**Development matters (Shape, Space and Measures)** Begin to use mathematical names for solid 3D shapes and flat 2D shapes, and mathematical terms to describe shapes. **ELG** Use language such as *circle* or *bigger* to describe the shape and size of solids and flat shapes.	**PD** Handle tools, objects, construction and malleable materials safely and with increasing control.
Lesson 29: 2D shapes	**Development matters (Shape, Space and Measures)** Begin to use mathematical names for flat 2D shapes, and mathematical terms to describe shapes. **ELG** Use language such as *circle* or *bigger* to describe the shape and size of solids and flat shapes.	**PD** Handle tools, objects, construction and malleable materials safely and with increasing control.
Lesson 30: Ordering by size	**Development matters (Shape, Space and Measures)** Order two or three items by length or height. **ELG** Use developing mathematical ideas and methods to solve practical problems.	**PD** Use a range of small and large equipment.

PSRN Lesson 1

Counting small objects

Learning objectives
- Development matters (Numbers as Labels and for Counting): Show curiosity about numbers by offering comments or asking questions.
- Development matters (Numbers as Labels and for Counting): Use some number names accurately in play.
- ELG: Count reliably up to ten everyday objects.

Resources
'Build your own' file; five small counting toys for each pair; photocopiable page 88 'Counting mat. Use the 'Build your own' file, which consists of a blank Notebook page and a collection of Gallery resources located in the My Content folder, to prepare a Noteboook file showing sets of one, two, three and four objects in different arrangements (save each set on a separate page).

Links to other ELGs
KUW
Investigate objects and materials by using all of their senses as appropriate.
- Use sets of natural materials such as fir cones and shells when sorting and counting.

Whiteboard tools
Use the Screen Shade to hide and reveal sets of objects.
- Pen tray
- Select tool
- Gallery
- Screen Shade

Introduction
Say the numbers one to five together. Keep a good pace. Then, in a circle, encourage the children to say the number names in turn, one after the other, so that each child has a turn at saying a number in order from one to five. Repeat this several times, keeping a good pace. If a child falters, say the number for them. Over time extend the range to up to ten.

Adult-focused whole-class activities
- Explain that you are going to show the children a set of objects for a few seconds and that you would like them to tell you how many there are.
- Open your prepared Notebook file (see Resources) and show the children the first set of objects. Display the first set for no more than five seconds, then use the Screen Shade to hide the objects.
- Ask: *How many did you see?* Reveal the set again and invite the children to check that they were correct. If they are unsure, count the set together, pointing to each item in turn.
- Repeat the process, using your other prepared Notebook pages. This activity encourages the children to use the skill of recognising small numbers without counting, so limit the display of each page to no more than five seconds.

Adult-focused group activity
- Arrange for the children to work in pairs. Provide each pair with five counting toys and a copy of photocopiable page 88.
- Explain that the children are to take turns to place some of the toys onto the counting mat. Their partner must look and, without counting by touching or pointing, say how many toys there are. The children may check by touching and moving if they disagree on the number of toys.
- Work with a group of younger or less confident learners, beginning with sets of one, two and three objects.
- Challenge older or more confident learners to place four and five objects in a variety of different ways.

Child-initiated activity
- Colour and laminate the counting mats and leave them in your counting area along with child-friendly sets of natural objects such as shells, feathers and shiny pebbles.

Plenary
- Use the 'Build your own' file to prepare some more Notebook pages with sets of up to five objects. Move to the next page with another set of objects. Hide the objects with the Screen Shade after four seconds.
- Ask the children how they worked out the number of objects that they saw. Discuss how they may recognise small quantities without counting. Emphasise that this is a very useful skill and that if they know how many there are by looking, then there is no need to count one at a time.
- Reassure the children that it is expected that they will need to count, by touching and moving or pointing, for sets larger than five.

PSRN Lesson 2

Counting more

Learning objectives
- Development matters (Numbers as Labels and for Counting): Count an irregular arrangement of up to ten objects.
- ELG: Count reliably up to ten everyday objects.

Resources
'Build your own' file; photocopiable page 88 'Counting mat' for each pair; up to ten counting toys for each pair; digital camera; mark-making tools.
Use the 'Build your own' file, which consists of a blank Notebook page and a collection of Gallery resources located in the My Content folder, to prepare a Noteboook file showing pictures of one to five items on the first five pages, then four to ten items on the next five pages.

Links to other ELGs
KUW
Investigate objects and materials by using all of their senses as appropriate.
- Sort and count items collected on a nature walk.

Whiteboard tools
Use the Screen Shade to hide and reveal sets of objects. Use a Highlighter pen to check the children's counting. To upload digital photographs to the Notebook file, select Insert, then Picture File, and browse to where you have saved the images. Use the Area Capture tool to separate objects in the digital photographs.

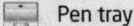

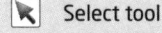

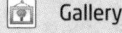

- Pen tray
- Select tool
- Gallery
- Screen Shade
- Highlighter pen
- Area Capture tool

Introduction
Open your prepared Notebook file (see Resources). Go the first page, showing up to five objects. Display the objects for five seconds, then use the Screen Shade to hide them. Invite the children to say how many objects they saw. Repeat for the other quantities up to five. Make a note of the children who 'knew' the number of items without counting.

Adult-focused whole-class activity
- Explain that you are going to reveal some objects for the children to count by pointing.
- Display the first quantity from the 'four to ten' pages of your prepared Notebook file. Demonstrate counting by pointing and agree how many items there are. Note which children are confident with this technique.
- Invite a child who finds this difficult to come to the board and count the items by touching, using a Highlighter pen to touch and count each one.
- Ask questions, such as: *What was the last number you said? So how many are there in this set?*
- Repeat this for other quantities. Ask: *Have you counted all the pictures? Count them in a different order? Are there still the same number? So how many are there in this set?*
- Explain that it is not always possible to count items by touching or moving objects, and that counting by pointing is a very useful skill to have.

Adult-focused group activity
- Arrange for the children to work in pairs. Give each pair a 'Counting mat' (photocopiable page 88) and up to ten counting toys.
- Invite them to take turns in placing a handful of counting toys onto their counting mat. Their partner should count how many toys there are, pointing at the toys rather than touching them. The first child should then check the count by using the touching, moving and saying the quantity strategy.
- Challenge older or more confident learners to count sets larger than ten.
- As the children work, ask: *How many are there? Count them again, starting with this toy. Is there still the same quantity?*

Planned independent activities
- Help the children to use a digital camera to take photos of their arrangements of counting toys.
- Provide mark-making tools and suggest that the children record their counting work in some way.

Plenary
- Upload the photographs from the digital camera and display one of these on a new Notebook page. Ask the following questions:
  - *How many toys can you see?*
  - *How did you count those?*
  - *Come to the front, and point to show us.*
  - *What was the last number you said as you pointed? So how many are there?*
  - *Who counted in a different way?*
  - *Does it matter in what order we count?*
- Use the Area Capture tool to separate the objects in the image by taking snapshots. Ask the children to count the objects again.

PSRN Lesson 3

Zero

Learning objectives
- Development matters (Calculating): Know that a group of things changes in quantity when something is added or taken away.
- Development matters (Calculating): Show an interest in number problems.
- ELG: Begin to use the vocabulary involved in adding and subtracting.

Resources
'Zero' Notebook file; photocopiable page 89 'Ten in the bed'; photocopiable page 88 'Counting mat' and ten counting toys for each child; selection of books and/or CDs of number rhymes.

Links to other ELGs
CLL
Listen with enjoyment, and respond to stories, songs and other music, rhymes and poems and make up their own songs, rhymes and poems.
- Listen to and join in with stories and rhymes which include zero.

Whiteboard tools
Use the Delete button to remove objects from the page.

- Pen tray
- Select tool
- Delete button

Introduction
Open the 'Zero' Notebook file and go to page 2. Tell the following story:
There were ten spots on the ladybird's back. His mother counted the spots. (Count the spots together.) *The next day she counted the spots and this time there were only nine.* (Repeat, counting down by one each time.) *At last the ladybird had no spots.*
At each stage remove one spot from the ladybird's back by using the Delete button (or choosing the Delete option from the dropdown menu).

Adult-focused whole-class activities
- Show the five stars on page 3 and ask the children to count them.
- Remove one of the stars and count again. Repeat, counting each time until there are no stars left.
- Introduce the word *zero*. Explain that the word means *none* or *nothing*. Use the Delete button to reveal the word and definition.
- Repeat the process using pages 4 and 5, counting down the different quantities on the board until zero is reached. (For page 5, drag the cakes into the cake tin instead of removing them.)
- Go to page 6 and press on the star to start playing the song *Ten in the bed*. Continue in this way, through pages 8 to 15, for the duration of the song. Invite the children to hold up their fingers to show how many are left each time. Draw their attention to the numbers displayed as the song counts down from ten.
- When the song ends (on page 15), ask the children how many would be left in the bed if the last one falls out.
- Reveal the answer on page 16: *zero*.

Adult-focused group activities
- Arrange the children to work in groups of four to six with an adult. Each child will need ten counting toys and a 'Counting mat' (photocopiable page 88).
- The adult should specify a number of objects to count out onto the counting mat, then say how many to remove, so that the children experience zero in context. For example: *Put out six onto your counting mat. Now move away four. How many are left? Move away one... and one more. What is left now?*
- Limit the number range to five or six for younger or less confident learners.
- Encourage older or more confident learners to say simple number sentences to describe the work, such as: *I put out six. Now I move away five. I move away one more. Now there is nothing left.*
- Provide each child with a copy of photocopiable page 89. Help them to repeat the counting rhyme with you, covering each person with a counter as they fall out of bed, one at a time!

Child-initiated activity
- Provide books and/or CDs of number rhymes that count down to zero for the children to listen to or look at freely.

Plenary
- Show the set of eight flowers on page 17 of the Notebook file. Invite a child to remove three of them, by selecting each and using the Delete button. Ask: *How many are there now?* Repeat this, asking the children to remove a given quantity each time until there is nothing left.
- Repeat singing or saying *Ten in the bed*, with actions so that the children show that they understand zero, none, or nothing.

PSRN Lesson 4

Estimating

Learning objectives
- Development matters (Numbers as Labels and for Counting): Estimate how many objects they can see and check by counting.
- ELG: Count reliably up to ten everyday objects.

Resources
'Estimating' Notebook file; photocopiable page 88 'Counting mat'; ten counting toys for each pair; transparent boxes and counting objects.

Links to other ELGs
KUW
Build and construct with a wide range of objects, selecting appropriate resources, and adapting their work where necessary.
- Invite the children to estimate how many pieces of a construction kit they have in front of them. Ask them to check by counting using touch, count and move, or point and count techniques.

Whiteboard tools
Use the Screen Shade to hide the images on the pages. Use a Pen from the Pen tray to strike through items on the screen as they are counted.

- Pen tray
- Select tool
- Screen Shade
- Delete button

Introduction
Open the 'Estimating' Notebook file and go to page 2. Explain that you will reveal a set of pictures on the whiteboard. Remove the circles to reveal the objects and ask the children to count how many they can see by pointing. Invite children who are younger or less confident to come and point with you to help them develop this skill. Repeat for page 3. Check the quantities by marking them with a Pen from the Pen tray. Continue this activity over time for quantities up to ten, using pages 4 and 5 of the Notebook file.

Adult-focused whole-class activity
- Explain that you will show the children a set of images on the whiteboard for just a little while.
- Display the set of three images on page 6 of the Notebook file for about five seconds. Then use the Screen Shade to hide the screen. Ask: *How many do you think there were?*
- Reveal the set again, and invite the children to count to check their estimates. Ask: *Did you make a good guess?*
- Now select the objects and press the Delete button to show a different way of organising them. Discuss whether it is easier to estimate and count the objects in this order.
- Repeat this for other quantities (up to ten), using pages 7 to 15 of the Notebook file.

Planned independent group activities
- Ask the children to work in pairs. Give each pair a 'Counting mat' (photocopiable page 88) and ten counting toys.
- Invite the children to take turns in scattering a handful of toys onto the counting mat. Encourage their partner to say straight away how many they think there are, so that there is no time to count.
- Now ask the children to check how many by counting, either by touch, move and count, or point and count (depending upon their skill level or experience of counting).
- As the children work, ask questions such as: *Did you make a good guess? Why did you think that there were five toys?*
- Consider limiting the number range to below six for younger or less confident learners, by providing them with larger counting toys so that they take fewer in a handful.
- For older or more confident learners, decide whether to provide slightly smaller counting toys in order to increase the number range.

Child-initiated activity
- In your counting area, provide transparent boxes with different numbers of objects for the children to explore. Provide extra counting objects and empty boxes and allow the children to play freely with them.

Plenary
- Pages 16 to 20 of the Notebook file contain larger sets of eight to ten images. Continue as before, displaying the page for about five seconds before enabling the Screen Shade and asking the children to make an estimate of how many items they saw.
- Now reveal the images again, this time asking the children to count. Ask: *Did you make a good guess?*
- Use different strategies to check and count. For example, mark the items with a Pen from the Pen tray as they are counted, or position them in a neater arrangement.

PSRN Lesson 5

Reading numerals

Learning objectives
- Development matters (Numbers as Labels and for Counting): Recognise numerals 1 to 5.
- ELG: Recognise numerals 1 to 9.

Resources
'Reading numerals' Notebook file; sorting toys; photocopiable page 88 'Counting mat'; photocopiable page 90 'Reading numerals' copied onto card and cut out to make sets of cards (decide on the range of numbers to provide for each group).

Links to other ELGs
KUW
Observe, find out about and identify features in the place they live and the natural world.
- Encourage the children to identify numbers of personal significance to them, such as their age, house numbers, numbers within their telephone numbers, car number plates and other numbers in their everyday environment.

Whiteboard tools
- Pen tray
- Select tool
- Delete button

Introduction
Go to page 2 of the 'Reading numerals' Notebook file and draw attention to the toys. Ask the children to count, by pointing, to find out how many there are. Invite children who find this skill difficult to come to the board and do this with you. Continue to pages 3 and 4 for other quantities between three and six.

Drag the toys into the toy box, counting one at a time, to confirm the quantities.

Adult-focused whole-class activities
- Display page 5 and ask the children to count by pointing at the images. Invite an individual to come to the whiteboard and use a Pen from the Pen tray to strike through the objects as the children count them. Ask: *What was the last number that you said? So how many are there?*
- Invite another child to use the Eraser from the Pen tray to rub over the first shape to reveal a number. Ask: *What number is this? Does this number match the number of objects?* Let the child rub over the remaining shapes until the matching number is found.
- Repeat for more sets of images and numbers on pages 6 to 9.
- If appropriate, continue with pages 10 to 12, which display sets of eight to ten objects. (You could use these pages in a later session.)
- Go to page 13. Use a Pen from the Pen tray to trace over the number on the page. Encourage the children to read it. Ask them to hold up that number of fingers.
- Repeat this for pages 14 to 17 to practise numbers one to five, and pages 18 to 23 for numbers zero to ten.

Adult-focused group activities
- Arrange for the children to work in groups of four. Provide each group with some counting toys and a set of number cards from photocopiable page 90. Provide each child with a counting mat (from photocopiable page 88).
- The number cards should be placed face down. Invite the children to take turns in turning over a number card. All the children should count out that quantity of toys onto their counting mat.
- After several turns, ask the children to spread their number cards out on the table. Let them take turns in placing some toys onto their mat, with the quantity matching one of the number cards. The other children must count the items and decide which number card matches the quantity.
- To start with, limit the children to numbers up to six (younger or less confident learners to four, and older or more confident to ten).

Child-initiated activities
- Make numbers a visible part of your classroom setting: chalk numbers onto the playground surface and post up numbers to indicate the number of children who may play in an area. Provide cards, chalks and counting materials and allow the children to experiment with them.

Plenary
- Provide each child with a set of 1-6 number cards. Display page 24 on the board. Ask the children to point and count. When you say *Show me*, they must hold up the number that matches the quantity counted.
- Use the Delete button to remove the box to reveal the number on the page for the children to check their answer. Press on the number to hear a cheer to show that it is correct.
- Repeat for different quantities on pages 25 to 29.

PSRN Lesson 6

Recording how many

Learning objectives
- Development matters (Numbers as Labels and for Counting): Begin to represent numbers using fingers, marks on paper or pictures.
- ELG: Recognise numerals 1 to 9.

Resources
'Reading numerals' Notebook file; photocopiable page 91 'Recording how many'; set of 1-10 number cards made from photocopiable page 90 'Reading numerals'.

Links to other ELGs
CLL
Attempt writing for different purposes, using features of different forms such as lists, stories and instructions.
- When the children make lists, encourage them to represent how many items there are by making marks.

Introduction
Choose a set of images from pages 2 to 4 of the 'Reading numerals' Notebook file. Ask the children to count by pointing. Check by counting together, and move each item to the toy box as it is counted so that it is clear what is still to be counted. Repeat for a different quantity.

Adult-focused whole-class activities
- Go to page 5. Ask the children to count how many items are on the page by pointing.
- After the set has been counted, invite a child to use the Eraser from the Pen tray to rub over the shapes on the page until they find the matching number. Use a Pen to draw a circle around the correct number.
- Next, draw a mark over each object on the page. Ask the children to count how many marks you made. Ask: *Are there the same number of marks as objects? So how many objects or marks are there?*
- Repeat the activity, using pages 6 to 12, and gradually build up to counting ten objects in a set. Invite individual children to make the marks to correspond to how many are in the set.
- Move on to page 13 and ask the children to read the number (3). Make three marks on the page and encourage the children to count them. Establish that the number of marks is the same as the number on the page.
- Use pages 14 to 23 to reinforce this concept.

Planned independent group activity
- Provide each child with a copy of photocopiable page 91. Explain that they must read the number and draw that number of marks. Alternatively, the children may like to draw some small pictures to represent how many.
- Ask an adult to work with younger or less confident learners as a group. Provide them with an A3 enlargement of the activity sheet. Suggest that the children count out some counting toys for each number before making marks to represent how many.
- Challenge older or more confident learners to choose their own quantities of counting toys, recording how many they have by making marks of their own choice on the back of the sheet.

Plenary
- Provide some further counting by pointing practice, using pages 24 to 29.
- Choose individuals to come to the board to count and make marks to represent the number of objects in the set. Ask them to choose a number card to represent the quantity. Delete the box to reveal the number on the page.
- Ask: *How many marks are there? How many are in the set?* Agree that the quantities of images and marks match, and that the number represents how many. Repeat for other quantities.
- Use the Random Number Generator from the Gallery to generate some random numbers for the children to count. Ask them to match the quantities to the correct number card.

Whiteboard tools
Use the Random Number Generator from the Gallery to generate some numbers in the Plenary session.

- Pen tray
- Select tool
- Delete button
- Gallery

PSRN Lesson 7

Writing numerals

Learning objectives
- Development matters (Numbers as Labels and for Counting): Sometimes match number and quantity correctly.
- Development matters (Numbers as Labels and for Counting): Begin to represent numbers using fingers, marks on paper or pictures.
- ELG: Recognise numerals 1 to 9.

Resources
'Writing numerals' Notebook file; set of number cards made from photocopiable page 90 'Reading numerals'; photocopiable page 92 'Writing numerals'; individual whiteboards and pens; counting toys; mark-making implements.

Links to other ELGs
CLL
Attempt writing for different purposes, using features of different forms such as lists, stories and instructions.
- Suggest that the children practise writing numerals when making lists. Similarly, when working with the sand, they can write numerals in the sand, using a finger or the handle of a spade.

Whiteboard tools
Use the Eraser from the Pen tray to reveal hidden answers.

- Pen tray
- Select tool
- Delete button

Introduction
Prepare sets of number cards provided on photocopiable page 90. Invite six volunteers to each hold a number card from 1 to 6. Reveal a set of one to six objects from pages 2 to 7 of the 'Writing numerals' Notebook file. Invite the children to count by pointing. Ask them to hold up the correct number card. Then delete the box to reveal the number on the page for them to check their answer. Press on the number to hear a cheer, indicating that the children are correct. Repeat for other quantities between one and six.

Adult-focused whole-class activities
- Go to page 8 and explain that you will write a number on the whiteboard. Invite the children to 'write' the same number, in the air, with large arm movements.
- Use the Eraser from the Pen tray to erase your writing and repeat for all the numbers one to six. Over time, extend to up to ten.
- Reveal the set on page 9 of the Notebook file. Ask the children to count the objects by pointing. Then write the number to match the quantity on the whiteboard. Ask the children to write it in the air with you.
- Repeat for other quantities and numbers on pages 10 to 13.
- Return to page 8 and erase your writing. Provide the children with individual whiteboards and pens. Ask them to write the number that you say on their whiteboards. Write it at the same time as they do, on page 8, to remind them how to form the number correctly.
- Repeat for other numbers up to seven.

Adult-focused group activities
- Ask the children to work in pairs. Provide each child with a copy of photocopiable page 92.
- Invite the children to take turns to take some counting toys and count them. They should then write the number and draw the toys or make marks to represent how many.
- Vary the number of counting toys to suit the children's different abilities. Most children should have six toys; fewer for younger or less confident learners and up to ten for older or more confident learners.

Child-initiated activities
- Equip your number area with mark-making implements such as chalk and boards, as well as a range of tactile numbers including plastic numbers, magnetic numbers, number stencils and number cards. Allow the children to explore the resources freely and independently.
- After a discussion about numbers all around us, pin up a display of photographs that show numbers in the environment, such as on number plates, house doors, buses, signposts and so on. Leave empty signs around – for example, on the home corner door, on large-wheeled toy vehicles and on posts in your outdoor area. Make a note of any children that make marks on these signs during free play.

Plenary
- Using page 14, invite children from each ability group to use a Pen from the Pen tray (set to a thick setting) to draw a given quantity of marks. Encourage them to write the corresponding number.

PSRN Lesson 8

Comparing quantities

Learning objectives
- Development matters (Calculating): Begin to make comparisons between quantities.
- Development matters (Calculating): Compare two groups of objects, saying when they have the same number.
- ELG: Use language such as *more* or *less* to compare two numbers.

Resources
'Comparing quantities' Notebook file; twenty counting toys and two set rings for each pair of children.

Links to other ELGs
CD
Use their imagination in art and design, music, dance, imaginative and role play and stories.
- In imaginative or small-world play, encourage the children to say which group of objects (such as play people, toy cars or plastic animals) has more or fewer. Challenge them to say how many more or fewer there are.

Whiteboard tools
- Pen tray
- Select tool
- Highlighter pen

Introduction
Start with some counting by pointing practice. Invite between five and ten children to stand at the front of the class. Ask the children to count by pointing to identify how many there are. Repeat for other quantities.

Adult-focused whole-class activities
- Display the four-column staircase of squares on page 2 of the 'Comparing quantities' Notebook file. (There is a small space between the columns to avoid any confusion with rows.)
- Ask the children to look at each column in turn and to count how many squares there are by pointing.
- Now point to the three- and four-square columns and ask: *Which has more? How many more?*
- Repeat this for columns two and four and ask: *Which has fewer? How many fewer?*
- Now invite a volunteer to come and make a bigger column of squares by dragging and dropping the squares from the ring to a new column next to the column of four squares. Count each square as it is dragged across. Ask: *How many squares does the new column have? How many more squares does it have than the four-square column?*
- Go to page 3, which shows a pair of sets. Discuss the set rings and how these separate the two sets. Count each set. Ask: *Which has more? Which has fewer?* Challenge older or more confident learners to say how many more or fewer there are.
- Repeat this using the sets on pages 4 to 9.

Adult-focused group activities
- Display page 10 of the Notebook file. Help the children to take turns dragging the blocks to make a staircase from one to five.
- Next, arrange for the children to work in pairs. Provide each pair with twenty counting toys and two set rings.
- Ask them to take turns to put two sets of toys into the set rings. Their partner must count each set and say which has more and which has fewer.
- Provide fewer counting toys for younger or less confident learners so that their quantity range is limited to no more than six in each set. Challenge older or more confident learners to compare their two sets and to say how many more or fewer there are each time.
- As the children work, ask questions such as: *Which has more/fewer? How many more/fewer? How do you know? How did you work that out?*

Plenary
- Use the one to ten staircase on page 11 for further practice in comparing quantities. Point to different columns and ask questions such as: *How many squares are in this column? How many more are there in this one? Are there more or fewer squares in this column?*
- Provide further practice of comparing sets by revisiting a selection of pages from 3 and 9.
- Note whether the children understand the vocabulary *more* and *fewer*. Plan further work for those who are still unsure.

PSRN Lesson 9

Learning objectives
- Development matters (Numbers as Labels and for Counting): Use some number language such as *more* and *a lot*.
- ELG: Use language such as *more* or *less* to compare two numbers.

Resources
'Number track' Notebook file; number cards made from photocopiable page 93 'What fits?'; two colours of counters and crayons for each pair of children.

Links to other ELGs
CD
Use their imagination in art and design, music, dance, imaginative and role play and stories.
- In a movement lesson, give ten children a number card, from 1 to 10. Ask the children to line up, saying, for example: *Number 1, stand by me. Now number 3 come up to the front too. Where will number 2 fit?*

Whiteboard tools
Use a Pen from the Pen tray to write numbers onto the number track and the Eraser to clear them.

- Pen tray
- Select tool

What fits?

Introduction
Display the two sets on page 2 of the 'Number track' Notebook file. Compare the quantities. Ask the children to count both sets by pointing and saying how many are in each. Ask: *Which set has more? Which set has fewer?* Repeat the activity using page 3.

Adult-focused whole-class activities
- Go to page 4 and invite a child to come and move some objects (up to six) into one of the set rings. Challenge another child to come up and move some objects into the other set ring. Ask: *Which set has more/fewer?*
- Continue in this way with the set rings and objects on pages 5 and 6. (Page 6 contains 17 objects, so the first child can move up to eight objects into the first set.)
- Next, reveal the blank number track on page 7. Explain that you will write the numbers from 1 to 10 on the track and that you would like the children to write each number in the air, using their whole arm, as you do this.
- Now ask the children to read the numbers as you point to them, in number order.
- Next, use the Eraser from the Pen tray to erase the numbers. Write most of them in again but leave one or two blank. Ask, for example: *Which number fits between 3 and 5?* (Write in *4*.) *Which number fits between 7 and 9?* (Write in *8*.)
- Repeat this game, erasing more of the numbers this time. Invite the children to say what each missing number is as you point to the spaces.

Planned independent group activities
- Provide each pair with coloured crayons, counters and a copy of photocopiable page 93.
- Tell the children to take turns to choose an empty square on the number track. Their partner must say the missing number. If they both agree, their partner should write in the number.
- Display the completed number track on page 8 of the Notebook file to provide support.
- Ask an adult to work with younger or less confident learners. Provide them with an A3 enlargement of the sheet, and suggest that the children take turns to choose a square on the track and say, then write, the number.
- Challenge older or more confident learners to play the game quickly, so that they recall the numbers, and their positions, as quickly as possible.

Child-initiated activity
- Draw number tracks in chalk on the playground surface. Leave chalks available for the children to choose.

Plenary
- Go back to page 7 and the blank number track. Invite individuals to come to the board and write numbers in the correct places.
- Complete the track in this way. Now erase the numbers and ask the children to work mentally. Say: *What number comes between 1 and 3... 5 and 7...* and so on.
- Show the children the jumbled-up track on page 9. Invite them to drag and drop the numbers into the correct positions on the blank number track above.

PSRN Lesson 10

Learning objectives
- Development matters (Numbers as Labels and for Counting): Count up to three or four objects by saying one number name for each item.
- ELG: Say and use number names in order in familiar contexts.

Resources
'Ordering numbers' Notebook file; twelve disposable cups or margarine pots and four sets of counting toys, such as cubes, beads, shape tiles and construction bricks, for each pair of children.

Links to other ELGs
KUW
Find out about and identify the uses of everyday technology and use information and communication technology and programmable toys to support their learning.
- Help the children to use a clipart program to create sets to count on a computer screen. Encourage them to compare and order their sets verbally.

Whiteboard tools
Move the Screen Shade to reveal the additional sets of objects in the Introduction. Use a Highlighter pen to strike through items as they are counted.

- Pen tray
- Screen Shade
- Highlighter pen
- Select tool

Ordering numbers

Introduction
Open the 'Ordering numbers' Notebook file and go to page 2. Ask the children to count each set by pointing. Then ask: *Which set has more stars? How many more? Which set has fewer stars? How many fewer?* When the children have agreed on the correct answer, move the Screen Shade to reveal the bottom pair of sets and repeat. Continue with the pairs of sets on pages 3 and 4.

Adult-focused whole-class activities
- Go to page 5. Drag and drop the three sets of images (a set of five, a set of three and a set of two) from the box onto the screen, so that they are not in quantity order.
- Ask the children to count each set and to agree how many stars are in each one. Ask: *Which set has fewest?* Invite a child to come and drag and drop that set to the left side of the page.
- Ask: *Which set has most?* Invite another child to drag that set to the right side of the page. Ask: *Where does the set with three stars belong?* Agree that it goes between the other two sets. Invite a third child to move this set into the middle.
- Discuss how the sets are now in number order.
- Repeat for the other sets of images on pages 6 to 8.

Adult-focused group activity
- Ask the children to work in pairs. They will need twelve disposable cups and four different sets of counting toys.
- Ask them to make three sets of different numbers of cubes (for example) by putting each set into a cup. Explain that they must order the sets, starting with the smallest number.
- Ensure that an adult works with younger or less confident learners, carrying out the task as a group. Encourage the children to use the vocabulary of ordering as they work.

Planned independent group activity
- Encourage the children to continue working with their partners to sort the other three sets of sorting toys.
- Challenge older or more confident learners to make four or five sets each time and to order these.

Plenary
- Invite some children of different ability to count out each of their sets and to explain how they have ordered them.
- Finish by going to pages 9 and 10 of the Notebook file. Drag and drop up to six sets out of the boxes and invite the children to count by pointing, and then order these from least to most.

PSRN Lesson 11

Ordering selected numbers

Learning objectives
- Development matters (Numbers as Labels and for Counting): Use some number names accurately in play.
- Development matters (Numbers as Labels and for Counting): Know that numbers identify how many objects are in a set.
- ELG: Say and use number names in order in familiar contexts.

Resources
'Ordering selected numbers' Notebook file; counting toys.

Links to other ELGs
KUW
Look closely at similarities, differences, patterns and change.
- Following a nature walk, ask the children to sort their collections. Suggest that they order these by quantity, putting the smallest quantity first, and so on. (For example, one fir cone, then two leaves, followed by three sticks.)

Whiteboard tools
Use the Undo button to erase any unsaved changes.

- Pen tray
- Undo button
- Select tool

Introduction
Go to page 2 and look at the empty number train together. Drag the numbers 1, 4, 7 and 10 into the correct places.

Ask the children to decide which numbers fit in the spaces. Drag and drop the numbers as the children say them. Repeat until the train is complete.

Press on the funnel when you've finished to hear the sound of a train tooting. Press the Undo button until the page is reset and start again with a different combination of numbers.

Adult-focused whole-class activity
- Display the set of images on page 3. Ask the children to count the number of triangles in each set by pointing. Ask: *How many are in each set?*
- Then ask: *Which is the smallest set?* Drag and drop this onto the empty set on the left side of the page. Ask: *Which is the largest?* Drag and drop this onto the empty set on the right. Can the children tell you where the last set goes? Agree that it belongs in the middle and that the sets are now in number order.
- Repeat for the sets on pages 4 to 6.
- Go to page 7. Look at the empty set in the middle and the sets at either side. Discuss what number of stars should go in the middle set. Invite a volunteer to come to the whiteboard and drag and drop a suitable number of stars into place.
- Repeat the activity on pages 8 and 9. (On page 9 there is more than one possible correct answer.)

Adult-focused group activities
- Go to page 10 of the Notebook file and look at the shirts on the washing line. Ask: *What numbers could go in the empty shirts?* Invite a child to come and select and drag the correct number to fill the empty shirt.
- Invite more children to do the same using pages 11 and 12.
- Arrange for the children to work in groups of four. They will need some counting toys.
- Ask each child to make a set of between one and ten toys. Each set in their group must have a different quantity of toys, so they will need to negotiate this with each other.
- Encourage them to order their sets of toys, putting the smallest quantity first. Repeat the activity three more times.
- As the children work, invite each group to explain how they know that their sets are in number order.
- Suggest that younger or less confident learners order quantities of up to six objects.
- Challenge older or more confident learners to order six sets.

Plenary
- Ask one group to choose one of their ordered sets, and to whisper the quantities to you. Write these numbers up, out of order, in the circles on page 13.
- Invite the other children to verbally order the numbers, from least to most.
- When the children agree, allow one child to drag the numbers into the correct order.
- Go to page 14 of the Notebook file. Invite individuals to come to the whiteboard, select a number and drop it in the right place on the washing line.

PSRN Lesson 12

Ordinal numbers

Learning objectives
- Development matters (Numbers as Labels and for Counting): Use ordinal numbers in different contexts.
- ELG: Say and use number names in order in familiar contexts.

Resources
'Ordinal numbers' Notebook file; photocopiable page 94 'Ordinal numbers'; pots of coloured crayons; counting toys.

Links to other ELGs
CD
Recognise and explore how sounds can be changed, sing simple songs from memory, recognise repeated sounds and sound patterns and match movements to music.
- Provide a group of six children with different musical instruments. Invite them to play their instruments in a given order, and use ordinal language to express this.

Whiteboard tools
- Pen tray
- Select tool

Introduction
Count from one to ten together, keeping the pace sharp.

Open the 'Ordinal numbers' Notebook file and go to page 2. Press on the image to watch the numbered procession of animals, counting together as the animals move across the screen. Look at the procession a second time, this time inviting the children to say the numbers from 1 to 10 in turn. If a child falters, pause the procession to allow them more time to focus on the number. Press Play to continue the procession.

Adult-focused whole-class activities
- Go to page 3 of the Notebook file and press on the image to open the animal parade labelling activity. Look at the numbered animals around the edge. Point to the numbers, in any order, one at a time, and ask the children to read the number.
- Still using page 3, ask the children to name the animals. Invite individuals to come to the board to drag and drop them into the correct number order. (Two of the animals have already been placed to start them off.)
- Encourage the use of ordinal number as they work, by asking questions such as: *Which one is first? Is the elephant second?*
- Go to page 4 of the Notebook file. Ask: *Which car is first? Which car is third?* and so on.
- Let individual children have fun moving the cars around the page. Keep asking them to describe the order, using the appropriate language.
- Repeat the activity, using the farm animals on page 5. Ask more searching questions such as: *Which animal is between the first and third? Which is between the third and fifth? How many animals are between the second and fifth?*
- Press on an animal to hear the sound that it makes.

Adult-focused group activities
- Arrange for the children to work in groups of four to six with an adult. Provide crayons and photocopiable page 94 for each child.
- Invite the children to point to the first car and colour it in blue. Repeat this for each of the other cars in turn (the second in green and so on).
- Now invite the children to point to specified cars: *Point to the fifth car. What colour is the car between the third and fifth cars?*
- Use counting toys (or beads on a lace) to support younger or less confident learners.
- Challenge older or more confident learners to put out ten different counting toys and repeat the activity using ordinal numbers to tenth.

Plenary
- Go back to the animal procession on page 2 and encourage the children to say which animal is first, second, third and so on. Check that they use and understand ordinal numbers (at this stage some children may just give the numbers, such as one, two and three).
- Organise the children into four teams to play the race game on page 6 as a fun way to conclude the session. Press on the button to view the rules of the game.

PSRN Lesson 13

Word problems

Learning objectives
- Development matters (Calculating): Compare two groups of objects, saying when they have the same number.
- Development matters (Calculating): Say the number that is one more than a given number.
- ELG: Find one more or one less than a number from one to ten.

Resources
'Number track' Notebook file; photocopiable page 95 'Word problems'; counting toys; drawing materials.

Links to other ELGs
PD
Move with confidence, imagination and in safety.
- Invite the children to develop a sequence of movements. Then ask them to make given numbers of movements, including one more/less than the number that you say. They will need to listen carefully and calculate the quantity before beginning the movements.

Whiteboard tools
Upload scanned images by selecting Insert, then Picture File, and browsing to where you have saved the images.

- Pen tray
- Select tool

Introduction
Open the 'Number track' Notebook file and press the button next to Lesson 13 to go to page 10. Encourage the children to read the numbers one to ten aloud as you write them into the number track. Ask questions such as: *Which number is between one and three? Which numbers are between two and five?*

Adult-focused whole-class activity
- Go to page 11 of the Notebook file and move four cars into one of the empty set rings. Ask the children to count by pointing, and tell you how many cars there are.
- Say: *There are four cars. Another car parks next to them* (drag one across). *How many cars are there now?* Agree that there are five. Now tell the children that one of the cars has driven away (drag one away). Ask: *How many are left?*
- Go to page 12 and drag six footballs into one of the set rings. Repeat the one more/one less questions for this set.
- Repeat the activity one more time on page 13.

Adult-focused group activities
- Arrange for the children to work in groups of four to six with an adult. Each group will need a copy of photocopiable page 95.
- Ask the adult to discuss with the children what there is in each picture, and how many. The adult should pose a word problem, such as: *There are four rabbits in the wood. One more joins/leaves them. How many rabbits are there now?*
- Ask the adult to repeat this for each of the pictures.
- Provide younger or less confident learners with counting toys so that they can count out the appropriate quantity of toys, and add one more, or remove one, to reflect the word problem.
- Challenge older or more confident learners to make up a word problem of their own for one more or one less. Invite them to draw suitable pictures for their problem. Check these problems before the Plenary, then scan their pictures and add them to page 14 of the Notebook file.

Child-initiated activity
- Encourage the children to monitor the numbers of children that may play in given areas. Investigate whether they can work out what would happen if one more child joins in or leaves.

Plenary
- Display a picture made by one of the older or more confident learners. Ask the child to explain the problem. Invite the other children to say the answer.
- Repeat this for some of the other problems that the older or more confident learners have made up.
- Create a set of eight cars using Notebook page 11. Ask: *How many cars can you see?* Point to one and say: *This one drove away* (drag the car from the set and drop it). *How many are left?*
- Continue, this time moving one more car to join the others.

PSRN Lesson 14

Combining two groups

Learning objectives
- Development matters (Calculating): Know that a group of things changes in quantity when something is added or taken away.
- Development matters (Calculating): Find the total number of items in two groups by counting all of them.
- ELG: Begin to relate addition to combining two groups of objects and subtraction to *taking away*.

Resources
'Set circles' Notebook file; photocopiable page 96 'Combining two groups'; blank dice marked 1, 2, 3, 3, 4, 4 and counting toys for each pair.

Links to other ELGs
KUW
Look closely at similarities, differences, patterns and change.
- When sorting items, invite the children to count and say how many there are in each of two groups, then to combine them and find the total by counting them all.

Whiteboard tools
Use the Undo button to erase unsaved changes, thereby resetting the page, after each number problem during the whole-class work.

- Pen tray
- Select tool
- Undo button

Introduction
Go to page 2 of the Notebook file and use the Eraser from the Pen tray to rub over the first yellow shape to reveal the hidden objects. Encourage the children to use the point and count technique and to say how many there are in total. Count again, together, with you pointing to (or highlighting) each item in turn. Repeat this for the next two sets of objects on the page.
Repeat the activity on page 3.

Adult-focused whole-class activity
- Go to page 4. Drag and drop three buttons into one empty set. Ask the children to count as you do this and agree that there are three buttons. Now drag two buttons into the second empty set and repeat.
- Ask: *How many are in this circle? And this one?* Explain that in order to find out how many there are altogether, the children should count on from one of the circles. Ask them to count with you as you count again: *one, two three; four and five*. So there are five altogether.
- Press the Undo button until the page is reset and repeat for other examples. Use vocabulary such as *add* and *makes*, *equals* and *totals*, as appropriate.

Adult-focused group activity
- Invite the children to work in pairs. They must take turns to roll the prepared dice twice (see Resources) and to count out the appropriate quantity of counting toys into each set circle on photocopiable page 96. They should then count how many there are in total, counting on from one set to the second.
- As the children work, encourage them to say the addition number sentences for the quantities in front of them. For example, for four and two they would say: *One, two, three, four; five, six. So four add two makes six.*
- Limit younger or less confident learners to dice marked 1, 1, 2, 2, 3, 3 and extend older or more confident learners by using a traditional 1-6 dice.

Child-initiated activity
- Set up a role-play shop in your setting and provide plenty of resources to encourage sorting, counting and combining during play.

Plenary
- Return to page 4 and repeat the activity from the whole-class work. This time, ask the children to say (from one to five) how many shapes to drag and drop into each circle.
- Invite confident learners to say the counting and the addition number sentence aloud.
- Display page 5 of the Notebook file and count the dots on the dominoes together. Encourage the children to say the number sentences with you.
- Finally, go to page 6 and invite volunteers to come and add spots to the blank dominoes to make a number that you specify (up to five). Encourage the child, and then the rest of the class, to say the number sentence that goes with the arrangement.

PSRN Lesson 15

Combining three groups

Learning objectives
● Development matters (Calculating): Count repeated groups of the same size.
● ELG: Begin to relate addition to combining two groups of objects and subtraction to *taking away*.

Resources
'Combining' Notebook file; ten counting toys for each pair (twelve for older or more confident learners); photocopiable page 97 'Combining three sets'.

Links to other ELGs
PSED
Select and use activities and resources independently.
● Encourage the children to put away the resources they have been using. Ask questions, such as: *How many bricks have you got, Peter? How many has Joe got? How many does that make altogether?*

Whiteboard tools
For the Plenary, add objects from the Gallery to create a new group of sets.

- Pen tray
- Select tool
- Delete button
- Gallery

Introduction
Go to page 2 of the 'Combining' Notebook file. Drag and drop objects into each of the set circles to make sets of three and four. Ask the children to count each set by pointing. Say: *This set has three; let's count on for the other set to find the total.* Point to each shape as the children count on and agree that three and four makes seven.

Repeat this for other combinations. If the children are confident with this, ask them to count on for themselves, then to say the addition sentence. For example, for four and two they should say: *Four, five, six. So four and two makes six.*

In subsequent sessions, repeat the activity using three sets on page 3 of the Notebook file.

Adult-focused whole-class activities
● Go to page 4 of the Notebook file to begin work on combining three groups. Ask the children to count each set, then to say how many there are altogether by counting all of the objects.
● Repeat the count for these three sets, this time asking the children to count on from the first set. Ask: *Is the total the same?* Establish that we can count on to find totals for three sets. Where children are not yet confident with counting on, accept that they will probably, at this stage, count all of the objects.
● Repeat this activity with further sets on pages 5 to 7.
● Use pages 4 to 7 to develop the work with older or more confident learners by asking them to use number sentences as they count and make the total. Encourage them to count the sets and then say the number sentence that matches the arrangement. Use the Delete button ☒ (or select Delete from the dropdown menu) to remove the shapes at the bottom of the page to reveal the number sentences hidden underneath.

Adult-focused group activity
● Arrange for the children to work in pairs. Provide some counting toys and copies of photocopiable page 97.
● Invite the children to take turns to take a handful of counting toys and place these on the sheet, dividing the toys between the three set circles. Their partner should count each set and finds the total.
● Suggest that younger or less confident learners count all the objects at this stage.
● Provide older or more confident learners with twelve counting toys.

Plenary
● Revisit pages 4 to 7 from the whole-class work. Ask the children how they could find the total.
● Invite those who count on from one set to demonstrate this.
● Repeat this for some other groups of three sets.
● Go to page 8 and add objects from the Gallery to create your own three sets. Invite individuals to come to the whiteboard and drag some shapes into each circle. Count them together.

PSRN Lesson 16

Counting on

Learning objectives
- Development matters (Calculating): Know that a group of things changes in quantity when something is added or taken away.
- ELG: Begin to use the vocabulary involved in adding and subtracting.

Resources
'Set circles' Notebook file; photocopiable page 96 'Combining two groups'; 1-6 dice; blank dice labelled 1, 2, 2, 3, 3, 4 and five counting toys for each pair.

Links to other ELGs
PSED
Work as part of a group or class, taking turns and sharing fairly.
- Use counting on to determine the total number of items, such as finding out how many biscuits there are to share out.

Introduction
Go to page 7 of the 'Set circles' Notebook file. Drag two buttons into one set circle and ask the children to count them. Drag three more buttons into the second set circle and repeat. Now find the total by counting all of the buttons. Encourage the children to say the addition sentence: *Two add three makes five.*

Press the Undo button until the page is reset and repeat for other quantities up to five in each set circle.

Adult-focused whole-class activities
- Go to page 8. Drag and drop some lollies into each set circle (such as four into one and two into the other).
- Ask the children to count the first set, then the second, and to say how many there are in each.
- Now count all: *One, two, three, four, five, six. So four add two makes six.*
- Repeat for other quantities.
- Move on to page 9. Drag four lollies into the left-hand circle and say: *I have put four lollies in this circle.* Drag two lollies into the right-hand circle and say: *I have put two lollies in this circle. How many lollies are there altogether?* Count on from four together to find out, saying: *Four, five, six. So four add two makes six.*
- Press the Undo button until the page is reset and repeat in the same way for other quantities, stating the quantity that is in the first circle, so that the children count on from that number each time.

Adult-focused group activity
- Provide each pair with a prepared dice (see Resources), a copy of photocopiable page 96 and five counting toys.
- Explain to the children that they must take it in turns to roll the dice and place the matching number of toys into one of the set circles. The other child takes some of the toys and places those into the other set circle.
- The children then count on from the number of spots on the dice to find the total for the two sets.
- Limit the number range for younger or less confident learners by using dice marked 1, 1, 2, 2, 3, 3.
- For older or more confident learners, provide standard 1-6 dice.

Plenary
- Go to page 10 and press the dice to roll it. Ask the children to count the spots on the dice. Draw some more spots in the circle using a Pen from the Pen tray.
- Ask the children to work out the total by counting on from the number of spots on the dice. Say the addition sentence together.
- Use the Eraser from the Pen tray to remove the spots from the circle and repeat the activity for other dice throws. Add different numbers of spots to the circle, keeping the total between eight and ten.

Whiteboard tools
Reset the page after each number problem by repeatedly pressing the Undo button.

- Pen tray
- Select tool
- Undo button

PSRN   Lesson 17

Doubling

Learning objectives
- Development matters (Calculating): Find the total number of items in two groups by counting all of them.
- Development matters (Calculating): Count repeated groups of the same size.
- ELG: Begin to relate addition to combining two groups of objects.

Resources
'Set circles' Notebook file; blank dice marked 1, 2, 3, 3, 4, 4; 1-6 dice; counting toys.

Links to other ELGs
PSED
Work as part of a group or class, taking turns and sharing fairly.
- When playing dice games, challenge the children to work out the double of the dice number.

Introduction
Open the 'Set circles' Notebook file and press on the button next to Lesson 17 to go to page 11. Say a number and ask the children to draw it in the air, making it as large as they can. Write the number on the Notebook file. Invite the children to repeat drawing the number in the air as you write on the board. Continue in this way, with other numbers between one and five.

Adult-focused whole-class activities
- Reveal the set circles on page 12. Drag and drop two stars into each circle, so that both circles contain the same quantity.
- Ask the children to count how many stars there are in each circle. Agree that there are two in each circle.
- Now count on from one circle to the other to find the total: *One, two, three, four. So two add two is four.*
- Repeat this for other quantities such as one add one; three add three.
- Move on to page 13. Write a number 2 (for example) in the space provided above the left-hand circle, and drag this number of spots into the circle. Repeat for the right-hand circle. Count the spots together from two saying: *Two and three, four. So two add two is four.* Use a Pen from the Pen tray or a Highlighter pen to strike through the spots in the right-hand circle as you count.
- Press the Undo button until the page is reset and repeat this for other doubles up to four. Encourage the children to count on to find the total, using their fingers to help with the counting on at this stage if appropriate.

Planned independent activities
- Arrange for the children to work in pairs. They will need a 1, 2, 3, 3, 4, 4 dice.
- Ask them to take turns to roll the dice and count on to find the total of the double. For example, if they roll a 3 they could count: *Three and four, five, six. So three add three is six.*
- Provide counting toys as well as the dice for younger or less confident learners to use. Suggest that they roll the dice, put out that quantity of toys and count on from the dice number using the toys as aids.
- Challenge older or more confident learners to use a standard 1-6 dice for finding doubles.

Plenary
- Challenge the children to explain how they worked out the doubles. Invite volunteers to say a number sentence for a double, such as: *Four add four makes eight.*
- Ask a child to roll the 1, 2, 3, 3, 4, 4 dice and say which number is shown. Encourage everyone to work out the double.
- Invite the children to take turns to say the number sentence. For example, for double 4 they might say: *Four and five, six, seven, eight. So four add four makes eight.*
- Challenge the older or more confident learners to find double five and double six and to explain to the others how they worked this out.

Whiteboard tools
Use a Pen from the Pen tray to strike through objects as you count them.

- Pen tray
- Select tool
- Undo button

PSRN Lesson 18

Totals

Learning objectives
- Development matters (Calculating): Find the total number of items in two groups by counting all of them.
- ELG: Begin to relate addition to combining two groups of objects.

Resources
'Combining' Notebook file; photocopiable page 96 'Combining two groups'; empty margarine tub (or similar) and ten counting toys for each pair.

Links to other ELGs
KUW
Investigate objects and materials by using all of their senses as appropriate.
- Count groups of objects that the children are exploring through natural discovery, such as sets of leaves or flowers. Ask questions such as: *If I have four leaves and three flowers, how many things do I have altogether?*

Whiteboard tools
Use the Undo button to reset the pages. Use a Pen from the Pen tray to write numbers, selecting a suitable thickness for the children to use.

- Pen tray
- Select tool
- Undo button

Introduction
Open the 'Combining' Notebook file and press on the button next to Lesson 18 to go to page 9.

Drag and drop the objects into the set circles to make sets of four and two. Ask: *How can we find out how many there are altogether?* Start by counting all the objects together and then count on from one set.

Press the Undo button until the page is reset and repeat the activity, changing the quantities to, for example, five and two.

Adult-focused whole-class activities
- Move on to page 10. Use the Eraser from the Pen tray to reveal the number hidden in the left-hand circle (3). Say the number together.
- Now drag and drop two lollies into the right-hand circle. Say the revealed number again (3) and then ask the children how many there are altogether.
- Together, with you pointing to the lollies in the right circle, count on from three. Then say: *Three add two makes five.*
- Repeat this for other quantities on pages 11 and 12, keeping the totals to up to ten, such as five and four; four and three.

Adult-focused group activities
- Arrange for the children to work in pairs. Provide each pair with a copy of photocopiable page 96, an empty margarine pot (or similar container) and ten counting toys.
- Invite the children to take turns to take some toys and hide them under the margarine pot, which they should then place on one of the circles on their sheet. They should tell their partner how many toys they have hidden. Next, they put some more toys onto the second circle. Their partner calculates the total by counting on from the known, but hidden, set.
- Limit the quantity of counting toys to up to six for younger or less confident learners.
- Challenge older or more confident learners to find several combinations for a larger total, such as nine. For example, seven (hidden) and two; five (hidden) and four; eight (hidden) and one.

Child-initiated activities
- Provide objects for the children to choose to hide in the sand pit.
- Leave pots and counters available for the children to use.

Plenary
- Go to page 13 of the Notebook file. Invite a volunteer to come to the whiteboard and write a number on the left-hand set circle. Drag and drop some objects into the right-hand set circle, keeping the totals to no more than ten.
- Ask: *How shall we find the total?* Invite a child to demonstrate counting on from the numeral to find the total. Say the addition sentence together.
- Press the Undo button until the page is reset and repeat the activity, using other numbers and quantities.

PSRN Lesson 19

Partitioning

Learning objectives
- Development matters (Calculating): Share objects into equal groups and count how many in each group.
- ELG: Begin to use the vocabulary involved in adding and subtracting.

Resources
'Partitioning' Notebook file; paper; pens; counting toys; drawing materials.

Links to other ELGs
KUW
Find out about their environment, and talk about those features they like and dislike.
- Ask the children to look at photographs of places in their local environment. Invite them to separate the photographs into two sets of their own choice, such as places they like or dislike. Count the number of photographs in each set as well as the total of the two sets.

Introduction
Go to page 2 and enable the Spotlight tool (so that the page is black, except for a small circle or rectangle). Move the spotlight and reveal one number at a time. Ask the children to hold up that number of fingers. Repeat for other quantities within the children's counting range.

Repeat this activity over time, extending the range up to ten.

Adult-focused whole-class activities
- Display page 3 and explain that you will move some teddy bears into one side of the circle. Encourage the children to count how many there are as you drag and drop them. Begin with all three teddy bears, and place them into one half of the circle. Ask: *How many are there?*
- Now move one of the teddy bears into the second part of the circle. Point to each part of the circle and ask: *How many are there here?* Then ask: *How many are there in total?* Agree that there are still three teddy bears. Say *two and one makes three*.
- Repeat this with the other partitions for three: one and two; two and one; three and zero; zero and three.
- Use pages 4 to 6 to repeat for other partitions (totals of four, five and six).

Adult-focused group activities
- Arrange for the children to work in pairs. Ask each pair to draw a circle with a line dividing it in half (like the one on the whiteboard). Provide some counting toys.
- Ask the children to show you one way of separating five toys on the circle they have drawn. Can they think of another way?
- Leave the toys in the first arrangement and suggest that the children draw another partitioned circle. Invite them to find another way to separate five toys. Continue to record the different ways by leaving the toys on the circles, drawing a new circle for each new way.
- Limit younger or less confident learners to finding partitions of three and four. Provide partitioned circles for them to use, rather than ask them to draw their own.
- Challenge older or more confident learners to find partitions for six, once they have completed those for five.

Plenary
- Invite children to describe their partitions for five. Demonstrate each one on the whiteboard using page 5 of the Notebook file.
- Ask the children to count each set, then to count all to confirm that, for example, three and two makes five.
- Invite older or more confident learners to describe their partitions for six and demonstrate these using page 6.

Whiteboard tools
Use the Spotlight tool to reveal the numbers on page 2 one at a time.

- Pen tray
- Spotlight tool
- Select tool

PSRN Lesson 20

Given totals

Learning objectives
- Development matters (Calculating): Select two groups of objects to make a given total of objects.
- ELG: Begin to relate addition to combining two groups of objects.

Resources
'Given totals' Notebook file; photocopiable page 98 'Given totals'; counters for each child (two of each colour available).

Links to other ELGs
CD
Recognise repeated sounds and sound patterns.
- Ask the children to count sounds when the sound source is hidden. Ask: *How many more sounds would we need to make...?* Keep the quantities small, such as totals of four or five.

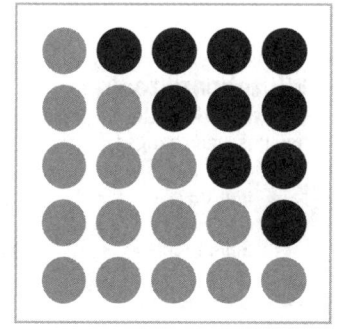

Whiteboard tools
Use the Eraser from the Pen tray to reveal concealed objects. Use the Undo button to reset the page in the whole-class activity.

- Pen tray
- Select tool
- Undo button

Introduction
Open the 'Given totals' Notebook file and go to page 2. Explain that you are going to clean the windows on the bus, one at a time (using the Eraser from the Pen tray), to find some hidden people. Tell the children to wait until the people are all revealed and then ask them to point and count to find the quantity.

Repeat for the other quantities that are concealed on pages 3 to 9 (including zero).

Adult-focused whole-class activity
- Display the dogs under the empty sets on page 10. Count them together and agree that there are five.
- Invite the children to suggest how the dogs could be placed into the two circles. (0 + 5; 1 + 4; 2 + 3; 3 + 2; 4 + 1; 5 + 0)
- Choose a suggestion and drag and drop the dogs into place. Say the addition sentence together for the relevant total of five.
- Repeat this for the other totals of five. Check by counting on from one set to the other. Reset the page by repeatedly pressing the Undo button after each example.

Adult-focused group activity
- Arrange for the children to work in pairs. They will need a copy of photocopiable page 98 and some counters (two counters in each colour available per child).
- Ask them to take turns to choose two sets of animals from the sheet, which they think will make a total of six. If their partner agrees, they may place matching counters onto each of the sets. (For example, if a child chooses a set of two elephants and a set of four camels to make a total of six, they should put one counter on the elephants and one counter of the same colour on the camels.)
- As the children work, encourage them to check their totals by counting on in ones from one set to the next.
- Arrange for an adult to work with a group of younger or less confident learners, with an A3 enlargement of the photocopiable sheet. Suggest that the children take turns to find two sets that make six. Ask them to check by counting as the adult points to the images.
- Challenge older or more confident learners to find different totals for seven. Allow them to use counters to represent their pairs of sets.

Plenary
- Go back to page 10 of the Notebook file. Explain that you will drag and drop some dogs into one set circle. Ask the children to decide how many more would be needed to make a total of, for example, four. They can count on, using their fingers to help if necessary, to find out what is missing.
- Drag the quantity of dogs that the children say into the other set circle. Check by counting on from the first set.
- Repeat this for other combinations for four.
- Move on to page 11. Replace some red counters with yellow counters to show the different combinations that make a total of five. Discuss the pattern that is made as you change the colour of one more counter in each row.

PSRN Lesson 21

Taking away

Learning objectives
- Development matters (Calculating): Show an interest in number problems.
- Development matters (Calculating): Know that a group of things changes in quantity when something is added or taken away.
- ELG: Begin to relate subtraction to *taking away*.

Resources
'Given totals' Notebook file; photocopiable page 88 'Counting mat'; counting toys.

Links to other ELGs
PSED
Work as part of a group or class, taking turns and sharing fairly.
- Count how many biscuits there are and how many will be left after giving some out to a group of children.

Introduction
Open the 'Given totals' Notebook file and press on the button next to Lesson 21 to go to page 12. Use a Pen from the Pen tray, on a thick setting, to write any number between 1 and 6 on the page. Ask the children to read the number, then to hold up that quantity of fingers. Repeat for other numbers from one to six. Extend this to up to ten over time.

Adult-focused whole-class activity
- Move on to page 13. Drag and drop four dogs into the left-hand ring. Now say: *I am going to take away one of these. How many do you think will be left? How did you work that out?*
- Drag and drop one of the dogs from the left- to the right-hand set circle. Now ask: *How many did we start with? How many have we taken away? So how many are left?*
- Count together what is left and say: *four take away one leaves three*.
- Repeat this for other subtractions from four, such as 4 - 2; 4 - 3; 4 - 4.

Adult-focused group activities
- Invite the children to work in pairs. They will need a counting mat (photocopiable page 88) and five counting toys.
- Ask the children to take turns to place all five toys on the counting mat. Their partner says how many to take away and they both predict how many are left, before counting. Encourage them to say the appropriate subtraction sentence after each turn.
- Help the children to repeat this for different subtractions from five: 5 - 0; 5 - 1; 5 - 2; 5 - 3; 5 - 4; 5 - 5.
- Show the children the five rows of five coloured counters on page 14. Demonstrate taking away different numbers from five by moving counters to the side of the page. Follow a pattern by taking away one, then two, three, four and five. What pattern do the children notice?
- Reinforce subtraction from two, three and four with younger or less confident learners.
- Challenge older or more confident learners to try this for subtraction from six.

Plenary
- Discuss what happens when subtracting zero. Agree that nothing changes because nothing has been taken away. Model this on page 13 by dragging five dogs into one set circle.
- Next, discuss what happens when subtracting all. Agree that all are taken away, so nothing (or zero) is left. Reset page 13 by repeatedly pressing the Undo button and demonstrate again with the dogs.
- Having shown the children what happens when subtracting all, reset the page again and demonstrate further examples. Each time, ask the children to say what will be left before the images are taken away.

Whiteboard tools
Use the Undo button to erase any unsaved changes.

- Pen tray
- Select tool
- Undo button

PSRN Lesson 22

Counting back

Learning objectives
● Development matters (Calculating): Know that a group of things changes in quantity when something is added or taken away.
● ELG: Begin to use the vocabulary involved in adding and subtracting.

Resources
'Counting back and up' Notebook file; photocopiable page 96 'Combining two groups'; ten counting toys for each pair.

Links to other ELGs
PSED
Work as part of a group or class, taking turns and sharing fairly.
● When children give out materials, encourage them to use counting back to say how many there were in total, how many have been given out, and what is left.

Whiteboard tools
Use images from the Gallery to model the group activity in the plenary session.

- Pen tray
- Select tool
- Undo button
- Gallery

Introduction
Go to page 2 of the 'Counting back and up' Notebook file. Drag and drop four objects into the left-hand circle. Say: *I am going to take away one of these. How many do you think will be left? How did you work that out?* Drag one of the images from the left- to the right-hand circle. Now ask: *How many did we start with? How many have we taken away? So how many are left?* Count together what is left and say: *Four take away one leaves three.*

Press the Undo button until the page is reset and repeat, keeping the total to no more than ten objects.

Adult-focused whole-class activity
● Reset the page using the Undo button and move five images into the left-hand circle. Encourage the children to count how many there are by pointing. Say: *I am going to take away two of the objects.* Drag two images into the other circle.
● Explain that another way to find out what is left after taking away is to count back from the larger number. Pointing to the images in the right-hand circle, count back two from five: *Four, three: so there are three left. Five take away two leaves three.* Check, by counting, what is in the left-hand circle.
● Repeat this for other starting quantities and amounts to take away.

Adult-focused group activity
● Ask the children to work in pairs. They will need ten counting toys and a copy of photocopiable page 96.
● Invite one child from each pair to take some counting toys (for example, six) and place them in one of the circles. The children should count the toys and agree how many there are.
● The second child should move some of the toys to the second circle (for example, three). They count back from the total (six) for the number in the second circle (three) to tell them how many are left. Encourage the children to say the subtraction sentence. For example: *Six take away three leaves three.*
● Invite the children to leave their final subtraction on the activity sheet in front of them so that these can be used in the Plenary.
● Limit younger or less confident learners to up to six counting toys.
● Challenge older or more confident learners to take away larger quantities from eight, nine or ten.

Child-initiated activities
● Provide board games that encourage the children to count back and forward.
● Chalk number lines in the playground area for the children to explore.

Plenary
● Invite a child to say how many counting toys they began with and how many they subtracted. Model this on the whiteboard, using page 3 of the Notebook file and images from the Gallery.
● Invite another child to demonstrate the counting-back procedure and to say the subtraction sentence.
● Repeat for other children's subtraction sentences.

PSRN Lesson 23

How many have gone?

Learning objectives
- Development matters (Calculating): Know that a group of things changes in quantity when something is added or taken away.
- ELG: Begin to use the vocabulary involved in adding and subtracting.

Resources
'Counting back and up' Notebook file; photocopiable page 96 'Combining two groups'; ten counting toys and an empty margarine pot for each pair.

Links to other ELGs
PD
Handle tools, objects, construction and malleable materials safely and with increasing control.
- When making models, the children count how many pieces there are, then check how many items have been used by counting up from what is left.

Whiteboard tools
Use the Eraser from the Pen tray to reveal the hidden numbers in the whole-class activity.

- Pen tray
- Select tool
- Undo button

Introduction
Open the 'Counting back and up' Notebook file and press on the button next to Lesson 23 to go to page 4. Drag and drop six shapes into the left-hand circle and ask: *How many shapes are there?* Now drag two of these into the right-hand circle. Say: *How many shapes have I taken away? How can we find out what is left?* Agree that the children can count these. Say together: *Six take away two leaves four.* Repeat for other quantities between three and ten.

Adult-focused whole-class activity
- Go to page 5 where the left-hand set circle contains a hidden number.
- Reveal the hidden number (3) using the Eraser from the Pen tray. Now drag and drop one object into the right-hand circle.
- Say: *How many were there in this?* (Point to the left-hand circle.) *How many have we taken away?* (Point to the right-hand circle.)
- Explain that in order to find out how many are left, the children can count up from what has been taken away. Suggest that they use their fingers to help them keep track of the count. So, for this example, say: *Two, three. So two are left. Three take away one leaves two.*
- Repeat this, using the other hidden numbers on pages 6 and 7 as starting points. (For example, for page 6 drag three objects into the right-hand circle and count up: *Four, five. So five take away three leaves two.*)
- Extend the activity by using the empty set circles on page 8. Write a chosen number in the left-hand circle and place some objects (a smaller amount) in the right-hand circle. Encourage the children to work out how many are left if you take the second number away from the first.

Adult-focused whole-class activity
- Arrange the children to work in pairs. Each pair will need an empty margarine pot, up to ten counting toys, and a copy of photocopiable page 96.
- The children take turns in taking some of the counting toys and counting how many they have, telling their partner the total. They should then hide some of the toys under the margarine pot on one of the circles and place the rest on the other circle. The other child calculates what is hidden by counting up from what they can see to the known total.
- Limit younger or less confident learners to up to six counting toys.
- Challenge older or more confident learners by giving them twelve counting toys.

Plenary
- Display page 9 of the Notebook file and tell the children that this time you will simply write the numbers into the set circles. Write *6* in the left-hand circle and *3* in the right-hand one. Say: *There were six cakes on the plate. Three cakes were eaten. How many were left?* Invite the children to find the answer by counting up.
- If necessary, drag and drop the cakes into the circles to check answers or to support younger or less confident learners.
- Repeat for other totals within ten, giving counting toys to children who need them.

PSRN Lesson 24

How many more?

Learning objectives
- Development matters (Calculating): Show an interest in number problems.
- ELG: Use language such as *more* or *less* to compare two numbers.

Resources
Prepare a Notebook file by using the Shapes tool to add two circles to the page, then select Lock in Place from the dropdown menu to place them in a set position on the page; photocopiable page 99 'How many more?'.

Links to other ELGs
CLL
Sustain attentive listening, responding to what they have heard with relevant comments, questions or actions.
- Encourage the children to invent their own, simple, word problems and to share these with others for them to solve.

Whiteboard tools
Use the Shapes tool to draw circles on a Notebook page and a Pen from the Pen tray to write numbers into the set circles.

- Pen tray
- Select tool
- Undo button
- Shapes tool

Introduction
Display your prepared Notebook file (see Resources). Use a Pen from the Pen tray to write a total into the left-hand circle and a smaller number into the right-hand one. Write, for example, the numbers 6 and 2 and say: *There are six rabbits in the hutch. Two of them go out into the garden. How many rabbits are left in the hutch?* Encourage the children to work out the answer by counting up. Suggest that they keep track on their fingers as they count, if necessary.

Adult-focused whole-class activity
- Explain to the children that today they will be learning about counting up in their heads to find the answers to some problems.
- Press the Undo button to reset the Notebook page and write 3 in the left-hand circle and 7 in the right-hand circle. Say: *We have three laces. There are seven children who want to make a necklace with the beads. How many more laces do we need?*
- Discuss how to solve this by counting up from three to seven. The children may find it useful, at this stage, to keep track of how many they count with their fingers. Say together: *Four, five, six, seven. We have counted four more. So we need four more laces.*
- Reset the page and repeat this for other examples of word problems where the children have to count up to find the answer.

Adult-focused group activity
- Organise the children to work in groups of four to six with an adult. Provide the adult with a copy of photocopiable page 99. The adult should read the problems to the children.
- Children who are still unsure about keeping a mental tally when counting up should be encouraged to use their fingers at this stage, to keep track of how many.
- Simplify the word problems with lower numbers for younger or less confident learners, and challenge older or more confident learners by increasing the higher number to up to twelve.

Child-initiated activity
- Provide resources for sharing in the home corner. Note whether the children solve problems (such as not having enough plates) during the context of role play.

Plenary
- Explain that you will ask some more problems. Again, write the numbers into the set circles on the whiteboard.
- Say the following problems out loud and invite the children to tell you the answer:
  - *There are four beakers. Eight children would like a drink. How many more beakers do we need?*
  - *Seven elephants would like a bun each. There are only three buns. How many more buns are needed?*
- Ask more questions like these. Again, if children at this stage find it helpful, they can use their fingers to keep a tally of how many they count up.

PSRN Lesson 25

Making patterns

Learning objectives
- Development matters (Shape, Space and Measures): Show an interest in shape and space by making arrangements with objects.
- ELG: Talk about, recognise and recreate simple patterns.
- ELG: Use developing mathematical ideas and methods to solve practical problems.

Resources
'Making patterns' Notebook file; photocopiable page 100 'Making patterns'; laces and shape beads (cubes, cuboids, cylinders, spheres) for each child.

Links to other ELGs
CD
Explore colour, texture, shape, form and space in two or three dimensions.
- Provide printing materials and ask the children to make their own patterns.

Whiteboard tools
Use the Fill Colour tool to change the colour of some shapes to create a repeating pattern.

- Pen tray
- Select tool
- Fill Colour tool
- Undo button

Introduction
Go to page 2 of the 'Making patterns' Notebook file and ask questions such as: *What colour is the second bead? Which bead is between the second and fourth? What colour would the next bead in the pattern be?*
Invite volunteers to come and drag the next bead into the sequence. Continue with two or three more beads and volunteers.

Adult-focused whole-class activity
- Move on to page 3. Invite the children to describe the pattern. Ask: *What would come next in the pattern? How do you know that? What is the third animal? What comes between the third and fifth animals?*
- Now go to page 4 and encourage the children to describe the pattern. Ask them to shut their eyes. Drag and drop a shape tile over the fourth element of the sequence. Invite the children to open their eyes and tell you what has been covered up. Repeat, covering other elements.
- Display the 3D shapes on page 5. Ask the children to describe the 3D shape pattern and then drag and drop some more shapes to continue the sequence. Repeat the activity from page 4 by using the blocks to cover different elements of the sequence.

Adult-focused group activity
- Show the children the shapes on page 6. Invite individuals to come to the whiteboard and use the Fill Colour tool to change the colour of some of the shapes to create a colour pattern.
- Next, provide each child with laces and beads, together with a copy of photocopiable page 100.
- Challenge the children to follow the patterns shown on the photocopiable page as they thread their laces. If the different-shaped beads are not available, ask the children to colour the beads on the sheet to make a colour pattern instead.
- As the children work, encourage them to describe the patterns.
- Work closely with younger or less confident learners and discuss the shape (or colour) of each bead.
- Challenge older or more confident learners to continue the patterns on their photocopiable sheets.

Child-initiated activities
- Put out beads, laces, coloured pasta pieces and string for the children to experiment with.
- Make pattern sheets and colouring materials available in your writing area.

Plenary
- Display page 7 of the Notebook file and explain that you will use the shapes provided to make some repeating patterns. Make the first pattern and ask the children to describe it.
- Use the Undo button to reset the page. Invite a child to come to the whiteboard and make a pattern of their own choice. Discuss and describe the pattern together.
- Repeat this activity several times.
- Make a pattern such as circle, square, circle, square, circle, square, by dragging and dropping shapes. Ask the children to look at the pattern, then shut their eyes. Insert another shape into the pattern.
- Invite the children to open their eyes and look at the pattern. Ask: *Is this a pattern? What has happened to it?* Correct it by removing the additional shape.

PSRN Lesson 26

Sorting

Learning objectives
- Development matters (Shape, Space and Measures): Sort objects, making choices and justifying decisions.
- ELG: Use developing mathematical ideas and methods to solve practical problems.

Resources
'Sorting' Notebook file; photocopiable page 88 'Counting mat'; sorting toys.

Links to other ELGs
KUW
Look closely at similarities, differences, patterns and change.
- Sort natural items, such as collections from a nature walk, by a given criteria.

Introduction
Drag and drop some images onto the counting mat on page 2 of the Notebook file. Ask the children to count how many there are. Now say: *If I add one more, how many will there be then?* Invite the children to tell you, then drag and drop one more image onto the counting mat. Ask the children to check by counting on.

Use the Undo button to revert the screen to the beginning and repeat for different totals (keep the totals to no more than about eight).

Adult-focused whole-class activity
- Move on to page 3. Look at the different types and colours of home. Encourage the children to describe each of the homes, by its colour, size and shape.
- Say: *We need to sort the homes. All the yellow homes need to go into the circle.* Following the children's instructions, drag and drop the homes that they suggest into the set ring.
- Ask: *Have we found all the yellow homes? Are all the yellow homes the same as each other? How are they different? What about the homes that are outside the circle? Are these yellow? Do they belong in the circle? Why not?*
- Repeat this using another sorting criterion, such as all the flats or all the bungalows. Invite volunteers to come and drag the objects into the set ring.

Planned independent activity
- Arrange for the children to work in pairs. Provide each pair with a 'Counting mat' (photocopiable page 88) and some toys to sort.
- Ask the children to find different ways to sort their toys.
- Limit the range of toys for younger or less confident learners so that they have fewer properties to sort.
- Challenge older or more confident learners to sort their toys by two properties, such as: *Is a house and is yellow*.
- Ask the children to keep their favourite way of sorting the toys for the plenary session.

Plenary
- Give the children a few minutes to look at each other's favourite sorting methods. Ask them to choose one of the other children's methods and to be ready to explain how the toys have been sorted.
- Invite the children to explain how other children have sorted their toys. Encourage them to express this as a sentence.
- Show the selection of objects and the set ring on page 4. Choose a sorting criterion, but do not tell the children what it is. Drag and drop some of the objects into the set ring and ask: *How have I sorted these?*
- Repeat for other criteria, or invite individuals to choose a criterion. Each time encourage the children to explain what the sorting is, in a sentence.

Whiteboard tools
Use the Undo button to clear the screen ready to sort in a different way.

- Pen tray
- Select tool
- Undo button

PSRN ▮ Lesson 27

Coins

Learning objectives
● Development matters (Calculating): Show an interest in number problems.
● ELG: Begin to use the vocabulary involved in adding and subtracting.

Resources 💿 📄
'Coins' Notebook file; photocopiable page 101 'Coins'; sets of coins for each group; pots to put the coins in.

Links to other ELGs
CLL
Attempt writing for different purposes, using features of different forms such as lists.
● Provide paper and pencils in the class shop. Ask the children to write price lists for the contents of the shop.

Introduction
Provide each group with a set of mixed coins. Open the 'Coins' Notebook file and go to page 2. Point to one of the coins on the page and ask the children to find that coin in their pot. Ask: *What is this coin called? What colour is it? What pictures can you see on it?* Press on the coin on the screen and use the Delete button ✖ (or select the Delete option from the dropdown menu) to reveal what is on the reverse.
Repeat for the other coins on the Notebook page.

Adult-focused whole-class activity
● Go to page 3. Point to the cherries and ask how much they are. Invite a volunteer to come to the whiteboard and drag the correct amount into the purse below the cherries. If the child suggests two 1p coins, accept this, but also point out that the 2p coin is worth the same as two 1p coins.
● Repeat the activity for the other items on the page.
● Point to the 5p apple. Ask: *Can you find some different ways to pay for this?* Encourage the children to show you the correct coins by placing them in front of them (five 1p coins; two 2p coins and a 1p coin; three 1p coins and a 2p coin; one 5p coin).
● Move on to page 4 and invite volunteers to come and show the different ways to pay for the 5p apple by dragging and dropping coins into the four purses.

Planned independent activity
● Arrange the children to work in pairs. Each pair will need pots of penny coins, a 1-6 dice and a copy of photocopiable page 101.
● Invite the children to take turns to roll the dice. Tell them to take their score in penny coins and place them on the stars. The first person to collect 10p wins the game.
● Arrange for an adult to work with younger or less confident learners to check that they can count how many coins they have for each throw of the dice, and for their total each time.
● Challenge older or more confident learners to say how many more coins they need each time to reach their goal.

Child-initiated activity
● Provide collections of real coins and a till for the children to play with in a role-play shop area.

Plenary
● Go to page 5, point to the cereal bar and read the price label. Ask the children to suggest ways that they could pay for the cereal bar.
● Invite individuals to come to the board and drag coins to the value of 10p into the purses. How many ways can they find? Press the Undo button 🔄 until the page is reset. Ask if the children can think of more than five ways to pay.
● Suggest that the children put out real coins in front of themselves for each new combination.

Whiteboard tools
Use the Delete button to reveal the images on the reverse of the coins on page 2.

🖥 Pen tray
➤ Select tool
✖ Delete button
🔄 Undo button

PSRN Lesson 28

3D shapes

Learning objectives
- Development matters (Shape, Space and Measures): Begin to use mathematical names for solid 3D shapes and flat 2D shapes, and mathematical terms to describe shapes.
- ELG: Use language such as *circle* or *bigger* to describe the shape and size of solids and flat shapes.

Resources
'Build your own' file; feely box or bag; selection of 2D shapes for the Introduction. Use the 'Build your own', which consists of a blank Notebook page and a collection of Gallery resources, to prepare a file as follows: page 1 to show a 2D shape of your choice; pages 2-5 to show a 3D shape of your choice on each page; sets of 3D shapes for each group (cylinders, cones, cubes, cuboids, spheres)

Links to other ELGs
PD
Handle tools, objects, construction and malleable materials safely and with increasing control.
- Make models of 3D shapes with malleable materials.

Whiteboard tools
The Screen Shade can be used to hide and then slowly show your chosen shapes.

- Pen tray
- Shapes tool
- Select tool
- Gallery
- Screen Shade

Introduction
Explain that you will show the children a shape on screen. Open your pepared Notebook file (see Resources) and show the children the 2D shape on page 1.

Provide the children with a selection of 2D shapes and ask them to look for the shape that you have displayed. Ask: *What is this shape called?* Provide the name if it is new to the children.

Adult-focused whole-class activity
- Organise the class into groups and provide each group with a box of 3D shapes to place in front of them.
- Explain that you will think of a shape and describe it. (Describe the shape that you have placed on page 2 of your prepared Notebook file, but do not show the page to the children yet.)
- The children must listen to the description and then sort out the shapes in front of them, putting back into the box any that do not fit the description. Continue to give one clue at a time, until the children have found the shape that you are thinking of. (For example, for a cube you could say: *My shape has flat faces. All its faces the same shape. All its faces are the same size.*)
- Activate the Screen Shade before going to page 2, where your shape will now be hidden. When the children have guessed, slowly reveal the image on the page.
- Repeat for the other shapes you have placed on pages 3 to 5 of the 'Build your own' Notebook file.
- At this stage, the children may call shapes by more familiar names such as *box* and *ball*. Introduce the mathematical names, but accept the more familiar names for the time being if the children do not remember the mathematical ones.

Adult-focused group activity
- Arrange for the children to work in groups with an adult. You may prefer to repeat this during the week until everyone has had a turn.
- The adult first places the 3D shapes inside the feely bag. The bag is then passed around the group from child to child. The adult should ask the child with the bag to find a named shape and take it out of the bag.
- Encourage the children to say its name and discuss its properties, such as: *it has flat faces, it is curved*, and so on.
- Limit the shapes for younger or less confident learners to cubes, spheres and cones.
- Include some pyramids for older or more confident learners.

Plenary
- Display page 3 of your Notebook file. Ask the children to look at the shape, name it, and find an example from the box of shapes in front of their group.
- Repeat this for the other shapes on pages 4 and 5.
- Encourage the children to describe a property of each shape.

PSRN Lesson 29

2D shapes

Learning objectives
- Development matters (Shape, Space and Measures): Begin to use mathematical names for flat 2D shapes, and mathematical terms to describe shapes.
- ELG: Use language such as *circle* or *bigger* to describe the shape and size of solids and flat shapes.

Resources
'2D shapes' Notebook file; tile sets of squares, circles, stars, triangles and rectangles; gummed paper shapes of squares, circles, stars, triangles and rectangles; paper.

Links to other ELGs
PD
Handle tools, objects, construction and malleable materials safely and with increasing control.
- Use 2D shape tiles as templates, drawing around these accurately, and naming the shape.

Whiteboard tools
Use the Spotlight tool to slowly reveal aspects of an image.

- Pen tray
- Select tool
- Spotlight tool
- Undo button

Introduction
Distribute the tile shapes among the children. Display the triangle on page 2 of the Notebook file. Ask the children to sort the shapes in front of them to find the shape that they see. Ask: *What is this shape called?* Agree that it is a triangle.

Select the shape and rotate it (by pressing and dragging the green circle) to change its orientation. Ask the children to decide whether or not it is the same shape.

Activate the Spotlight tool before moving to the next page of the Notebook file.

Adult-focused whole-class activity
- Invite the children to work in groups, with a box of 2D shapes in front of them.
- Explain that you will think of a shape and describe it. The children must listen to your clues and sort out the shapes in front of them, putting back into the box, one at a time, any that do not fit the description.
- Give the first clue, revealing a little of the square on page 3 with the spotlight. Keep giving clues and providing glimpses of the shape until the children have found the shape that you are thinking of. You could say, for example: *My shape has four sides. All the sides are the same length.*
- When the children have guessed, turn off the Spotlight tool to reveal your shape.
- Repeat for the circle on page 4. Say, for example: *My shape is curved. It has just one line, which goes all around my shape.*
- The children may use everyday language to name shapes such as *round* instead of *circle*. Introduce the mathematical names, but accept the more familiar names at this stage. Make sure, however, that the children do not confuse the names of 3D and 2D shapes, such as *square* and *cube* or *box*.

Adult-focused group activity
- Go to page 5 and show the children the house made from shapes. Ask them to help you to copy the picture by directing you as you move the shapes provided into place.
- Once you have completed the picture, press the Undo button until the page is reset. Invite volunteers to come to the whiteboard and try to make the house shape themselves.
- Next, provide pairs of children with some gummed paper shapes and paper.
- Invite them to choose some shapes to make a picture of their own choice, such as a face, an animal, a house and so on.
- As the children work, encourage them to name and describe the shapes that they choose. Encourage them to use mathematical vocabulary as they describe their shapes.
- Support younger or less confident learners by providing ideas of pictures to create.
- Challenge older or more confident learners to be more explicit in their descriptions.

Plenary
- Go to page 6 of the Notebook file. Ask the children to look in their boxes of shapes to find the shapes that they can see on the screen.
- Invite volunteers to use the shapes to create a picture of their own choice on the Notebook page.

PSRN Lesson 30

Ordering by size

Learning objectives
- Development matters (Shape, Space and Measures): Order two or three items by length or height.
- ELG: Use developing mathematical ideas and methods to solve practical problems.

Resources
Plasticine or play dough, boards and tools; 2D shape tiles; photocopiable page 102 'Ordering by size'. Prepare a Notebook file as follows - page 1: a 2D shape; pages 2 onwards: a page of 2D shapes such as three triangles, the same shape, but different sizes (ensure that the shapes are not in size order). Prepare further pages, using other shapes, and increase the number of shapes to be ordered to four or five for the Plenary.

Links to other ELGs
PD
Use a range of small and large equipment.
- Provide construction materials and ask the children to make models of different heights. Order the models by height.

Whiteboard tools
Use the Shapes tool to select and add shapes to Notebook pages.

- Pen tray
- Shapes tool
- Select tool

Introduction
Distribute the shape tiles among the children. Open the first page of your prepared Notebook file (see Resources). Ask the children to sort out their shape tiles and to find the shape displayed. Invite them to take turns to name the shape and to tell you one of its properties.

Adult-focused whole-class activity
- Reveal the first set of three shapes on page 2. Ask: *What are these shapes? Are they all the same? What is different about them?* Discuss the different sizes of the shapes and how the children know which is the smallest and which is the largest.
- Ask the children to tell you which is the smallest shape. Place this one first, on the left side of the page. Now ask: *Which is the largest shape?* Place this to the right side of the page. Ask: *Where does the remaining shape go?* Place this in the middle of the other two.
- Discuss how the shapes are in size order, from smallest to largest. Ask: *How can we change the shapes around so that the largest is first?* Follow the children's suggestions, moving the shapes so that they are now ordered with the largest first.
- Repeat for the other shapes on your subsequent Notebook pages.

Adult-focused group activity
- Arrange for an adult to work with a group of four to six children. (Repeat this activity during the week so that each group has time to work with an adult.) Each child will need some Plasticine or play dough, a board and some tools.
- Invite the children to make a shape like the first animal on photocopiable page 102.
- Ask the children to make another animal, but this time larger. Repeat for one larger still.
- Now invite the children to order their animals, smallest first, then largest first. Ask the children to describe the shapes of their animals, including the sizes.
- This activity is accessible for all levels of confidence in learning. Help younger or less confident learners with mathematical vocabulary and challenge older or more confident learners to be more explicit in their descriptions.

Plenary
- Display your prepared Notebook page showing four shapes of different sizes. Invite the children to describe each shape, including its size.
- Ask the children to help you to order these, smallest first.
- Repeat, this time ordering the shapes with the largest first.

PSRN LESSONS 1–5, 21 & 26   Name _____

Counting mat

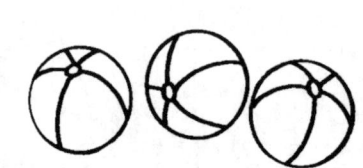

PSRN LESSON 3   Name _____

Ten in the bed

0 | 1 | 2 | 3 | 4 | 5 | 6 | 7 | 8 | 9 | 10

PSRN LESSONS 5, 6 & 7

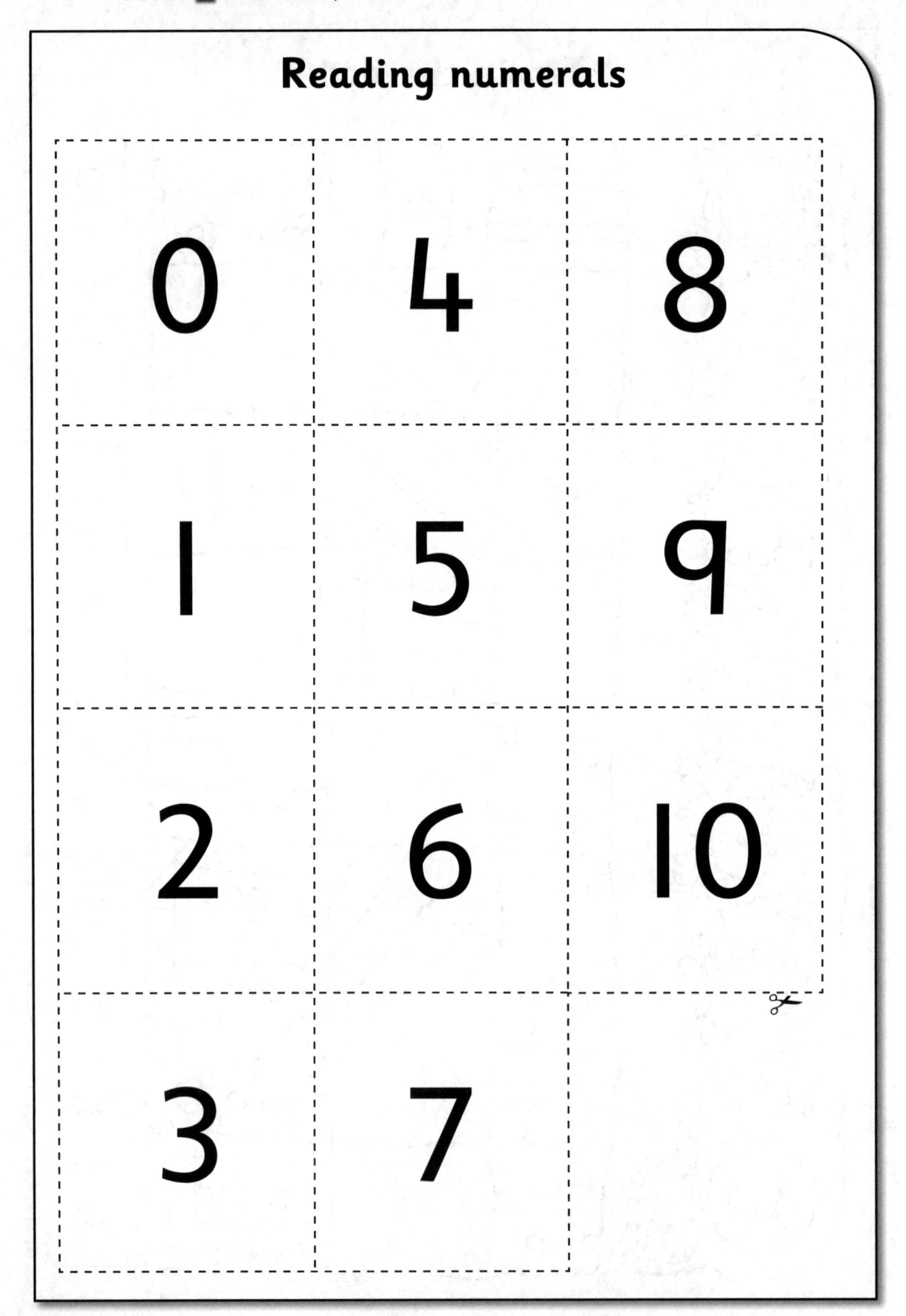

Reading numerals

0	4	8
1	5	9
2	6	10
3	7	

Recording how many

■ Draw some marks to match the number.

1	
2	
3	
4	
5	
6	

PSRN LESSON 7   Name _____

Writing numerals

- Take turns with your partner to take some counting toys.
- Count and draw the toys. Write how many there are.

Number	Draw the toys

PSRN LESSON 9   Name _____

What fits?

- Work with a partner.

  - You will each need a coloured crayon and a counter.

  - Take turns to put a counter on an empty square on the number track.

  - Ask your partner to say what number belongs in this square.

  - If you both agree then your partner writes in the number.

  - Repeat until all the numbers are written onto the track.

PSRN LESSON 12   Name _____

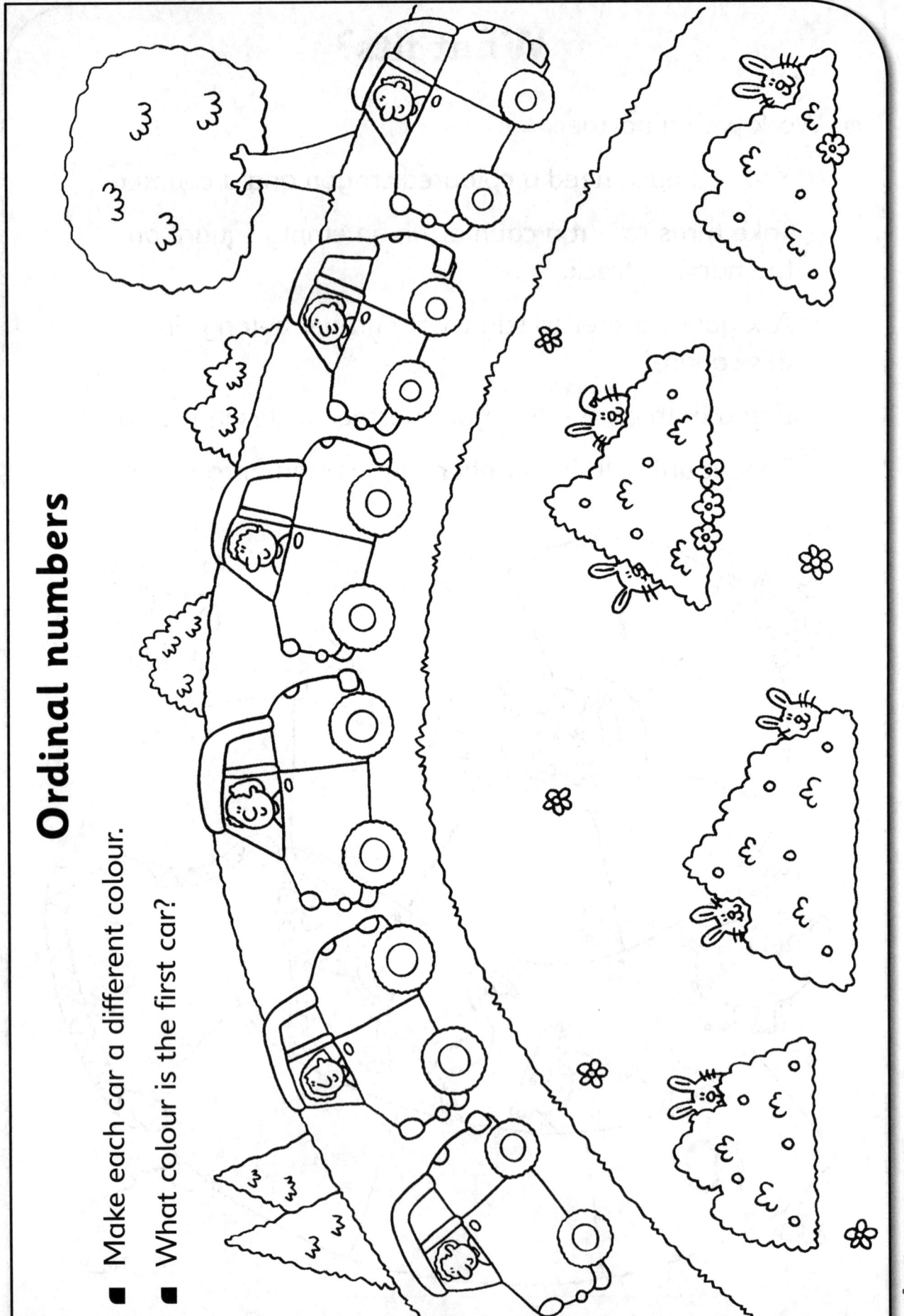

Ordinal numbers

- Make each car a different colour.
- What colour is the first car?

94 PHOTOCOPIABLE
100 SMART Board™ LESSONS • YEAR R

PSRN LESSON 13   Name _____

Word problems

- Count how many animals are in each picture.
    - How many are there if one goes away?
    - How many are there if another one arrives?

PSRN LESSONS 14, 16, 18 & 22   Name _____

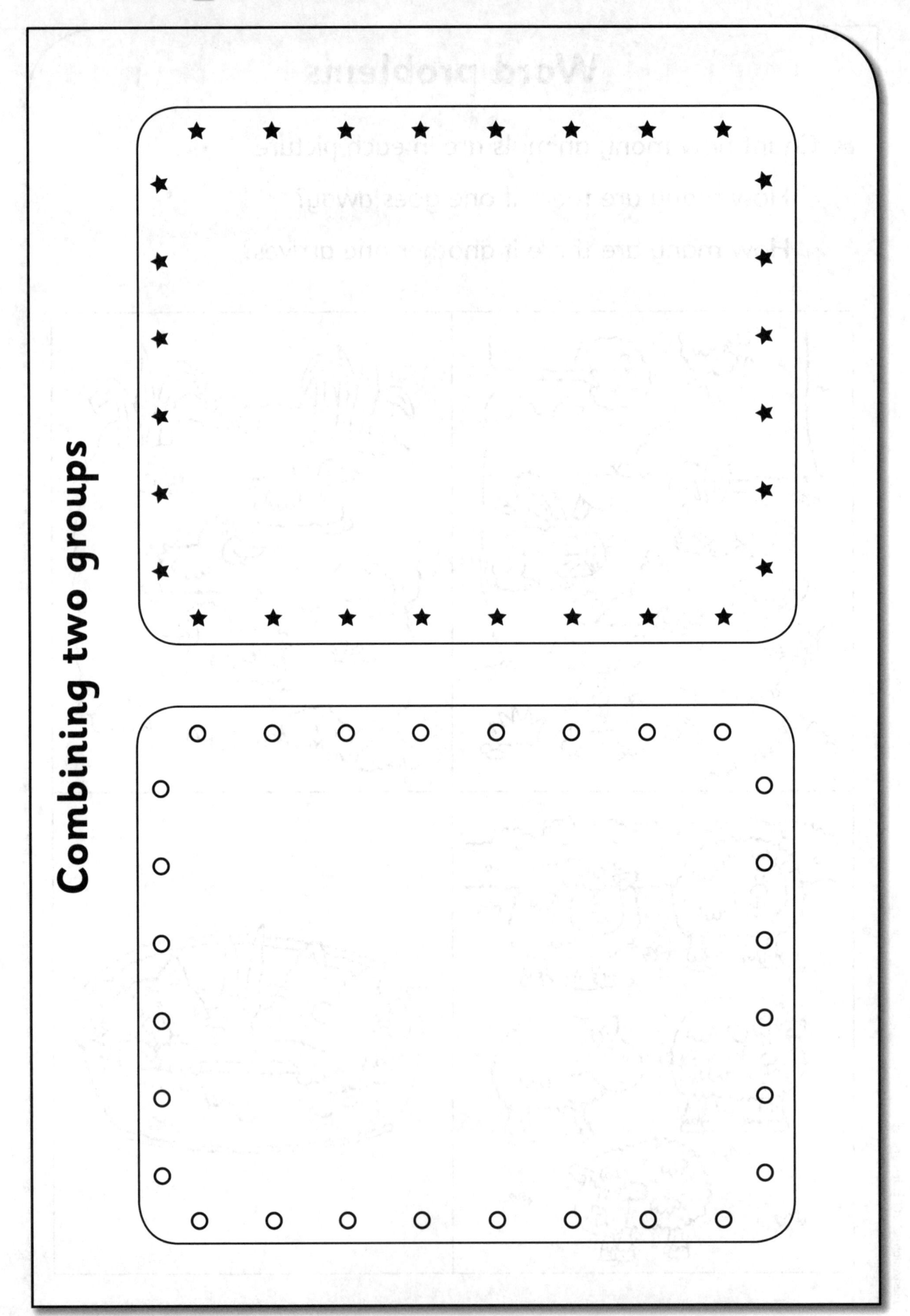

Combining two groups

PSRN LESSON 15   Name _____

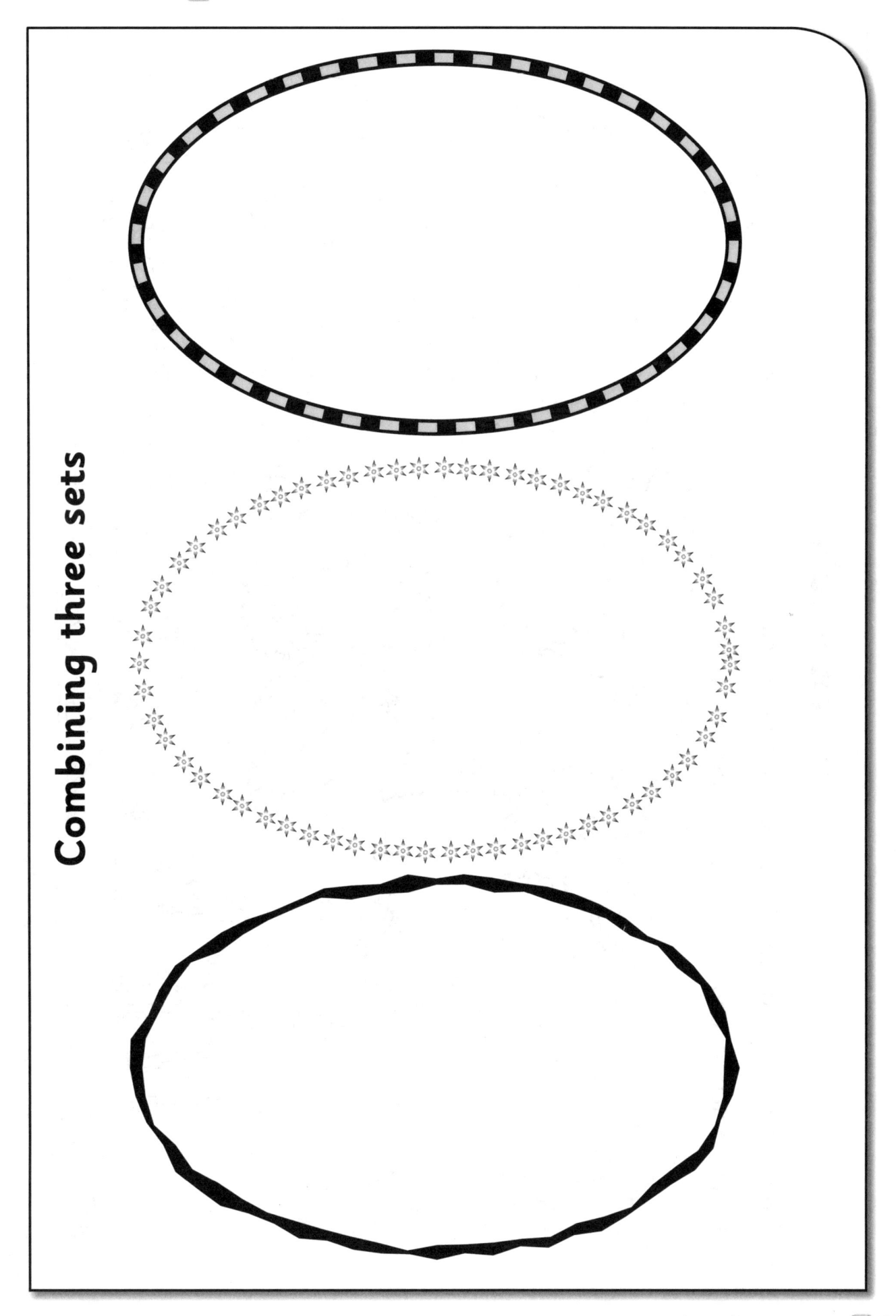

Combining three sets

PSRN LESSON 20   Name _____

Given totals

- Find two sets of animals that make a total of six.
- Place matching counters on each pair of sets.

How many more?

- Read each problem to the children.
- Ask them to solve it by counting up from the lower to the higher number.

1. There are four ducks on the pond. There are six chickens in the barn. How many more chickens than ducks are there?

2. There are seven raisins in Molly's lunchbox. There are four raisins in Peter's lunchbox. Who has more? How many more?

3. There are four apples on the plate. Eight children would like an apple. How many more apples do we need?

4. There are seven dogs. There are only three kennels. But every dog would like a kennel. How many more kennels do we need?

5. Nine cats are hungry. There are only six bowls of cat food. How many more bowls of cat food do we need?

6. Eight children want to play in the snow. There are only six pairs of mittens. How many more pairs of mittens do we need?

7. There are four bowls of ice cream. Ten children would like some ice cream. How many more bowls of ice cream do we need?

8. Nine children want to paint a picture. There are only two easels. How many more easels do we need?

PSRN LESSON 25   Name _____

Making patterns

- You will need: beads and laces.
  - Make the patterns.
  - Continue the patterns.

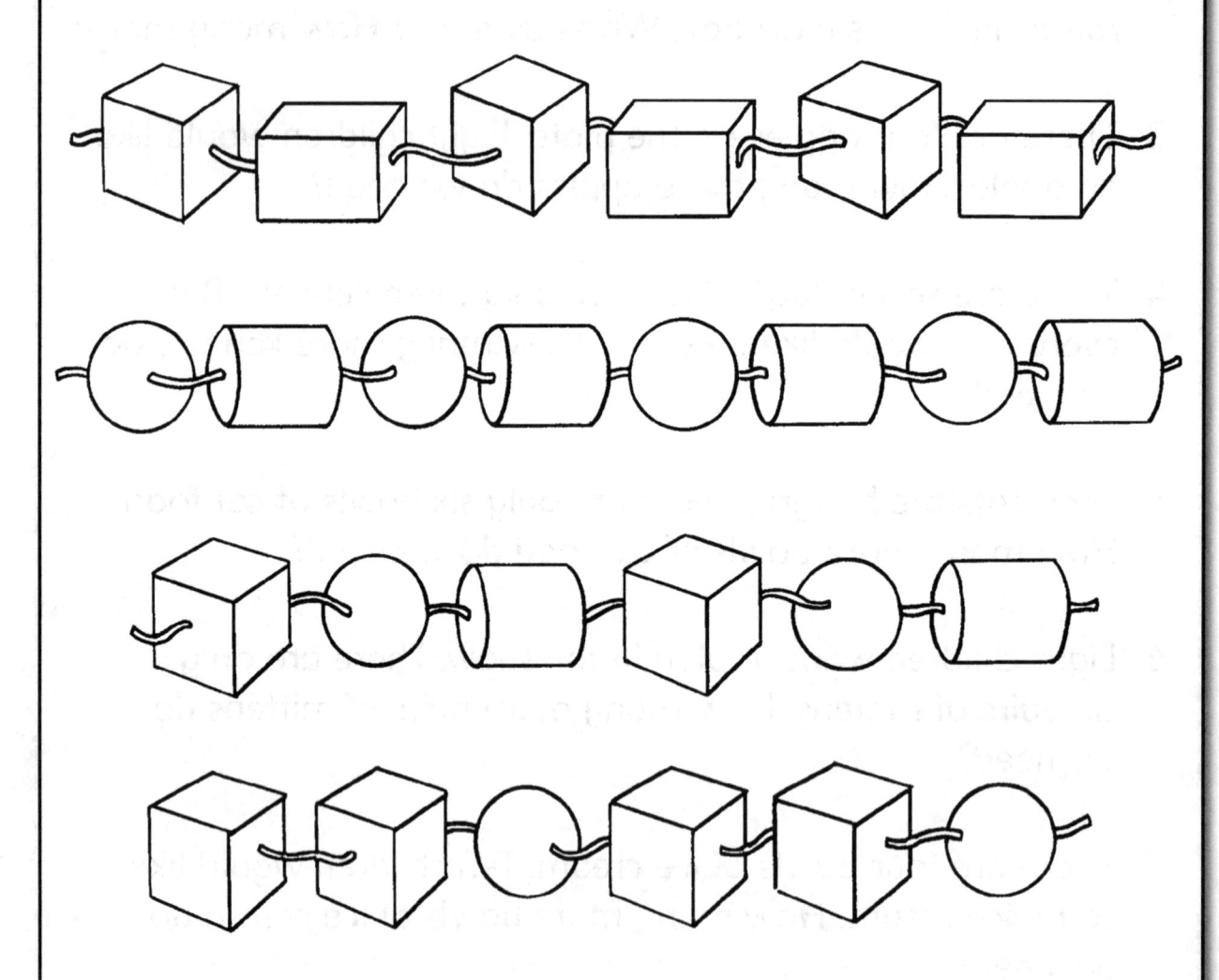

PSRN LESSON 27

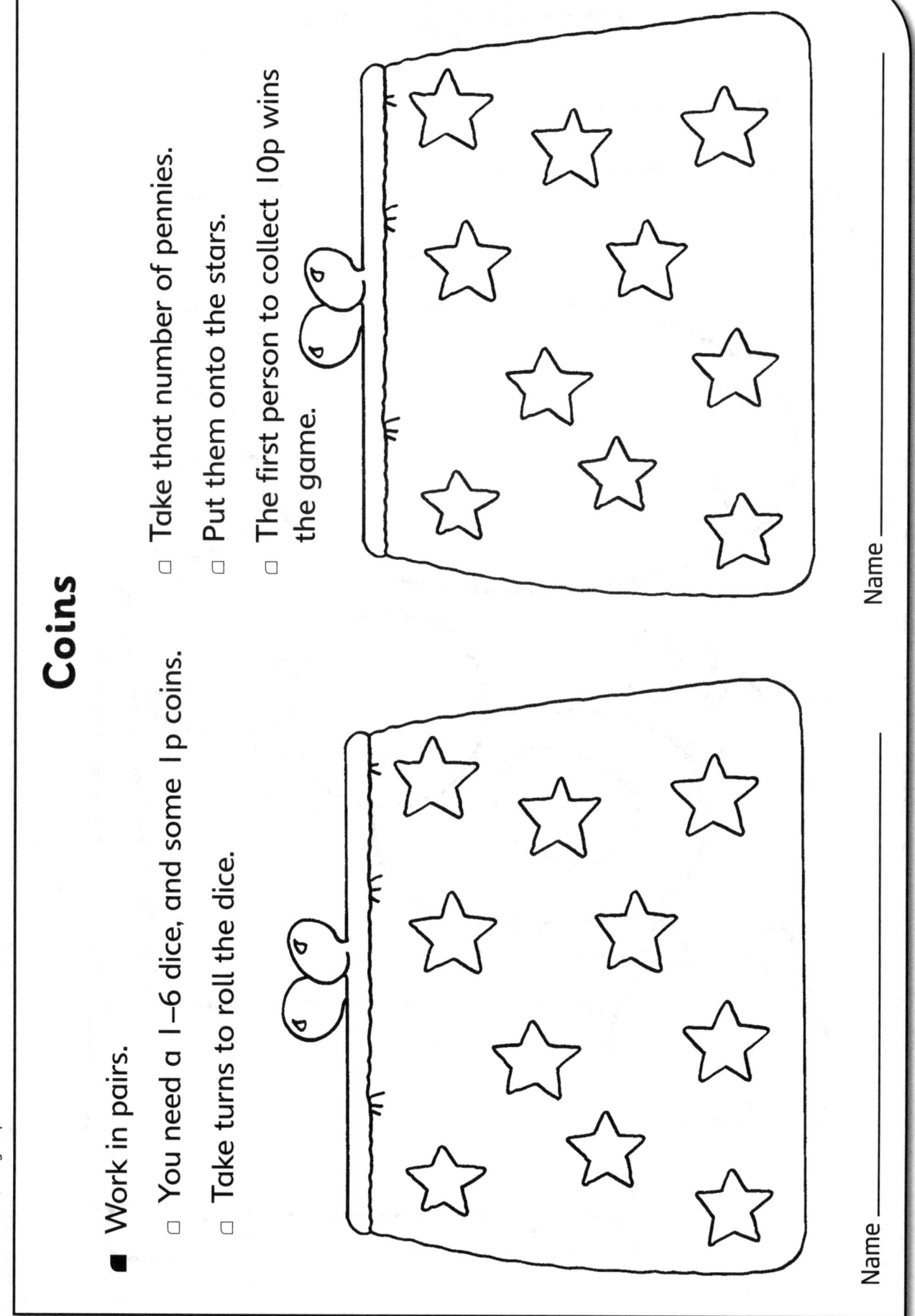

Coins

- Work in pairs.
- ☐ You need a 1–6 dice, and some 1p coins.
- ☐ Take turns to roll the dice.
- ☐ Take that number of pennies.
- ☐ Put them onto the stars.
- ☐ The first person to collect 10p wins the game.

Name

Name

PSRN LESSON 30 Name _____

Ordering by size

■ Make these animals.

KUW Chapter 3

Knowledge and understanding of the world

Introduction
This chapter provides 20 activities based on objectives taken from the Early Learning Goals for Knowledge and understanding of the world in the *Early Years Foundation Stage*. The lessons are divided into four themes, each lesson focusing on a broad aspect of this area of learning (science, geography, history, and design and technology). The themes are: Minibeasts, Early mapping skills, Children long ago and Planning a picnic.

Throughout these inspiring lessons, the children will become actively involved by using the interactive software which enables them to explore, observe, problem solve, predict, make decisions and discuss the world around them. Throughout, they will also learn about the everyday uses of ICT.

Title	Learning objectives	Cross-curricular links
Minibeasts		
Lesson 1: How many legs?	**Development matters (Exploration and Investigation)** Describe and talk about what they see. **Development matters (Exploration and Investigation)** Notice and comment on patterns. **ELG** Look closely at similarities and differences.	**PSRN** Use language such as *more* or *less* to compare two numbers.
Lesson 2: Where do animals live?	**Development matters (Exploration and Investigation)** Describe and talk about what they see. **Development matters (Exploration and Investigation)** Notice and comment on patterns. **ELG** Look closely at similarities, differences, patterns and change.	**CLL** Write their own names and other things such as labels and captions. **KUW (ICT)** Use information and communication technology to support their learning.
Lesson 3: What is the same?	**Development matters (Exploration and Investigation)** Describe and talk about what they see. **Development matters (Exploration and Investigation)** Notice and comment on patterns. **ELG** Look closely at similarities, differences, patterns and change.	**CLL** Write their own names and other things such as labels and captions.
Lesson 4: How do animals move?	**Development matters (Exploration and Investigation)** Show curiosity and interest in the features of objects and living things. **ELG** Find out about, and identify, some features of living things.	**PD** Recognise the changes that happen to their bodies when they are active.
Lesson 5: Life cycles	**Development matters (Exploration and Investigation)** Describe and talk about what they see. **Development matters (Exploration and Investigation)** Show curiosity and interest in the features of objects and living things. **ELG** Find out about, and identify, some features of living things.	**CLL** Attempt writing for different purposes.

KUW Chapter 3

Lesson title	Objectives	Cross-curricular links
Early mapping skills		
Lesson 6: What is a map?	**Development matters (Place)** Comment and ask questions about where they live. **ELG** Observe, find out about and identify features in the place they live and the natural world.	**CLL** Use talk to organise, sequence and clarify thinking, ideas, feelings and events.
Lesson 7: Aerial view	**Development matters (Place)** Comment and ask questions about where they live. **ELG** Observe, find out about and identify features in the place they live and the natural world.	**KUW (ICT)** Use information and communication technology to support their learning.
Lesson 8: Where is the hall?	**Development matters (Place)** Comment and ask questions about where they live. **ELG** Observe, find out about and identify features in the place they live and the natural world.	**PSRN** Use everyday words to describe position.
Lesson 9: Mapping the classroom	**Development matters (Place)** Comment and ask questions about where they live and the natural world. **Development matters (Place)** Notice differences between features of the local environment. **ELG** Find out about their environment, and talk about those features they like and dislike.	**PSED** Have a developing awareness of their own needs, views and feelings, and be sensitive to the needs, views and feelings of others.
Lesson 10: Following directions	**Development matters (ICT)** Know how to operate simple equipment. **Development matters (ICT)** Use ICT to perform simple functions. **ELG** Use information and communication technology and programmable toys to support their learning.	**PSRN** Use developing mathematical ideas to solve problems.
Children long ago		
Lesson 11: Timelines	**Development matters (Time)** Show interest in the lives of people familiar to them. **Development matters (Time)** Begin to differentiate between past and present. **ELG** Find out about past and present events in their own lives, and in those of their families and other people they know.	**CLL** Attempt writing for different purposes.
Lesson 12: Games long ago	**Development matters (Time)** Show interest in the lives of people familiar to them. **Development matters (Time)** Begin to differentiate between past and present. **ELG** Find out about past and present events in their own lives, and in those of their families and other people they know.	**CLL** Write their own names and other things such as labels or captions and begin to form simple sentences, sometimes using punctuation.

KUW Chapter 3

Lesson title	Objectives	Cross-curricular links
Lesson 13: Clothes long ago	**Development matters (Time)** Show interest in the lives of people familiar to them. **Development matters (Time)** Begin to differentiate between past and present. **ELG** Find out about past and present events in their own lives, and in those of their families and other people they know.	**PSED** Have a developing awareness of their own needs, views and feelings, and be sensitive to the needs, views and feelings of others.
Lesson 14: Homes long ago	**Development matters (Time)** Show interest in the lives of people familiar to them. **Development matters (Time)** Begin to differentiate between past and present. **ELG** Find out about past and present events in their own lives and in those of their families and other people they know.	**CLL** Show an understanding of how information can be found in non-fiction books.
Lesson 15: When did they live?	**Development matters (Time)** Show interest in the lives of people familiar to them. **Development matters (Time)** Begin to differentiate between past and present. **ELG** Find out about past and present events in their own lives, and in those of their families and other people they know.	**PSRN** Use developing mathematical ideas and methods to solve practical problems.
Planning a picnic		
Lesson 16: Is it healthy?	**Development matters (Exploration and Investigation)** Show curiosity and interest in the features of objects and living things. **ELG** Investigate objects and materials by using all of their senses as appropriate.	**PSED** Have a developing awareness of their own needs, views and feelings. **PD** Use a range of small and large equipment.
Lesson 17: Where shall we go?	**Development matters (Place)** Comment and ask questions about where they live and the natural world. **ELG** Find out about their environment, and talk about those features they like and dislike.	**CLL** Attempt writing for different purposes. **KUW (ICT)** Use information and communication technology to support their learning.
Lesson 18: What shall we eat?	**Development matters (Exploration and Investigation)** Describe and talk about what they see. **Development matters (Exploration and Investigation)** Notice and comment on patterns. **ELG** Look closely at similarities, differences, patterns and change.	**CD** Explore colour, texture, shape, form and space in two, or three dimensions. **PD** Move with control and coordination.
Lesson 19: How do we use these tools?	**Development matters (Designing and Making)** Begin to try out a range of tools and techniques safely. **Development matters (Designing and Making)** Use simple tools and techniques competently and appropriately. **ELG** Select the tools and techniques they need to shape, assemble and join materials they are using.	**PD** Handle tools, objects, construction and malleable materials safely and with increasing control.
Lesson 20: Making pizza	**Development matters (Designing and Making)** Begin to try out a range of tools and techniques safely. **Development matters (Designing and Making)** Use simple tools and techniques competently and appropriately. **ELG** Select the tools and techniques they need to use to shape, assemble and join materials they are working with.	**PSRN** Use developing mathematical ideas to solve problems.

KUW Lesson 1

Learning objectives
- Development matters (Exploration and Investigation): Describe and talk about what they see.
- Development matters (Exploration and investigation): Notice and comment on patterns.
- ELG: Look closely at similarities and differences.

Resources
'How many legs?' Notebook file; photocopiable page 126 'How many legs?'; plastic animals; sorting hoops; texts involving a variety of animals; Plasticine and pipe-cleaners; tray of sand or earth and leaves; magnifying glasses, paper and clipboards.

Links to other ELGs
PSRN
Use vocabulary such as *more* or *less* to compare two numbers.
- Suggest that the children extend the hoop activity by sorting according to whether an animal has more or less than a given number of legs.

Whiteboard tools
Reveal the answers in the Introduction by pressing on the blue rectangles and then pressing the Delete button (or select the Delete option from the dropdown menu). Alternatively move the rectangles to the bottom of the page.

- Pen tray
- Select tool
- Delete button

How many legs?

Introduction
Display page 2 of the 'How many legs?' Notebook file, showing photographs of animals. Ask the children to name them. Use the Delete button ✖ (or select the Delete option from the dropdown menu) to remove the boxes to reveal the names as the children identity each animal.

Adult-focused whole-class activity
- Talk about the different animals on page 2 together. Encourage the children to tell you what they notice about them.
- Arrange the children in pairs to discuss where they might have encountered the animals before.
- Steer the discussion to the number of legs of each animal. Can the children think of any animals with an odd numbers of legs? Notice how, generally, legs tend to be arranged in pairs.
- Go to page 3 of the Notebook file and, together, drag the animal photographs from the box in the middle, and sort them by the number of legs.

Adult-focused group activity
- Provide each child with a copy of photocopiable page 126. Invite them to cut out the animals and stick them onto the table in the top half of the sheet, sorting them according to the number of legs. Ask: *How many legs has this animal? How can you find out?*
- Support younger or less confident learners by limiting the sort to *four legs* and *other*.
- Extend the activity by asking children to sort into *two, four, six, eight legs* and *other*.

Planned independent activities
- Provide plastic animals with hoops in which to sort them.
- Bury some plastic animals in the sand tray or in a tray of earth and leaves. Encourage the children to find and identify them, and to count the number of legs.
- Read some non-fiction animal books with the children.
- Leave Plasticine and pipe-cleaners on the creative table and challenge the children to use them to make minibeasts.
- Provide magnifying glasses, paper and clipboards to hunt minibeasts in the outside classroom.

Plenary
- Review the group activity and go back to page 3 of the Notebook file to check the answers.
- Display the pictures of the animals on page 4 and drag and drop the number of legs onto each.
- Use the pictures to establish the fact that insects have six legs; minibeasts with more than six legs are not insects.

KUW Lesson 2

Where do animals live?

Learning objectives
- Development matters (Exploration and Investigation): Describe and talk about what they see.
- Development matters (Exploration and Investigation): Notice and comment on patterns.
- ELG: Look closely at similarities, differences, patterns and change.

Resources
'Where do animals live?' Notebook file; photocopiable page 127 'Where do animals live?'; plastic animals; texts containing a variety of animals; digital photographs of parts of the outside classroom; a variety of collage materials and painting equipment.

Links to other ELGs
CLL
Write their own names and other things such as labels and captions.
- Give the children pictures of the animals used in the Introduction activity and ask them to write labels for them.
KUW (ICT)
Use information and communication technology to support their learning.
- Extend the photo activity by inviting the children to take their own digital photographs of the areas, showing any minibeasts they found there.

Introduction
Show the children page 2 of the Notebook file, which contains a number of different animals in a garden. Encourage them to name the animals. Ask questions such as: *Which animals do not belong in the garden? Where do they belong and why?* Delete ✖ the misplaced animals.

Adult-focused whole-class activity
- Using page 3 of the Notebook file, ask: *Which of these animals does not live in the sea?*
- Encourage the children to use talk partners to discuss where the animals live.
- Ask: *How do you know where the animals live? Have you seen any of them before? Does an octopus always live in the sea? What about zoos?*
- Decide where each animal lives and delete any that don't live in the sea.

Adult-focused group activities
- Using photocopiable page 127, ask the children to cut out and sort the animals shown into their different habitats.
- Support younger and less confident learners by having a choice of only two habitats and limiting the number of animals to farm or pond animals.
- Extend the activity by challenging the children to sort all the animals into one of four habitats: farm, pond, garden and jungle.
- Read some non-fiction books involving animals and minibeasts with the children. Focus on the habitats in which the animals live.
- Take digital photographs of parts of your outdoor area where minibeasts might be found and challenge the children to find where the photos were taken. Ask: *Is anything living there now?*

Child-initiated activity
- Provide plastic animals and minibeasts, paints and collage materials and leave them available on the creative table. Allow the children to explore and experiment with them.

Plenary
- Review the group activity.
- Display page 4 of the Notebook file. Ask: *Can we put the right animals into the right habitats?*
- Wait for the children's responses, then drag the animals into the habitats according to their instructions (farm, pond, wood).
- Press on the speaker icons once all the animals are sorted to hear the sounds that they make.

Whiteboard tools
- Pen tray
- Select tool
- Delete button

KUW Lesson 3

What is the same?

Learning objectives
- Development matters (Exploration and investigation): Describe and talk about what they see.
- Development matters (Exploration and investigation): Notice and comment on patterns.
- ELG: Look closely at similarities, differences, patterns and change.

Resources
'What is the same?' Notebook file; plastic animals; picture of ants; minibeast writing paper; names of minibeasts on card for children to copy; magnifying glasses; minibeast maths game; laminated pictures of animals cut up into jigsaws.

Links to other ELGs
CLL
Write their own names and other things such as labels and captions.
- Ask the children to write the names of the minibeasts they found, matching them to the places located during the hunt.

Whiteboard tools
Use the Eraser from the Pen tray to reveal possible answers in the Introduction. Use the Undo button to erase any unsaved changes.

- Pen tray
- Select tool
- Undo button

Introduction
Display page 2 of the 'What is the same?' Notebook file, which shows pictures of a woodlouse and a ladybird. Ask: *What is the same about these two animals? What is different?* Using the Eraser from the Pen tray, rub over the purple area below each picture to reveal some possible answers.

Adult-focused whole-class activity
- Using page 3 of the Notebook file, draw the children's attention to the ant (circled).
- Discuss the main characteristics of an ant: for example, they have six legs, no wings and they run rather than fly.
- Organise the children into talk partners. Ask: *Which of these animals is like the ant? Which of these animals is different to the ant? Why?*
- Use a Pen from the Pen tray to record the children's responses around the pictures on the Notebook page. Move the yellow circle to highlight the various animals.

Adult-focused group activity
- Take the children on a minibeast hunt around the school. Remind them of the different habitats that animals might be found in. When you find a minibeast, ask: *How is this like the ant?*
- Support younger or less confident learners by taking a picture of an ant with you to compare to any animals you find.
- Extend the activity by asking the children to complete a record sheet, drawing or writing the name of the animals they find.
- Back in the classroom, display page 4 of the Notebook file and invite the children to help you to sort the minibeasts according to a criteria they specify, such as *number of legs* or *colour*.

Planned independent activities
- Provide non-fiction books for the children to identify anything found in the hunt.
- Supply attractive minibeast writing paper in the writing corner with names of minibeasts to copy.
- In the maths corner, provide a beetle drive game or similar.
- Cut up laminated pictures of different minibeasts into jigsaw puzzles for the children to construct. Challenge them to name the minibeasts and decide how they are similar or different to each other.

Plenary
- Discuss the minibeast hunt. Ask: *What did we find? How did we know the names of the minibeasts?*
- Go to page 4 of the Notebook file again and press the Undo button until the page is reset. This time, write the names of two of the places where the children found the minibeasts above each set ring (such as *soil* and *plants*). Sort the pictures into the places you found them, or where you would expect to find them.
- Ask: *Where did we find the most animals? Why do you think they were found there? Were all the similar animals found in similar places?*

KUW Lesson 4

How do animals move?

Learning objectives
- Development matters (Exploration and Investigation): Show curiosity and interest in the features of objects and living things.
- ELG: Find out about, and identify, some features of living things.

Resources
'How many legs?' Notebook file; a large space to move around in, such as a hall; a variety of classical music at different speeds and played on different instruments; variety of sound makers; video of animals moving (if available), including walking, running, slithering, flying, swimming, gliding, crawling, jumping; plastic animals and play mat; painting resources.

Links to other ELGs
PD
Recognise the changes that happen to their bodies when they are active.
- Question the children about how they felt when they moved in the various ways during the activity.

Introduction
Open the 'How many legs?' Notebook file and press on the button next to Lesson 4 to go to page 5. Discuss the variety of animals shown. Ask: *How do these animals move? Can you think of any other ways that animals move? Which animals move in the same way as a cat? What do we call the different ways that horses move? Do all animals with wings fly? Are there any other animals that move like the slug?*

If possible, show the children a video of animals moving. Use a Pen from the Pen tray to write the names of the movements next to the animals on the Notebook page.

Adult-focused whole-class activity
- Take the children into the hall or other large space and challenge them to move like different animals.
- Play some music to help the children to think of different animals (such as *Carnival of the Animals* by Saint-Saëns or *Peter and the Wolf* by Prokofiev). Include different short pieces of music that are suggestive of various animal movements. If these pieces are not available, most classical music can be applied to animal movement: for example, slow cello music for snails; fast strings for insects; trumpets played loudly for lions; full orchestra playing slowly for elephants.

Planned independent activities
- Provide a variety of sound makers and encourage the children to recall the movement work that they have just done. Invite them to make their own minibeast music.
- Clear an open space in the classroom or in your outdoor area for the children to move to music played on the class CD player.
- In the creative area, supply paints and paper for the children to paint a picture of their favourite animal moving.

Child-initiated activity
- Provide plastic animals and a play mat for the children to explore and experiment with.

Plenary
- Ask: *Which animals did we pretend to be? Did they move by flying, slithering or crawling? Were they fast or slow? Do all animals with wings always fly? Do all animals with no legs slither?*
- Go to page 6 of the Notebook file. Invite volunteers to come to the whiteboard and take a turn to select and drag an animal from the box in the middle and sort them by the way they move (fly, slither, walk and swim).

Whiteboard tools
Use a Pen from the Pen tray to write down the ways that the animals move.

- Pen tray
- Select tool

KUW Lesson 5

Life cycles

Learning objectives
- Development matters (Exploration and Investigation): Describe and talk about what they see.
- Development matters (Exploration and Investigation): Show curiosity and interest in the features of objects and living things.
- ELG: Find out about, and identify, some features of living things.

Resources
'Build your own' file; photocopiable page 128 'Life cycle of a frog'; frogspawn (if possible); water tray with plastic frogs and pond creatures; jelly in small trays; magnifying glasses. Open the 'Build your own' file, which consists of a blank Notebook page and a ready-made collection of resources located in My Content in the Gallery, and use it to prepare a Notebook file. On the first page add photographs of people of different ages. On the second page add a picture of a frog and on the next page add images to illustrate the life cycle of a frog (but muddle them up so that they are not in the correct order). Add the complete life cycle of a frog to page 4 of your Notebook file.

Links to other ELGs
CLL
Attempt writing for different purposes.
- Invite the children to write their feelings about the jelly activity. For example: *It is cold and runny.*

Whiteboard tools
- Pen tray
- Select tool

Introduction
Ask the children to discuss with a talk partner how they have changed since they were babies. Ask: *Have you always been this tall? Had all those teeth? Been able to run fast?*

Adult-focused whole-class activity
- Open your prepared Notebook file (see Resources). Show the children the first page, showing pictures of babies, toddlers and children of their own age, as well as older people.
- Ask: *How will you change as you get older?* Draw the children's attention to increases in height, changing hair colour, skin getting wrinkly and so on.
- Mix up the pictures and ask the children to tell you in which order they should go. Invite volunteers to come to the whiteboard and drag the pictures into the correct order on the screen.
- Display the picture of the frog on page 2 and ask: *Has this always been a frog? How has this changed since it was born?*
- Ensure that the children know that a frog began life as frogspawn, changed into a tadpole and then became a frog.
- Now go to page 3 to show the children the different stages in the life cycle of a frog.
- Challenge the children to tell you in which order the pictures should go. Invite individuals to move the images to show the correct order of the life cycle. The completed life cycle on page 4 can be used to check the children's work.
- If possible, show the children some real frogspawn or arrange a visit to a pond under close supervision.

Adult-focused group activity
- Provide each child with a copy of photocopiable page 128. Ask them to cut out the pictures of the life cycle of a frog and order them correctly.
- Encourage the children to talk about the pictures and use the correct vocabulary for the life cycle. Ensure that they know that adult frogs lay more frogspawn to continue the cycle.

Planned independent activities
- If possible, supply real frogspawn and magnifying glasses to examine it closely. Challenge the children to find some tadpoles with the beginnings of legs. Supply pencils and sketching paper and encourage the children to draw what they can see from close observation.
- Supply plastic frogs, toads, newts and rocks in the water tray to make a pond habitat. Ask: *What else might a frog need to make it feel at home?*
- Provide small trays of jelly for the children to feel with their hands. Ask: *Do you think frogspawn feels like this?* (**Important note:** Ensure that the children know that they should not touch real frogspawn in ponds in case they fall in or harm the eggs.)

Plenary
- Refer back to the life cycle of the frog and ensure that the children have understood its cyclical nature. Order the pictures on your Notebook page again.
- Ask: *Are there any other animals you can think of that start life in a different form?* (For example, a caterpillar becomes a butterfly.)

KUW Lesson 6

What is a map?

Learning objectives
- Development matters (Place): Comment and ask questions about where they live.
- ELG: Observe, find out about and identify features in the place they live and the natural world.

Resources
'Maps and views' Notebook file; photocopiable page 129 'What is a map?'; selection of maps at different scales (such as a road map, a street-names map, map of a local zoo or park); plan of the school; globe; road playmats and cars; pencils; travel brochures.

Links to other ELGs
CLL
Use talk to organise, sequence and clarify thinking, ideas, feelings and events.
- Invite the children to discuss with a partner how they would represent other features on a map. For example, what symbol would they use for a church, park, playground or swimming pool?

Introduction
Show the children the map of the British Isles on page 2 of the Notebook file. Ask: *Do you know what this is? Where on the map do we live?* Invite children to move the country names to the correct parts of the map.

Adult-focused whole-class activity
- Using page 3 of the Notebook file, demonstrate how the map shown (Wales) is just one part of the map on page 2. Ask: *Do we live anywhere shown on this map?* If not, go back to page 2 and use a Pen from the Pen tray to mark where the home town or city is.
- Move on to the world map on page 4. Explain that this map shows the whole world laid out flat. Encourage the children to try to locate the British Isles.
- Show the children a globe and match some of the country shapes on the globe to those on the map. Ask: *Do you know the names of any countries in the world?* Find these countries on the globe and map and write the names on the Notebook page.

Adult-focused group activities
- Provide the children with a selection of maps of different scales. Ask: *What can you see? What do the lines and pictures mean?* Draw the children's attention to the different types of graphics used on the various maps.
- Support younger or less confident learners by showing them just a couple of maps of places they might know.
- Extend the activity by giving children more maps including one of the world. Ask: *Which countries do you know? Which is nearer to where we live – France or Australia?*

Planned independent activities
- Provide each child with a copy of photocopiable page 129. Challenge them to colour the countries and cut out and stick the country names into the correct places.

Child-initiated activities
- Supply road playmats and cars for the children to explore.
- With the children's help, set up your role-play area as a travel agency. Supply holiday brochures, maps and a globe for the children to use in their free play.

Plenary
- Review the group activities. Ask: *What do people use maps for?*
- Go to page 5 of the Notebook file. Ask: *What do you think these map symbols mean?*
- Once the children have made guesses for all of the symbols, use the Eraser from the Pen tray to reveal the answers in the boxes underneath the symbols.

Whiteboard tools
Use the Eraser from the Pen tray to reveal the answers in the Plenary.

- Pen tray
- Select tool

KUW Lesson 7

Aerial view

Learning objectives
- Development matters (Place): Comment and ask questions about where they live.
- ELG: Observe, find out about and identify features in the place they live and the natural world.

Resources
'Maps and views' Notebook file; photocopiable page 130 'Aerial view'; everyday objects such as mugs, cups, toy cars, books, tins; objects in a large cardboard box; construction equipment; drawing materials; road playmats and cars.

Links to other ELGs
KUW (ICT)
Use information and communication technology to support their learning.
- Help the children to take digital photos of their constructions or of other parts of the classroom from an aerial viewpoint.

Whiteboard tools
Use a Pen from the Pen tray for drawing aerial views of objects.

- Pen tray
- Select tool

Introduction
Open the 'Maps and views' Notebook file and press on the button next to Lesson 7 to go to page 6. Show the children the objects on the page, and have similar real objects available, if possible. Encourage the children to describe the objects to a partner, with particular emphasis on the shapes.
   Ask the children to consider what the objects might look like from above. Allow them to come out and look more closely if necessary.
   Draw a simple aerial view of each object next to it on the Notebook page.

Adult-focused whole-class activity
- Remind the children of the previous session about maps and the fact that when we draw a map of something we can only draw it flat, even though places are not flat. We therefore draw places from above as though we were hovering above them. This is called an *aerial* or *plan view*.
- Use page 7 of the Notebook file to show the children how everyday objects can be viewed from the side and above. Drag the correct object to the matching aerial view.

Adult-focused group activities
- Provide some everyday objects such as those shown in the Notebook file for the children to draw from above. Encourage them to imagine themselves hovering above the objects and to only draw what they can see from above, rather than what they know is hidden underneath or at the sides.
- Support younger or less confident learners by providing objects with simple, regular outlines.
- Extend the activity by placing several objects together or by using objects with a more complicated aerial outline.

Planned independent activities
- Place objects in a large cardboard box for the children to view from above. Provide paper for them to draw the shapes.
- Put road playmats and cars on the floor for the children to explore. Challenge them to describe the shapes of the places on the mats. Ask: *Is this map drawn from an aerial view?* (Often they are not.)
- Provide building blocks and 3D shapes in the construction area for the children to build castles. Ask: *What shape does your castle look like from above?*
- In the writing corner, provide the children with copies of photocopiable page 130 to match the side and aerial views of common objects.

Plenary
- Review the group activities. Keep any construction castles that provide interesting shapes from above for all the children to discuss.
- Go to page 8 of the Notebook file and invite the children to help you to drag each object to its correct aerial or side view.
- Show the children page 9, followed by the aerial photograph on page 10 of the Notebook file. Explain how mapmakers use these photographs to help ensure that the roads are shown accurately.
- Annotate the map with labels of recognisable features such as roads, trees and houses.

KUW Lesson 8

Where is the hall?

Learning objectives
- Development matters (Place): Comment and ask questions about where they live.
- ELG: Observe, find out about and identify features in the place they live and the natural world.

Resources
Map or plan of the school scanned and uploaded onto a blank Notebook page (if possible); smaller photocopies of the school plan; doll's house models; digital photographs of key features of the school; Pelmanism game of objects in side and aerial view; outlines of an island.

Links to other ELGs
PSRN
Use everyday words to describe position.
- Ask the children to guide a doll or toy around their construction of the school, using vocabulary such as *forward, next to, left, right, turn* and so on.

Introduction
Ask: *Why do people use maps?* Remind the children that they are primarily used for people to find their way from one place to another without getting lost.

Adult-focused whole-class activity
- Show the children the scanned plan of the school on the whiteboard. (If this is not possible, show them an enlarged plan on paper.)
- Ask: *What is this? Where is our classroom? How do you know? Where is the main entrance? The playground? The ICT suite? The library? The hall?* Use a Pen from the Pen tray to mark key features on the plan.

Adult-focused group activities
- Take the children on a walk to the school hall, noticing features on the way (such as the office and the toilets).
- On returning to the classroom, show the children the plan of the school and ask them to follow the route you took to the hall. Ask questions such as: *Where on the plan are the office and toilets?*
- Give each child a photocopy of the school plan and encourage them to draw the route you followed.
- Support younger or less confident learners by giving them a doll's house model person to 'walk' round the route on the plan.
- Extend the activity by asking older or more confident learners to mark the main features on the map and to begin to use a key (such as blue for toilets; green for offices).

Planned independent activities
- Provide bricks for the children to build a model of the school in the construction area. Challenge them to show the route from the classroom to the hall in their model.
- Provide digital photographs of key features of the school for the children to identify and locate. Ask: *Where in the school would you see this?*
- Supply a Pelmanism game of photographs of matching objects taken from above, and from the side, to reinforce understanding of aerial views.
- In the writing and drawing area, supply outlines of an island for the children to use to create their own treasure maps.

Plenary
- Return to your scanned plan of the school on the whiteboard. Ask the children to mark on it any further features they have found as a result of having seen the digital photographs.
- Ask: *If a new child joined our class, how could you direct him or her to the hall?* Encourage the use of directional language and suggest that they mention key features along the route.

Whiteboard tools
Upload scanned images by selecting Insert, then Picture File, and browsing to where you have saved the images.

- Pen tray
- Select tool

KUW Lesson 9

Mapping the classroom

Learning objectives
- Development matters (Place): Comment and ask questions about where they live and the natural world.
- Development matters (Place): Notice differences between features of the local environment.
- ELG: Find out about their environment, and talk about those features they like and dislike.

Resources
A very large sheet of paper or piece of cardboard; smaller boxes and collage resources; construction equipment; glue; outlines of classroom plan; sand tray with construction bricks; digital photographs of partially obscured parts of the classroom; outline of the classroom plan on the whiteboard.

Links to other ELGs
PSED
Have a developing awareness of their own needs, views and feelings, and be sensitive to the needs, views and feelings of others.
- During circle time discuss how a new child would feel knowing that the class have considered their feelings. Ask: *What do new children feel like? Have any of the class recently joined?*

Whiteboard tools
Use the Lines tool or a Pen from the Pen tray to create a basic outline of the classroom's shape. Use the Shapes tool to add shapes (such as squares for tables).

- Pen tray
- Select tool
- Lines tool
- Shapes tool

Introduction
Display an outline of the classroom's basic shape on a blank Notebook page. (Use the Lines tool or a Pen from the Pen tray to draw this.)
Explain to the children that they are going to produce a map of the classroom, showing all the important features, so that a new child could find everything they need.

Adult-focused whole-class activity
- Ask the children to discuss, with a talk partner, which are the most important features of the classroom. For example, the tables, writing corner, role-play area and sink.
- Encourage the children to think of what to put on the map (for example, they should not include people on maps, usually only objects or fixed features).
- List the children's ideas and then ask: *Where on this outline map should we draw the tables? The writing corner? The role-play area?*
- Compile a map of the classroom together, using the Shapes tool and a Pen from the Pen tray, ensuring that the features are shown in aerial view.

Adult-focused group activity
- On a very large sheet of paper or cardboard, invite the children to draw or stick on key features of the classroom. Use boxes for tables, draw chairs, use pieces of construction equipment for cupboards (especially if the cupboards depicted usually store that particular piece of construction equipment). Build up a three-dimensional model of the classroom, with every child contributing.
- Support younger or less confident learners by giving them boxes to stick in the correct positions.
- Extend the activity by asking older or more confident learners to decide where the features should go, considering the distances between the tables and the scale of the boxes used.

Planned independent activities
- Give each child their own copy of the classroom outline, as shown on the whiteboard. Invite them to draw their own map of the room. Challenge them to include every table in the correct position.
- Supply digital photographs of obscure parts of the classroom (such as a keyhole, a cupboard handle or a corner of a display board). Ask the children to locate the areas.
- In the sand tray, supply construction equipment for the children to model the classroom, a town or the hall.

Plenary
- Look at the outline of the classroom on the whiteboard again. Is there anything the children want to add to it following the structured play activity?
- Gather the children around the 3D map of the classroom. Ask: *Does this look like our classroom? Why/why not? Which parts do you like best? Are there any parts you don't like? Why not?*
- Allow the children to use the 3D map in future structured play, with small dolls to represent themselves and the teacher.

KUW Lesson 10

Following directions

Learning objectives
- Development matters (ICT): Know how to operate simple equipment.
- Development matters (ICT): Use ICT to perform simple functions.
- ELG: Use information and communication technology and programmable toys to support their learning.

Resources
'Routes' Notebook file; programmable floor robot or similar; large sheets of paper; robot floor mat or prepared map on which to guide the robot; cardboard boxes for robot masks; CD-ROMs focusing on position and direction.

Links to other ELGs
PSRN
Use developing mathematical ideas to solve problems.
- Pose further problems using the floor robot, such as: *How could we get the robot to draw a square?'*

Whiteboard tools
Use a Highlighter pen to mark the routes taken.

- Pen tray
- Select tool
- Highlighter pen

Introduction
Go to page 2 of the 'Routes' Notebook file. Ask: *How can Nisha get to the windmill?* Establish the number of steps that she needs to move forwards and to the right. Move her along the route and then use a Highlighter pen to trace her route.

Adult-focused whole-class activity
- Invite the children to sit in a circle on the floor. Show them the floor robot and explain that it can be made to move around the floor when people tell it what to do. Tell the children that it can only do what we tell it to and nothing else.
- Ask: *How can we get the robot to move from my chair to James?* (for example). Encourage the children to discuss this with a partner, using directional language such as *forwards*, and a measure of distance.
- Gather the children's ideas. Try one of the ideas to see if the robot moves where the children wanted it to.
- Pose several more questions of this type, showing the children clearly how to program the robot, step by step.

Adult-focused group activity
- Using a robot floor mat, or a large sheet of paper with different destinations drawn onto it, allow small groups of children to program the floor robot to reach each destination.
- Encourage the use of positional and directional language as they program the robot, saying each step as they go along.
- Support younger or less confident learners by focusing on forwards and backwards for a certain distance only.
- Extend the activity to include directing the robot to make turns in order to reach the features on the map.

Planned independent activities
- Supply cardboard for the children to make robot masks. Suggest that they pretend to guide each other round the classroom.
- Provide some positional and directional software for the children to consolidate their understanding of the concepts.
- Supply the children with large sheets of paper. Invite them to work in pairs to produce a map for the floor robot to move around.

Child-initiated activity
- Have programmable toys available for the children to choose during free play. Provide floor mats and chalks for the outside area and leave the rest up to the' children's imaginations!

Plenary
- Review the children's learning by challenging them to talk in pairs and decide on how to direct the floor robot to another feature of the classroom. Alternatively, use one of the child-produced large maps to guide the robot around (if one has been produced on a large enough scale).
- Display page 3 of the Notebook file. Encourage the children to tell you how the robot will get home, using directional language. Move him along the children's suggested path, then use a Highlighter pen to highlight his route home.

KUW Lesson 11

Timelines

Learning objectives
- Development matters (Time): Show interest in the lives of people familiar to them.
- Development matters (Time): Begin to differentiate between past and present.
- ELG: Find out about past and present events in their own lives, and in those of their families and other people they know.

Resources
'What is happening now?' Notebook file; paper and pens; stories set in the past or with an element of time in them; small-world people and doll's house; laminated pictures of daily events for sequencing; story to read in the Plenary such as *Peepo* by Janet and Allan Ahlberg (Viking Kestrel Picture Books).

Links to other ELGs
CLL
Attempt writing for different purposes.
- Help the children to write their daily activities in the form of a simple diary.

Whiteboard tools
Use a Pen from the Pen tray to write and draw events on the timelines.

- Pen tray
- Select tool

Introduction
Introduce the theme by telling the children about two or three important events that have happened to you over the previous few weeks, such as a family birthday, a visit to a nearby town or a holiday. Model the vocabulary of time, such as *last week, a few days ago, before/after that*.

Display page 2 of the Notebook file and ask the children to help you to decide how to order the pictures. Model the language used (*last summer, in December* and so on).

Adult-focused whole-class activity
- Ask the children to talk to a partner about something they have done in the recent past. Choose three or four children to share their ideas with the whole class. Encourage the use of time-related vocabulary and model good listening skills, showing an interest in the speaker.
- Using page 3, draw or write down three of the events in chronological order.

Adult-focused group activity
- Encourage the children to tell you some interesting things they have done recently.
- Provide the children with paper and pens and help them to draw the events along a timeline, with today at the far right-hand side and the earliest event on the left.
- Support younger or less confident learners by sequencing only three events during a day, such as waking up, eating breakfast and coming to school.
- Extend the activity for older or more confident learners by including much earlier events, such as family holidays or starting school.

Planned independent activities
- Read stories to the children that are set in the past or involve events over a long period of time.
- Suggest that they use the role-play home corner to act out a day in their life.
- Challenge the children to remember the order in which they do things.
- Provide pictures of daily events for the children to put in the right sequence and talk about.

Child-initiated activity
- Provide small-world people and a dolls' house for the children to play with freely.

Plenary
- Look at the timelines that the children have made. Discuss them together, practising the relevant time-related vocabulary.
- Go to page 4 of the Notebook file. Ask the children to help you order the pictures along the timeline, based on a morning in the life of a child.
- Model the language used. For example: *In the morning; at lunchtime* and so on.
- Read the children a story set in the past (such as *Peepo* by Janet and Allan Ahlberg) to discuss the similarities and the differences between children's lives now and then.

KUW Lesson 12

Games long ago

Learning objectives
- Development matters (Time): Show interest in the lives of people familiar to them.
- Development matters (Time): Begin to differentiate between past and present.
- ELG: Find out about past and present events in their own lives, and in those of their families and other people they know.

Resources
'Games long ago' Notebook file; a selection of games and toys from the past 50 to 100 years (such as hoops, marbles and train sets); non-fiction books about toys and games in the past; pictures of toys from the past and their modern-day equivalents.

Links to other ELGs
CLL
Write their own names and other things such as labels or captions and begin to form simple sentences, sometimes using punctuation.
- Provide pictures of toys or pictures of children playing with them and ask the children to write a simple sentence to match a chosen picture.

Whiteboard tools
Use the Eraser from the Pen tray to reveal hidden answers.

- Pen tray
- Select tool

Introduction
Ask the children: *What is your favourite game or toy?* Listen to a few suggestions, then ask: *Did children long ago play with these games and toys? Why? Why not?*

Adult-focused whole-class activity
- Go to page 2 of the Notebook file and show the children the pictures of the old toys and games. Ask: *What are these called?* Once they have all been guessed, use the Eraser from the Pen tray to reveal the answers in the yellow boxes. Ask: *Do these toys look like anything we play with now?*
- Move on to page 3 and ask the children to decide which of the two toys shown is old or new. Select the items and drag them aside to reveal the answers hidden underneath.
- Repeat this activity on pages 4 and 5 of the Notebook file.
- Ask: *How can you tell if the object is old or new?* Draw the children's attention to the colour, material and whether the object looks faded or broken.

Adult-focused group activities
- Read non-fiction books about how children played in the past. Discuss any pictures showing children playing games and using toys.
- Show the children a small selection of games or toys from long ago (50 to 100 years if possible). Encourage them to handle the games carefully and to describe what they feel and look like (discuss their colours and the materials from which they are made).
- Support younger or less confident learners by limiting the objects to two and having a modern-day equivalent for them to compare them to.
- Extend the activity by hiding the games and describing them first to see if the children can guess what they are.

Planned independent activities
- Provide hula hoops and sticks, marbles, spinning tops, chalk and blackboards, teddies, train sets, wooden bricks and dolls for the children to use when role playing 'being in the olden days'.
- Supply pictures of toys from the past and their modern-day equivalents for the children to match. Ask: *Which goes with which?*

Plenary
- Go to page 6 of the Notebook file and show the children the variety of games and toys. Ask them to decide which is the odd one out. (The Jack-in-the-box is the odd one out, as it is much older than the other toys.) If they press on each toy they will hear either a groan or a cheer, to indicate a right or wrong answer.

KUW Lesson 13

Clothes long ago

Learning objectives
- Development matters (Time): Show interest in the lives of people familiar to them.
- Development matters (Time): Begin to differentiate between past and present.
- ELG: Find out about past and present events in their own lives, and in those of their families and other people they know.

Resources
'Clothes and homes long ago' Notebook file; photocopiable page 131 'Clothes long ago'; dressing-up clothes (including some in the style of the past); water tray with dolls' clothes to wash and hang up; cut-out paper clothes; cardboard dolls.

Links to other ELGs
PSED
Have a developing awareness of their own needs, views and feelings, and be sensitive to the needs, views and feelings of others.
- During circle time, extend the idea of what it might have felt like to live long ago. For example, ask: *Were the clothes comfortable? Were the toys and games fun? Would you like to have lived long ago?*

Whiteboard tools
Use a Pen from the Pen tray to annotate the pictures.

- Pen tray
- Select tool

Introduction
Ask: *What are you wearing today? Are these clothes comfortable? What happens when they get dirty?* Talk about the different types of clothes the children wear.

Adult-focused whole-class activity
- Show the children page 2 of the Notebook file and ask them to decide whether the photograph is modern or old. How can they tell? (The photograph was taken in 1918.)
- Ask: *Why does the child look different? What is she wearing?* Notice the girl's dress, the bow in her hair, her shoes and her necklace. Note some comments in the space around the picture. Ask: *Do you think the children were comfortable in these clothes?*
- Move on to page 3 of the Notebook file and ask the children to decide if this picture is older or newer than the first one. Ask questions such as: *Were the family who lived here rich or poor? How can you tell?*
- Ask the children the same questions as for page 2, and annotate the picture in the same way.

Adult-focused group activities
- Give each child a copy of photocopiable page 131, which shows clothes from three time periods. Ask them to number the clothes in chronological order (1 being the oldest and 3 the most modern).
- Support younger or less confident learners by limiting the choice to two pictures: one old and one from the present day.
- Extend the activity for older or more confident learners by giving them four pictures including Victorian, 1930s, 1970s and modern day.

Planned independent activities
- If possible, provide some Victorian or Edwardian-style pinafores, aprons, mob caps, braces, flat caps and knee britches in your dressing-up clothes box in the role-play area. This will give the children experience of different clothes other than their own. Ask: *Which clothes do you like the most or least?*
- In the writing corner, supply paper cut-outs of historical clothes and cardboard dolls to stick them onto.
- In the water tray, provide dolls' clothes for the children to wash and a line to peg them onto. Include some made of cotton, nylon and wool. Ask: *Which ones are easiest to wash and dry?*

Plenary
- Go to page 4 of the Notebook file. Ask the children to decide which is the oldest picture, based on what they have learned about clothes. Ask: *Which order shall we put these pictures in?* Drag and drop them on the screen into the correct chronological order.
- Go to page 5, which shows the correct order. Ask the children to guess the dates of the pictures before moving the red box at the foot of the page to reveal the answers.

KUW Lesson 14

Homes long ago

Learning objectives
- Development matters (Time): Show interest in the lives of people familiar to them.
- Development matters (Time): Begin to differentiate between past and present.
- ELG: Find out about past and present events in their own lives and in those of their families and other people they know.

Resources
'Clothes and homes long ago' Notebook file; flour and water to mix in basins with wooden spoons; role-play area set up as a bedroom from Victorian times; drawing materials.

Links to other ELGs
CLL
Show an understanding of how information can be found in non-fiction books.
- Show children an old-fashioned cookery book with some traditional recipes in it. Choose, read and make a recipe together.

Introduction
Ask the children: *What do you have in your bedroom at home?* Encourage them to discuss this with a partner and then take suggestions to share with the whole class.

Adult-focused whole-class activity
- Show the children the picture of a modern-day bedroom on page 6 of the 'Clothes and homes long ago' Notebook file. Encourage them to notice the similarities between it and their own rooms. Annotate the page with the main features (for example, bed, television and so on).
- Next, go to page 7 of the Notebook file and show the children what a bedroom belonging to their great-grandmother (their grandparent's mother) might have looked like long ago.
- Ask: *What is different? What is the same?* Annotate the picture with the children's suggestions.

Adult-focused group activity
- Using page 8 of the Notebook file, encourage the children to discuss what they can see in the Victorian kitchen and in the modern kitchen/dining area. Help them to write down or highlight on the Notebook file what is the same and what is different.
- Support younger or less confident learners by recording their findings as a group.
- Supply older or more confident learners with labels so that they can copy the words for objects they might discuss in the pictures.

Planned independent activities
- Set up the role-play area as an old-fashioned bedroom with crocheted blankets, a potty under the bed, a stone hot-water bottle, train set and dolls to play with, jug and basin to wash with. Model how to use these objects to extend the play.
- In the writing and drawing area, challenge the children to draw their bedroom, including any objects they think would not have been in a bedroom long ago, such as a TV or a games console.
- Provide flour and water for the children to mix in basins with wooden spoons to role play cooking in a Victorian kitchen. Ask: *What would we use now to cook?*

Plenary
- Go to page 9 of the Notebook file and ask the children to decide which features of the old kitchen are similar to those in the new one. Use the Eraser from the Pen tray to reveal some possible answers.

Whiteboard tools
Use the Eraser from the Pen tray to reveal the answers during the Plenary.

- Pen tray
- Select tool

KUW Lesson 15

When did they live?

Learning objectives
- Development matters (Time): Show interest in the lives of people familiar to them.
- Development matters (Time): Begin to differentiate between past and present.
- ELG: Find out about past and present events in their own lives, and in those of their families and other people they know.

Resources
'Clothes and homes long ago' Notebook file; photocopiable page 132 'When did they live?'; blank timeline (either on a Notebook page or paper); games from the past (hoops, marbles, wooden bricks and so on); dressing-up clothes from the past.

Links to other ELGs
PSRN
Use developing mathematical ideas and methods to solve practical problems.
- Extend the idea of past and present or earlier and later by discussing activities that the children have participated in recently. Ask them to order them and explain what they have done.

Introduction
Remind the children of the previous sessions on games, clothes and houses from long ago. Reintroduce the idea of a timeline, as used on page 5 of the 'Clothes and homes long ago' Notebook file.

Adult-focused whole-class activity
- Explain that a timeline can be any length and start at any time, but often finishes with the present day.
- Show the children the pictures from three different eras on page 10 of the Notebook file. Ask them to help you to order them correctly on the timeline.
- Continue to encourage the use of sequential vocabulary such as *first, then, later* and *longer ago*.

Adult-focused group activities
- Read stories that are set in the past or have an element of time in them.
- Provide each child with a copy of photocopiable page 132. Ask them to cut out and stick pictures from three different eras along a timeline in the correct order.
- Support younger or less confident learners by only giving them the toys to sequence.
- Extend the activity by giving children all three types of objects (toys, bedrooms and kitchen equipment) to sequence. Ask them to express opinions about which of the three eras they would like to live in.

Child-initiated activities
- Provide a range of dressing-up clothes from the past for the children to play with freely.
- Provide a range of toys from the past such as hula hoops and sticks, marbles, spinning tops, chalk and blackboards, teddies, train sets, wooden bricks and dolls. Notice whether the children use them for role playing 'in the olden days'.

Plenary
- Remind the children that people they know may have been born during some of the times they have been learning about.
- Using the blank timeline on page 11 of the Notebook file, insert the dates that the children in the class were born. Insert yours and your adult helpers' dates of birth and those of your parents. If any children know how old a senior relative is, insert this date too.

Whiteboard tools
Use a Pen from the Pen tray to add dates in the Plenary.

- Pen tray
- Select tool

KUW Lesson 16

Is it healthy?

Learning objectives
- Development matters (Exploration and Investigation): Show curiosity and interest in the features of objects and living things.
- ELG: Investigate objects and materials by using all of their senses as appropriate.

Resources
'Food' Notebook file; photocopiable page 133 'Is it healthy?'; selection of fruit and vegetables to taste; hoops and skipping ropes; drawing and painting equipment.

Links to other ELGs
PSED
Have a developing awareness of their own needs, views and feelings.
- During circle time, discuss how the children felt when faced with new foods. How did they feel after they had tried something new?

PD
Use a range of small and large equipment.
- Provide skipping ropes and hula hoops to use as warm-ups during a PE or games session. Ask questions about how the children's bodies feel during PE sessions and encourage them to consider this each time they exercise.

Introduction
Start off this lesson by checking for any food allergies that the children may have. Display the range of foods that they will probably be familiar with on page 2 of the Notebook file. Ask: *Which of these are good for us? How do you know? Which are not good for us? Why?* Remind them not to try eating anything unless a trusted adult has said that it is all right to do so.

Invite the children to tell you which pieces of food are good for us, and check by pressing on each item: you will hear a cheer for healthy foods and a groan for unhealthy foods.

Adult-focused whole-class activity
- Pass round a selection of fruit and vegetables for the children to feel, smell and then taste.
- Stress that these foods are all good for us, but that does not mean that everyone will like them!
- Praise the children for trying these foods, but do not put pressure on them to try something they do not wish to.

Adult-focused group activity
- Provide each child with a copy of photocopiable page 133. Ask them to sort familiar foods into 'healthy' and 'not so healthy' categories. Ask: *Is it good for you?*
- Support younger or less confident learners by limiting the number of foods they are asked to sort.
- Extend the activity by including some foods that might or might not be healthy, such as cereals and yoghurts which may have had sugar added to them.

Planned independent activities
- Set up the role-play area as a fruit and vegetable shop. Encourage the children to buy food for making a healthy snack.
- In the creative corner, supply paints and paper for the children to paint fruit and vegetable pictures, or to print with them.
- Cut open some fruit or vegetables and encourage the children to observe the patterns inside. Sketch the fruits using pencils or pastels.
- Provide skipping ropes, hula hoops and mark up a hopscotch court if possible. Remind the children of the importance of exercise in keeping healthy.

Plenary
- Using page 3 of the Notebook file, invite individuals to come to the whiteboard and help you to sort the foods into 'healthy' and 'not healthy' groups by dragging and dropping the images into the appropriate circles.

Whiteboard tools
- Pen tray
- Select tool

KUW Lesson 17

Planning a picnic

Learning objectives
- Development matters (Place): Comment and ask questions about where they live and the natural world.
- ELG: Find out about their environment, and talk about those features they like and dislike.

Resources
'Planning a picnic' Notebook file; photograph of your preferred picnic site; teddies; cloth, utensils and play food for a teddy bears' picnic; paper and pencils in the writing corner; pre-loaded graphics software.

Links to other ELGs
CLL
Attempt writing for different purposes.
- Invite the children to write about their perfect picnic or a picnic they have really been on.
KUW (ICT)
Use information and communication technology to support their learning.
- Print out the pictures that the children made using the graphics software and look at them together in a large group or as a class. Discuss which places look good for a picnic.

Whiteboard tools
Use the Select tool to drag and drop shapes. Use a Pen from the Pen tray to annotate the Notebook pages.

- Pen tray
- Select tool

Introduction
Open the 'Planning a picnic' Notebook file. Tell the children that they will be going on a picnic, but that you have not decided where yet. Use pages 2 to 5 of the Notebook file to make suggestions as to a suitable location. Add some of the children's comments to the page.

Adult-focused whole-class activity
- Go to page 6 of the Notebook file and choose the features of an environment that will make for a pleasant picnic: for example, away from traffic, flat ground to sit on and flowers. Ask: *What things might spoil the picnic?* (Too much noise, bad weather and so on.)
- Ask: *Are there any other good or bad features of places that we should consider?* For example, the absence of litter and a nice view.
- Now ask the children to suggest a suitable place nearby or within the school grounds. Ask: *Why would this be a good place for a picnic?*

Adult-focused group activity
- Suggest the place that you think the children should go to for their picnic. Show them a photograph of the place and ask them to describe the good and bad features of the location. Make a list of their suggestions.
- Support younger or less confident learners by giving them a choice of features, and ask them to decide whether they are good or bad.
- Extend the activity by asking the children to choose between two possible sites, giving reasons for their choices.

Planned independent activities
- Provide paper and pencils for the children to draw a perfect picnic environment. Ask: *What would make this place good for a picnic?*
- Provide a cloth, utensils, teddies and play food for the children to hold a teddy bears' picnic.
- Load a graphics software package ready for the children to use to draw a pleasant or unpleasant picnic site.

Child-initiated activity
- Have play food, utensils and picnic baskets available for free play in your outdoor area.

Plenary
- Take a class vote between two possible sites for the picnic.
- Display page 7 of the Notebook file. Demonstrate how to tally the vote by dragging the pentagons and triangles from the right-hand side of the page and dropping them onto the relevant side of the blank table. Ask: *Which site is most popular?* Discuss possible reasons for any differences of opinion.

KUW Lesson 18

What shall we eat?

Learning objectives
- Development matters (Exploration and Investigation): Describe and talk about what they see.
- Development matters (Exploration and Investigation): Notice and comment on patterns.
- ELG: Look closely at similarities, differences, patterns and change.

Resources
'Build your own' file; photocopiable page 134 'What shall we eat?'; play food and plastic knives; paper plates and collage materials; range of food-themed books.

Links to other ELGs
CD
Explore colour, texture, shape, form and space in two or three dimensions.
- The children could print with some of the foods discussed to make their own wrapping paper or paper plate to eat their picnic from.

PD
Move with control and coordination.
- Help the children to use needles and thread to stitch round the outlines of food.

Whiteboard tools
Use the Gallery to find images of favourite foods.

- Pen tray
- Select tool
- Gallery

Introduction
Make sure that you have checked for food allergies or any religious considerations.

Ask: *What is your favourite food?* Encourage the children to discuss their opinions with a partner and then share several ideas with the class. Try to steer the children away from chocolate and sweets towards main dishes and picnic foods.

Adult-focused whole-class activity
- Open the 'Build your own' file, which contains a blank Notebook page and a ready-made Gallery collection of resources saved under My Content. Choose pictures of some of the children's favourite foods, and drag and drop them from the KUW folder under My Content, onto the page. (Use a Pen from the Pen tray to draw any additional items if necessary.)
- Ask the children to consider whether this combination of foods would make a good picnic. Encourage them to consider the colours of the foods (*Do they look good together?*); their shapes (*Is there an interesting variety?*); their flavours (*Will they taste nice?*). Ask: *Are the foods healthy?*
- Tell the children that they will be making a pretend picnic pizza. Ask them what sorts of pizza they like. Which of the displayed foods could be used as toppings?
- Select some of these foods and move them to one side of the screen, so that you have a selection of possible toppings.

Adult-focused group activities
- Provide each child with a copy of photocopiable page 134. Ask them to choose the food that they would like to have on their pizzas. Make some suggestions to help them to decide.
- Help them to complete the planning sheet (including the tools they will use to make the food with).
- Now ask them to draw a picture of their picnic plate.
- Support younger or less confident learners by only asking them to choose the foods.
- Extend the activity by considering whether the foods look good together, and how healthy the completed pizza would be.

Planned independent activities
- In the creative corner, provide paper plates and collage materials for the children to use to make a pretend picnic plate of food.
- Read some fiction and non-fiction books about picnics or food to the children. Ask: *Which picnic foods look the tastiest? Are the picnic foods in the story healthy?*

Child-initiated activity
- Make play food and plastic knives available for the children to choose during free play.

Plenary
- Share some of the completed planning sheets with the class. Draw the children's attention to those pizzas that show colour or taste contrasts, or those that are particularly healthy.

KUW Lesson 19

How do we use these tools?

Learning objectives
- Development matters (Designing and Making): Begin to try out a range of tools and techniques safely.
- Development matters (Designing and Making): Use simple tools and techniques competently and appropriately.
- ELG: Select the tools and techniques they need to shape, assemble and join materials they are using.

Resources
'Food' Notebook file; a selection of table knives, plates, spoons, peelers and graters; vegetables and fruit suitable for practising peeling, cutting and grating skills on (such as carrots, apples and bananas); unusual and interesting fruits and vegetables for the children to draw (such as kiwis, lemons cut in half, passion fruit); drawing equipment; play dough and toy knives; role-play cutlery and pretend food.

Links to other ELGs
PD
Handle tools, objects, construction and malleable materials safely and with increasing control.
- Practise using the kitchen tools with increasing control.
- Encourage the children to make meals from dough, Plasticine and construction kits.

Whiteboard tools
Upload scanned images by selecting Insert, then Picture File, and browsing to where you have saved the images.

- Pen tray
- Select tool
- Delete button

Introduction
You will need to check your own school's food-technology policy before starting this activity, to make sure that you are following the rules for safety and hygiene.

Remind the children of the picnic pizza planning sheets they completed in the previous session (photocopiable page 134). If possible, scan one or two into the computer to show on the interactive whiteboard

Display page 4 of the 'Food' Notebook file and ask the children which of the items are used for peeling, grating or chopping. Use the Delete button (or select the Delete option from the dropdown menu) to remove the red boxes to reveal the answers.

Adult-focused whole-class activity
- Move on to page 5. Ask the children to help you to sort the foods into those that need chopping, grating and peeling. Explain that some foods could belong in more than one category. Demonstrate all three actions if you have the tools available.
- Show the children the tools provided for them to practise their cutting, grating and peeling skills. Ask: *What must we remember to do before we handle food?* (Wash hands, clean the table, put on an apron.)
- Model how to use each tool correctly and safely, ensuring that the children know how to pass tools to each other and that they understand the necessity for keeping them pointing away from people, towards the ground.

Adult-focused group activity
- In small groups, allow the children to practise cutting soft fruits such as bananas, and grating and peeling vegetables such as carrots.
- Ensure that the children hold the foods firmly onto the table and cut towards the chopping board with all their fingers on top of the knife for safety.
- When grating, ensure that the children hold a large piece of carrot near the end so as to avoid the risk of grating their fingers. (Graters that consist of a metal lid on top of a fitted bowl are easier for the children to use than the stand-up cuboid-shaped graters with a handle on top.)
- Support younger or less confident learners by helping them to hold the fruit and vegetables while they cut and peel them.
- Extend the activity by including more varieties of food to practise on and by asking the children to try to make their pieces of an equal size.

Planned independent activities
- Provide role-play cutlery and food for pretend cooking. Challenge the children to remember the safety rules for cooking with real food.
- Cut open some unusual fruit or vegetables to show the children the patterns inside. Encourage the children to make detailed observational drawings using pencils or pastels.
- Supply play dough and toy knives or tools for the children to practise cutting skills. Challenge them to cut the dough into equal-sized pieces.

Plenary
- Recap on the safety and hygiene rules for handling food. Ask: *How do we keep ourselves safe when we cook?*
- Discuss the skills that the children practised. Ask questions such as: *Which foods were easiest to cut? Why? What do we need to remember when we are grating?*
- Display page 6 and invite the children to help you to order the pictures.

KUW Lesson 20

Making pizza

Learning objectives
- Development matters (Designing and Making): Begin to try out a range of tools and techniques safely.
- Development matters (Designing and Making): Use simple tools and techniques competently and appropriately.
- ELG: Select the tools and techniques they need to shape, assemble and join materials they are using.

Resources
'Food' Notebook file; photocopiable page 135 'Making pizza'; food and kitchen implements; recipe for pizzas of your choice and pizza bases (if you would prefer not to make these); access to oven or grill; aprons; the children's planning sheets (from the activity on photocopiable page 134); teddies and play food for pretend picnic; 2D shapes and hoops; potatoes cut in half with patterns marked into them; paint and paper for printing.

Links to other ELGs
PSRN
Use developing mathematical ideas to solve problems.
- Ask the children to find out which topping was the most popular. Demonstrate how to illustrate this using a chart or a pictogram.

Whiteboard tools
- Pen tray
- Select tool

Introduction
Open the 'Food' Notebook file and press the button next to Lesson 20 to go to page 7.
Remind the children about where you are going for the picnic, and why (see Lesson 17); what you are going to make (see Lesson 18), and the safety and hygiene rules you practised in the last session. Summarise the points on the Notebook file.

Adult-focused whole-class activity
- Show the children the recipe you have selected to make pizzas. (Pizza bases or basic cheese and tomato individual pizzas could be used if you prefer not to make the bases yourselves.)
- Talk through the available toppings and remind the children that they have planned their pizzas, although they could adjust their choices if required. Give them their completed planning sheets (photocopiable page 134) to remind them of their ideas.
- Use page 8 of the Notebook file to practise building pizzas using the toppings available.
- Discuss with the children which fruit they would like to take as a dessert, and what they are going to drink on their picnic. Suggest healthy options such as water, fruit juice or milk.

Adult-focused group activity
- Make pizza bases (if appropriate). Spread tomato sauce or puree on the bases, chop the vegetables and fruit to put on the top, and grate the cheese.
- Support younger or less confident learners by restricting the number of cooking activities they try, and provide ingredients that have already been chopped or grated. Let them spread the tomato paste.
- Extend the activity by encouraging the children to grate or chop all the ingredients themselves. Challenge them to make pieces of an equal size, and suggest that they distribute the different ingredients evenly around the pizza.

Planned independent activities
- Once the children have made their pizzas, give each child a copy of photocopiable page 135 to use to evaluate their finished meals.
- Provide a cloth, utensils, teddies and play food for the children to hold a teddy bears' picnic.
- Using 2D shapes and hoops, challenge the children to make large pretend pizzas.
- In the painting area, provide cut potatoes for printing. Challenge the children to make a repeating pattern.

Plenary
- Take the pizzas, fruit and drinks to the picnic site and eat them.
- Talk about how the pizzas taste and what they look like. Ask: *How many marks out of five do you give your pizza? Would you change anything if you made one again?*
- Take a look at the pizza recipes that scored five and ask the children what made them so good.
- Record some of these points on page 9 of the Notebook file, or build the pizzas with the images available on the screen.

KUW ☐ LESSON 1   Name _____

How many legs?

- How many legs do the animals have?
- Cut out them out and stick them in the spaces below.

0	2	4	6	8

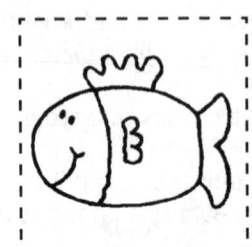

KUW LESSON 2

Where do animals live?

- Cut out and sort the animals.
- Match each animal to its home.

KUW LESSON 5 Name _____

Life cycle of a frog

- Cut out the stages of the life cycle of a frog.
- Stick them in the correct order around the circle.

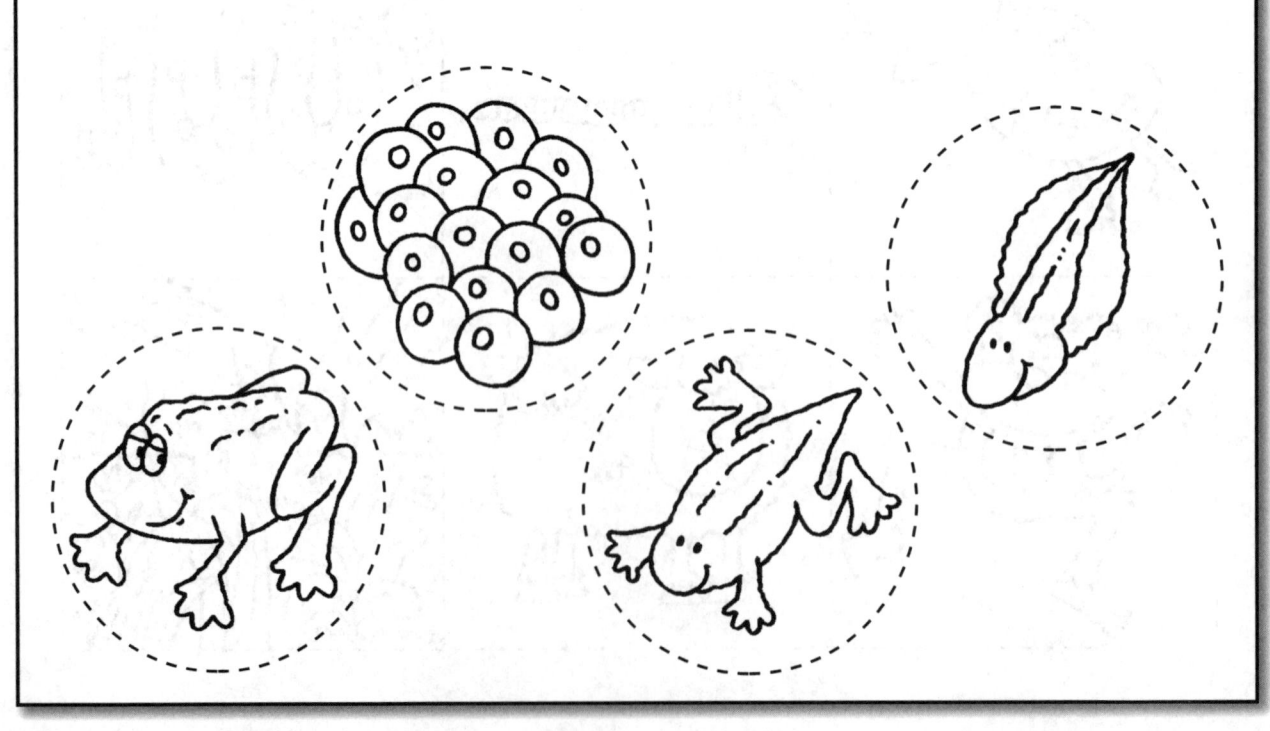

KUW LESSON 6   Name _____

What is a map?

■ Colour and label the countries of the British Isles.

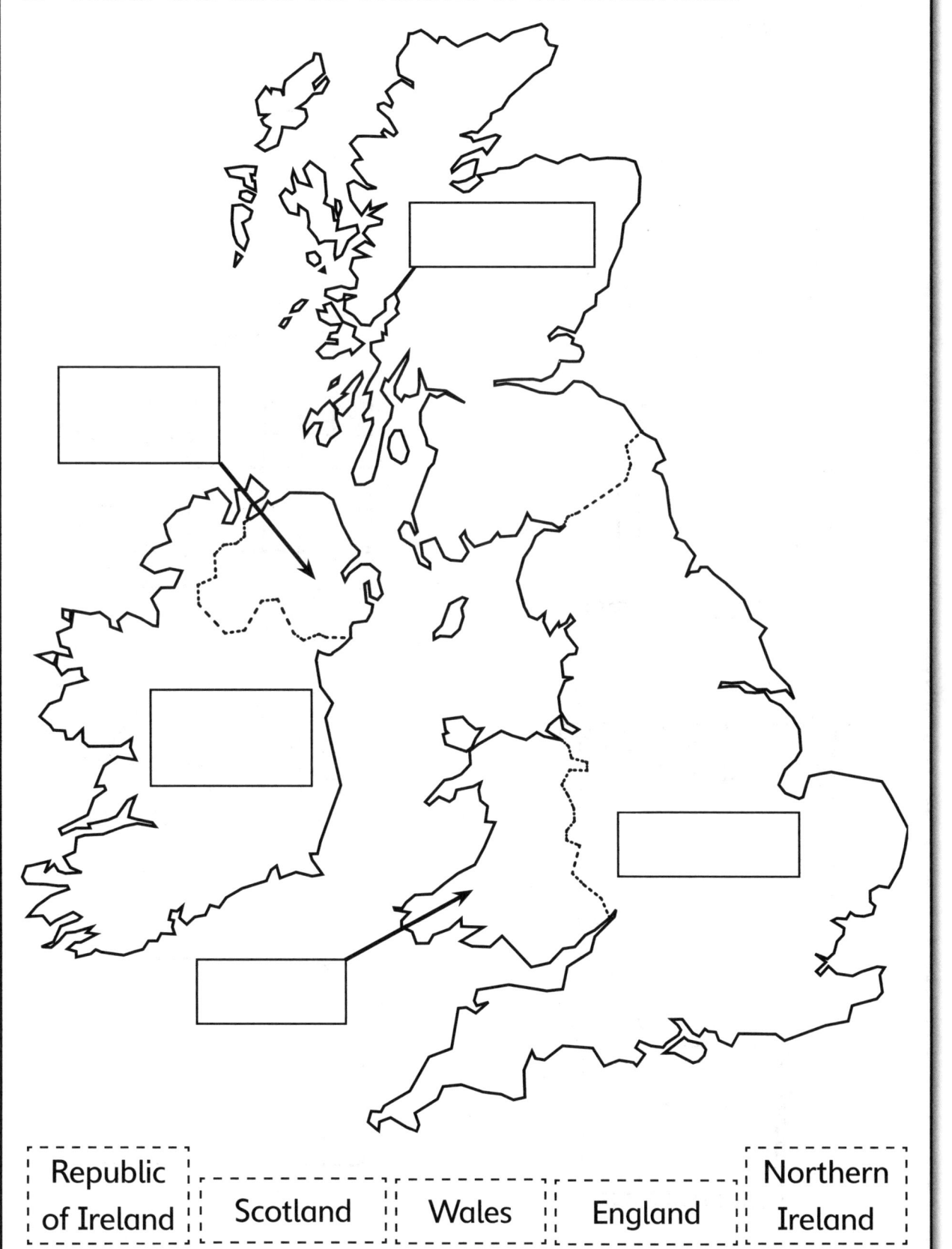

| Republic of Ireland | Scotland | Wales | England | Northern Ireland |

Aerial view

- Draw arrows to match the side view of the object with the aerial view.

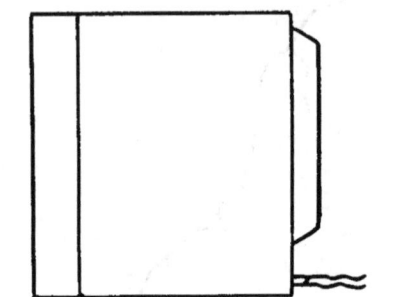

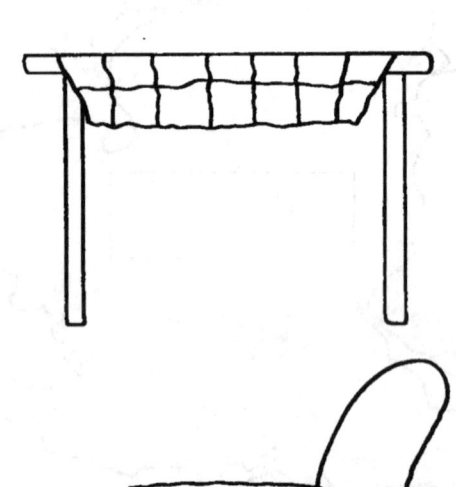

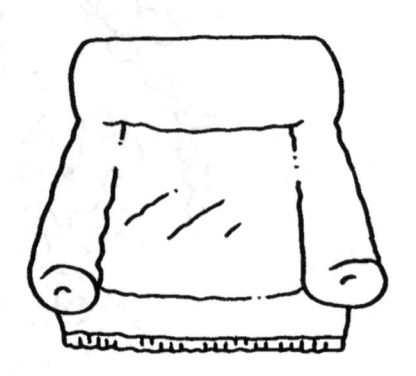

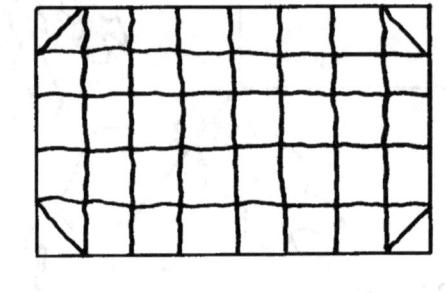

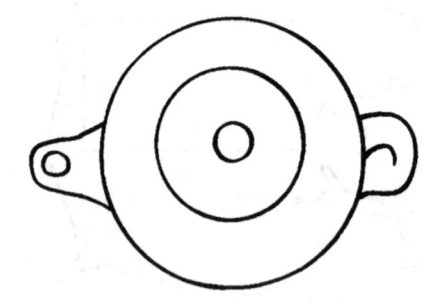

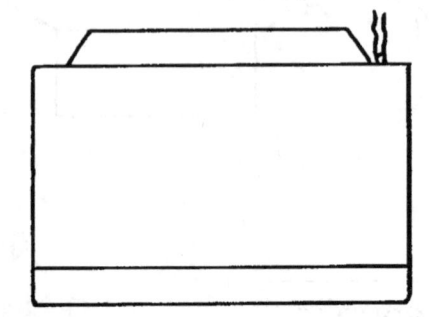

KUW LESSON 13   Name _____

Clothes long ago

- Which clothes are the oldest?
- Number the pictures 1, 2 and 3 to show the correct order.

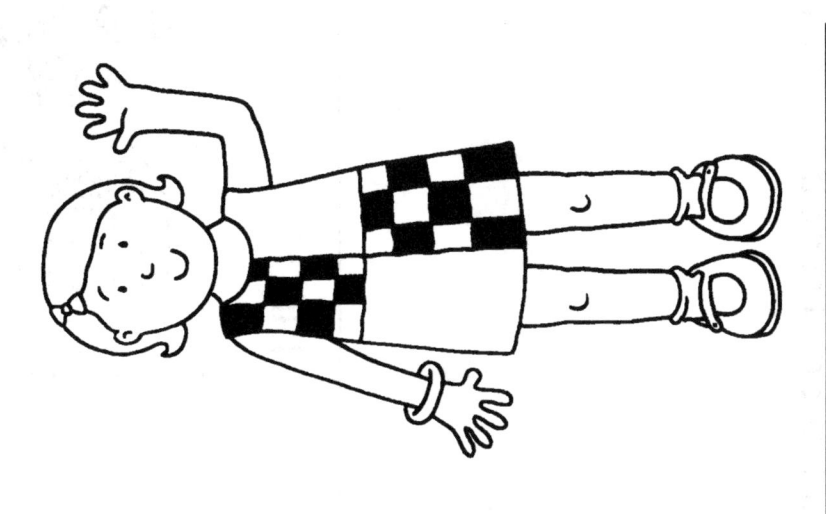

KUW LESSON 15   Name _____

When did they live?

- Cut out and stick the pictures onto the timeline.

1900   1960   2005

132 PHOTOCOPIABLE
100 SMART Board™ LESSONS • YEAR R

Illustrations © 2006, Jenny Tulip

SCHOLASTIC
www.scholastic.co.uk

KUW LESSON 16   Name _____

Is it healthy?

- Cut out and stick the foods in the boxes.

Unhealthy

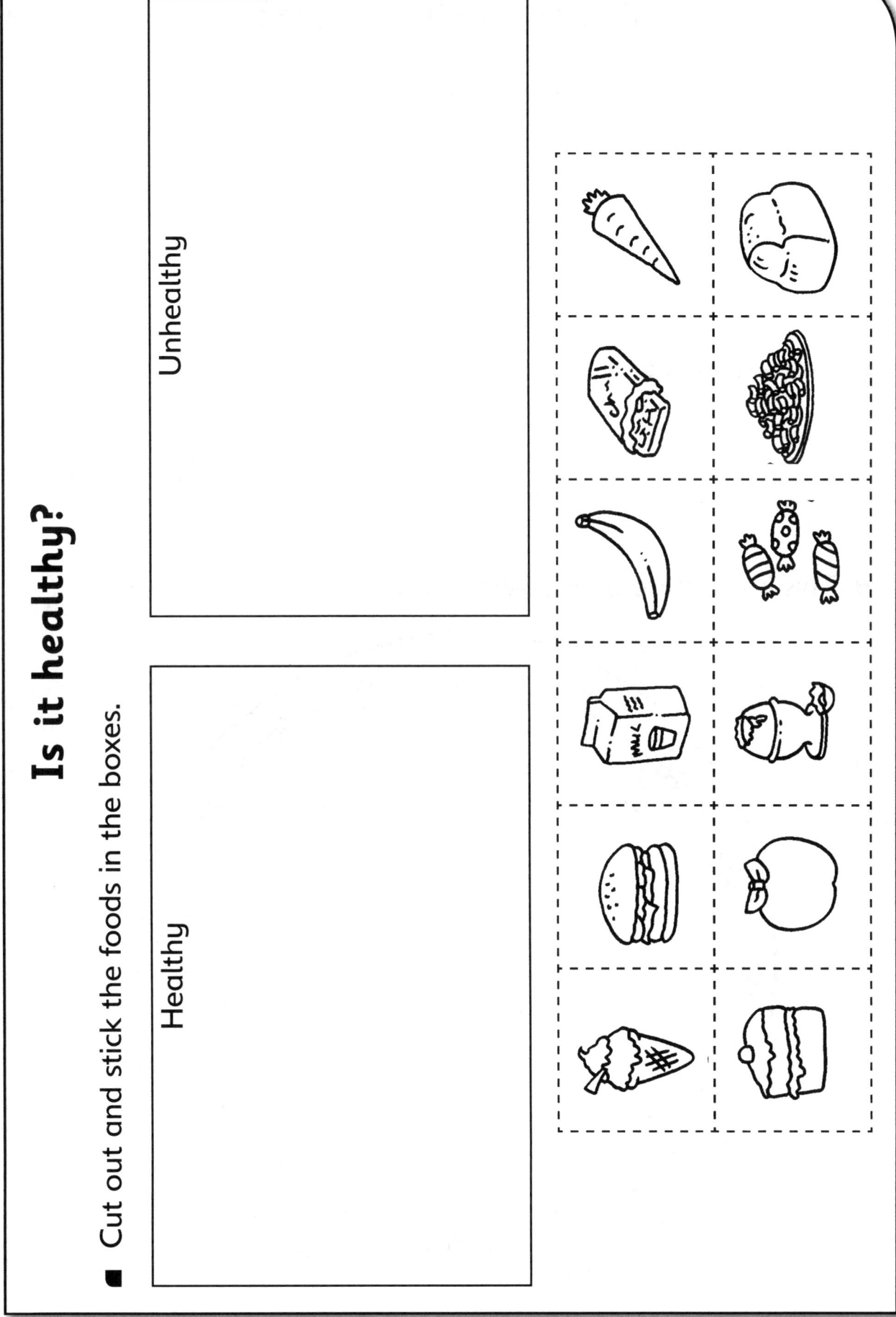

Healthy

KUW LESSON 18   Name _____

What shall we eat?

- On my pizza I am going to have:

- The tools I will need are:

- This is a picture of my picnic plate:

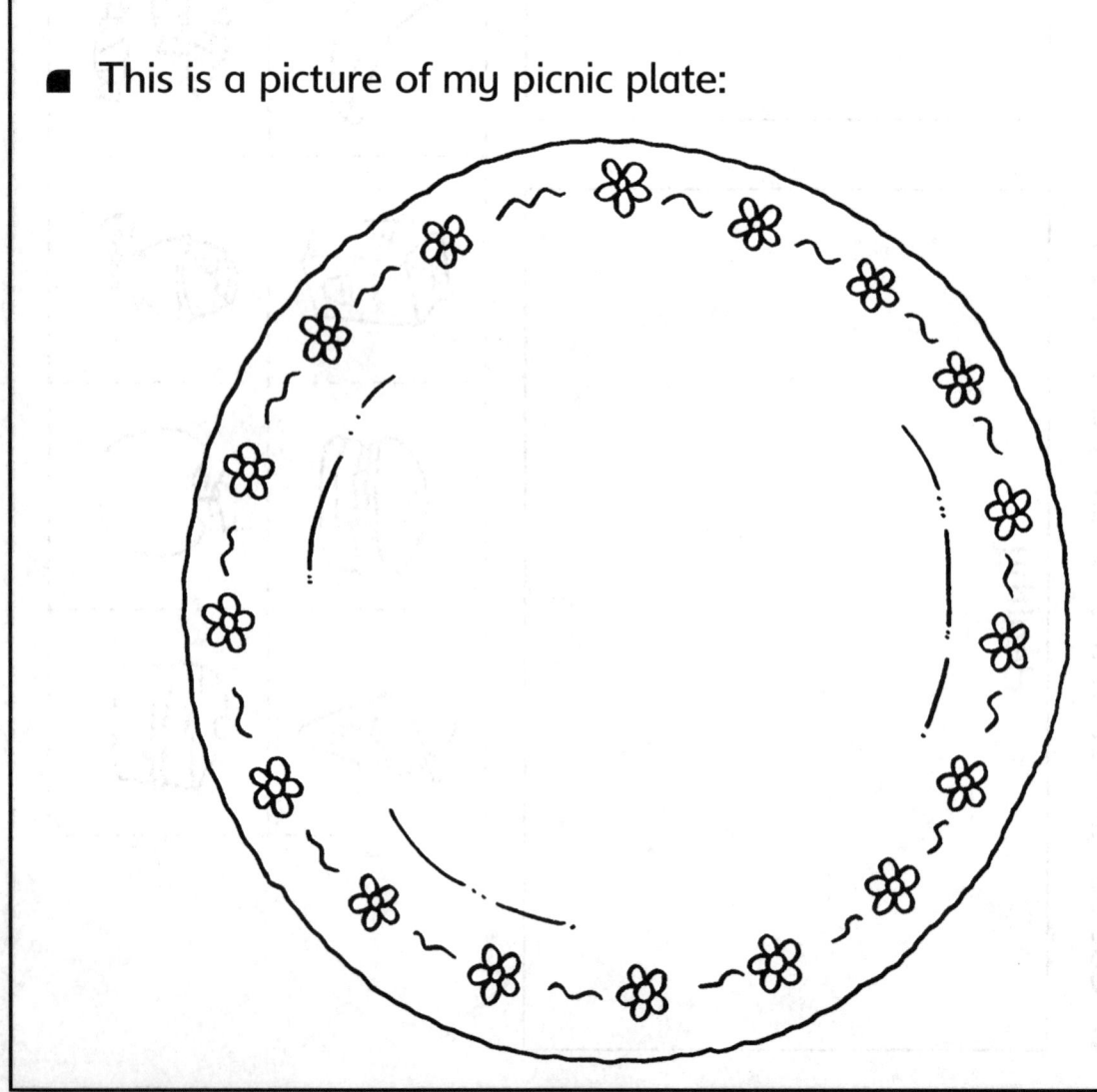

134 PHOTOCOPIABLE
100 SMART Board™ LESSONS • YEAR R

SCHOLASTIC
www.scholastic.co.uk

Illustration © 2006, Jenny Tulip

KUW LESSON 20   Name _____

Making pizza

- Draw a picture of your finished pizza.

Does the pizza look good?   Yes/No

Does the pizza taste good?   Yes/No

How happy are you with your pizza?

Other areas Chapter 4

Other areas of learning

Introduction
This chapter covers the Personal, social and emotional development, Physical development and Creative development areas of learning from the *Early Years Foundation Stage*.

Many of the activities for each of these areas of learning are based around a common theme. The theme for the first six lessons in the chapter is 'Celebrations'. Lessons 7-9, also in this area of learning, focus on the early foundation stage skills and social and emotional development.

Lessons 10-12 cover aspects of the Physical development area of learning using the interactive whiteboard, with the Introduction to the lessons acting as stimuli for the main parts of the lessons.

Lessons 13-17 provide five activities based on objectives taken from Creative development in the curriculum guidance for the Foundation Stage. The lessons are based on the familiar and well-loved story *We're Going on a Bear Hunt* by Michael Rosen (Walker Books).

Lessons 18-20 provide three further activities based on objectives taken from the Creative development curriculum guidance for the Foundation Stage. The lessons are based on the topic 'Shape and patterns'.

Lesson title	Objectives	Cross-curricular links
Personal, social and emotional development (PSED)		
Lesson 1: Diwali	**Development matters (Sense of Community)** Have an awareness of, and an interest in, cultural and religious differences. **ELG** Understand that people have different needs, views, cultures and beliefs that need to be treated with respect. **ELG** Understand that they can expect others to treat their needs, views, cultures and beliefs with respect.	**CD** Use their imagination in art and design, music, dance, imaginative and role play and stories.
Lesson 2: Hanukkah	**Development matters (Sense of Community)** Have an awareness of, and an interest in, cultural and religious differences. **ELG** Understand that people have different needs, views, cultures and beliefs that need to be treated with respect. **ELG** Understand that they can expect others to treat their needs, views, cultures and beliefs with respect.	**PSRN** Count reliably up to ten everyday objects.
Lesson 3: Christmas around the world	**Development matters (Sense of Community)** Have an awareness of, and an interest in, cultural and religious differences. **ELG** Understand that people have different needs, views, cultures and beliefs that need to be treated with respect. **ELG** Understand that they can expect others to treat their needs, views, cultures and beliefs with respect.	**CD** Explore colour, texture, shape, form and space in two or three dimensions. **CD** Respond in a variety of ways to what they see, hear, smell, touch and feel.
Lesson 4: Chinese New Year	**Development matters (Sense of Community)** Have an awareness of, and an interest in, cultural and religious differences. **ELG** Understand that people have different needs, views, cultures and beliefs that need to be treated with respect. **ELG** Understand that they can expect others to treat their needs, views, cultures and beliefs with respect.	**CLL** Enjoy listening to and using spoken and written language, and readily turn to it in their play and learning.

Other areas — Chapter 4

Lesson title	Objectives	Cross-curricular links
Lesson 5: Birthdays	**Development matters (Sense of Community)** Have an awareness of, and show an interest in, cultural and religious differences. **ELG** Understand that people have different needs, views, cultures and beliefs that need to be treated with respect. **ELG** Understand that they can expect others to treat their needs, views, cultures and beliefs with respect.	**PD** Handle tools, objects, construction and malleable materials safely and with increasing control.
Lesson 6: Easter	**Development matters (Sense of Community)** Have an awareness of, and show an interest in, cultural and religious differences. **ELG** Understand that people have different needs, views, cultures and beliefs that need to be treated with respect. **ELG** Understand that they can expect others to treat their needs, views, cultures and beliefs with respect.	**CD** Explore colour, texture, shape, form and space in two or three dimensions.
Lesson 7: Washing and dressing	**Development matters (Self-care)** Seek to do things for themselves, knowing that an adult is close by, ready to support and help if needed. **ELG** Dress and undress independently and manage their own personal hygiene.	**PD** Recognise the importance of keeping healthy, and those things which contribute to this. **KUW** Look closely at similarities, differences, patterns and change. **KUW** Use programmable toys to support their learning.
Lesson 8: How do I feel?	**Development matters (Self-confidence and Self-esteem)** Express needs and feelings in appropriate ways. **ELG** Have a developing awareness of their own needs, views and feelings, and be sensitive to the needs, views and feelings of others.	**CD** Use their imagination in art and design, music, dance, imaginative and role play and stories.
Lesson 9: Golden rules	**Development matters (Making Relationships)** Value and contribute to own well-being and self-control. **ELG** Understand that there need to be agreed values and codes of behaviour for groups of people, including adults and children, to work together harmoniously.	**CLL** Write their own name and other things such as labels and captions.
Physical development (PD)		
Lesson 10: Firework night	**Development matters (Movement and Space)** Move freely with pleasure and confidence. **ELG** Move with confidence, imagination and in safety.	**CD** Express and communicate their ideas, thoughts and feelings by using a widening range of materials. **KUW** Find out about and identify the use of everyday technology to support their learning.
Lesson 11: What happens to our bodies as we exercise?	**Development matters (Health and Bodily Awareness)** Observe the effects of activity on their bodies. **ELG** Recognise the changes that happen to their bodies when they are active.	**KUW** Ask questions about why things happen and how things work.
Lesson 12: Curly caterpillar letters	**Development matters (Using Equipment and Materials)** Demonstrate increasing skill and control in the use of mark-making implements. **ELG** Handle tools, objects, construction and malleable materials safely and with increasing control.	**CLL** Use a pencil and hold it effectively to form recognisable letters, most of which are correctly formed. **KUW** Find out about and identify the use of everyday technology and use information and communication technology to support their learning.

Other areas — Chapter 4

Lesson title	Objectives	Cross-curricular links
Creative development (CD)		
Lesson 13: Going on a bear hunt	**Development matters (Being Creative)** Capture experiences and responses with music, dance, paint and other materials and words. **ELG** Use their imagination in art and design, music, dance, imaginative and role play and stories. **ELG** Respond in a variety of ways to what they see, hear, smell, touch and feel.	**CLL** Use language to imagine and recreate experiences and roles.
Lesson 14: Making sounds	**Development matters (Creating Music and Dance)** Show an interest in the way musical instruments sound. **ELG** Recognise and explore how sounds can be changed; recognise repeated sounds and sound patterns.	**PD** Use a range of small and large equipment.
Lesson 15: Creating a role play	**Development matters (Being Creative)** Capture experiences and responses with music, dance, paint and other materials or words. **ELG** Explore colour, texture, shape, form and space in two or three dimensions. **ELG** Respond in a variety of ways to what they see, hear, smell, touch and feel. **ELG** Express and communicate their ideas, thoughts and feelings by using a widening range of materials, suitable tools, imaginative and role play.	**KUW** Observe, find out about and identify features in the place they live and the natural world.
Lesson 16 Using our imagination	**Development matters (Being Creative)** Explore and experience using a range of senses and movement. **ELG** Use their imagination in art and design, music, dance, imaginative and role play and stories. **ELG** Respond in a variety of ways to what they see, hear, smell, touch and feel. **ELG** Express and communicate their ideas, thoughts and feelings by using a widening range of materials, suitable tools, imaginative and role play.	**PD** Handle tools, objects, construction and malleable materials safely and with increasing control.
Lesson 17: Making a map	**Development matters (Exploring Media and Materials)** Work creatively on a large or small scale. **ELG** Explore colour, texture, shape, form and space in two or three dimensions.	**KUW** Find out about and identify the uses of everyday technology and use information and communication technology and programmable toys to support their learning.
Lesson 18: Mondrian	**Development matters (Exploring Media and Materials)** Work creatively on a large or small scale. **ELG** Explore colour, texture, shape, form and space in two or three dimensions.	**PSRN** Use language such as *circle* or *bigger* to describe the shape and size of solids and flat shapes.
Lesson 19: Repeating patterns	**Development matters (Exploring Media and Materials)** Explore colour and begin to differentiate between colours. **ELG** Explore colour, texture, shape, form and space in two or three dimensions.	**PSRN** Use everyday words to describe position.
Lesson 20: Symmetrical patterns	**Development matters (Being Creative)** Begin to use representation as a form of communication. **ELG** Respond in a variety of ways to what they see, hear, smell, touch and feel.	**KUW** Use information and communication technology to support their learning.

PSED Lesson 1

Diwali

Learning objectives
- Development matters (Sense of Community): Have an awareness of, and an interest in, cultural and religious differences.
- ELG: Understand that people have different needs, views, cultures and beliefs that need to be treated with respect.
- ELG: Understand that they can expect others to treat their needs, views, cultures and beliefs with respect.

Resources
'Diwali' Notebook file; photocopiable page 159 'Rangoli pattern'; outline masks of story characters (use the images provided on the CD-ROM for mask templates); diva lamps (or images of them); modelling clay and clay tools; collage materials; crayons; traditional Diwali dress (optional).

Links to other ELGs
CD
Use their imagination in art and design, music, dance, imaginative and role play and stories.
- If Diwali dress is available, let the children wear the outfits to act out the story of Rama and Sita. Alternatively, suggest that they role play celebrating the festival of Diwali.

Whiteboard tools
Help children use the grid on page 8 and the Shapes, Lines and Fill Colour tools to create their own rangoli patterns.

- Pen tray
- Select tool
- Screen Shade
- Fill Colour tool
- Shapes tool
- Lines tool

Introduction
Explain that Hindus celebrate the festival of Diwali, the *festival of light*, because of the story of Rama and Sita. Read the story on page 2 of the Notebook file. Emphasise the names of the main characters in the story as they appear, and prepare a list of them.

Adult-focused whole-class activity
- Use pages 3 to 6 to show some of the characters from the story.
- After displaying each picture, ask the children (with their talk partners) to discuss what the character's role was in the story, and to decide if they like them or not.
- Invite the children to discuss the reasons why they like or dislike each character.
- Go on to discuss how people celebrate Diwali. Use page 7 to show a variety of simple rangoli patterns. Press on the red box to find out about Rangoli patterns. Explain to the children that *rangoli* is the name given to a pattern made by people on the doorsteps of their houses to celebrate the festival of Diwali.
- Discuss the shapes used in each of the patterns shown on page 7.

Adult-focused group activity
- Show the children some diva lamps (or images of them). Explain that you are going to help them to make their own lamps. Look at examples of the decorations used on them.
- Provide modelling clay and clay tools for the children to use to create and decorate their lamps. Encourage them to discuss the shapes they are creating (curved, round, flat, and so on).
- Ask: *Why do people use diva lamps to celebrate Diwali?* (Re-read the story on page 2 of the Notebook file if necessary.)
- Discuss how the people of the kingdom lit oil lamps to show Rama and Sita the way home.
- Extend the activity by asking the children to create repeating patterns to decorate their lamps.

Planned independent activities
- Use page 8 of the Notebook file to model a rangoli pattern, using the Lines and Shapes tools (or the shapes already provided on the page). Experiment with different colours by changing objects' colours with the Fill Colour tool.
- Give each child a copy of photocopiable page 159. Challenge them to create their own rangoli pattern. Display page 7 of the Notebook file to help them.
- Provide the children with mask shapes (these are available in PDF format on pages 3 to 6) and suitable collage materials and crayons. Invite them to create a mask based on their chosen character from the story.

Plenary
- Enable the Screen Shade and look back at the Notebook file of the characters on pages 3 to 6. Pull up the screen from the bottom of the page but don't show the headings with the characters' names. Ask: *Can you remember who this is?* Then reveal the names to check whether the children remembered correctly.
- Use page 9 of the Notebook file to record the children's comments about what they have learned about the festival of Diwali.

PSED Lesson 2

Hanukkah

Learning objectives
- Development matters (Sense of Community): Have an awareness of, and an interest in, cultural and religious differences.
- ELG: Understand that people have different needs, views, cultures and beliefs that need to be treated with respect.
- ELG: Understand that they can expect others to treat their needs, views, cultures and beliefs with respect.

Resources
'Hanukkah' Notebook file; photocopiable page 160 'Dreidel'; counters; glue; paper and writing materials.

Links to other ELGs
PSRN
Count reliably up to ten everyday objects.
- The children will be counting the coins, counters or sweets into and out of the pots as they play the dreidel game.

Whiteboard tools
Use the On-screen Keyboard, accessed through the Pen tray or the SMART Board tools menu, to label the artefacts on page 3. Use a Highlighter pen to highlight the Hebrew letters.

- Pen tray
- Select tool
- On-screen Keyboard
- Highlighter pen

Introduction
Revise what the children have learned about Diwali during the previous lesson. Explain that today they are going to learn about another festival of light – the Jewish festival called Hanukkah.

Use the electronic book on page 2 to tell the story of Hanukkah. Point out important words in the story.

Adult-focused whole-class activity
- Go to page 3 of the Notebook file, and talk about the pictures of artefacts used to celebrate Hanukkah: the dreidel, menorah and the Star of David.
- Explain to the children that a dreidel is a four-sided top with a Hebrew letter on each side. A menorah is a nine-candle candle holder. The Star of David is the most famous symbol of the Jewish faith.
- Encourage the children to ask questions to find out information about what the artefacts are and what they are used for.

Adult-focused group activities
- Provide each child with a copy of photocopiable page 160, copied onto card. Work with the children to help them create their own dreidel.
- Explain to the children that a dreidel is like a four-sided spinning top used to play a game. Tell them that in Israel, dreidels have the letters *nun, gimel, hay, pay*. These stand for *Nes Gadol Haya Po* which means *a great miracle happened here*.
- Ask the children to colour the four symbols on their photocopiable sheet.
- Then help them to cut out the outline of the dreidel and fold along the lines. Glue the tabs together and attach the handle.
- The children can then play the game in which all players start with the same number of counters, coins or sweets. They spin the dreidel and act on the instruction given:
  - *Nun* means the player neither wins nor loses.
  - *Gimel* means the player takes the whole pot.
  - *Hay* means the player takes half the pot.
  - *Pay* means the player must put a counter/coin/sweet in the pot.

Planned independent activity
- Suggest that the children draw or make a collage of their own menorah. Encourage them to label each of the candles with the correct number.
- Invite them to explore the story of Hanukkah using the whiteboard.
- Show the children how to use the On-screen Keyboard to label the artefacts on page 3.

Plenary
- Look at the copy of the Hebrew alphabet on page 4 of the Notebook file. Ask the children if they can identify some of the letters on the screen as you name them. Use a Highlighter pen to highlight these.
- Provide the children with paper and writing materials. Invite them to try to write some of the Hebrew letters. They may also like to have a go at writing their own names or simple words in Hebrew.

PSED Lesson 3

Christmas around the world

Learning objectives
- Development matters (Sense of Community): Have an awareness of, and an interest in, cultural and religious differences.
- ELG: Understand that people have different needs, views, cultures and beliefs that need to be treated with respect.
- ELG: Understand that they can expect others to treat their needs, views, cultures and beliefs with respect.

Resources
'Christmas and New Year' Notebook file; photocopiable page 161 'Dear Santa'; fruit (oranges, apples, lemons or limes); cloves; cinnamon; ribbon; glue; toothpicks; fabric/netting or tissue paper; star templates (printed from Notebook page 7); paper; card; glitter; writing and painting materials; computer-based art program such as 'Dazzle'.

Links to other ELGs
CD
Explore colour, texture, shape, form and space in two or three dimensions.
Respond in a variety of ways to what they see, hear, smell, touch and feel.
- Provide collage materials, glue, card and ribbons and allow the children to experiment creating some colourful Christmas decorations for your setting.

Whiteboard tools
If a microphone is available, use Windows® Sound Recorder (accessed through Start>Programs>Accessories>Entertainment) to record the children's Christmas greetings.

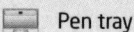

- Pen tray
- Highlighter pen
- Select tool
- On-screen Keyboard

Introduction
Ask the children how they celebrate Christmas. Discuss how and why we celebrate Christmas. Ask: *Does anyone celebrate differently?*

Use pages 2 to 6 of the Notebook file to explain how other countries celebrate in different ways. Read the text to the children and explain the pictures. Use a Highlighter pen to highlight important words.

Adult-focused whole-class activity
- Discuss the different greetings we use to wish people a happy Christmas. Explain that in different countries people speak different languages and so say different things to celebrate Christmas.
- Go back through pages 3 to 6 of the Notebook file, asking the children to practise saying some of the greetings shown in red at the foot of each page.
- Attach a microphone to your computer and use Windows® Sound Recorder to record the children saying *Merry Christmas* in several different languages.
- Play the greetings back for the children to hear.

Adult-focused group activity
- Tell the children they are going to make their own pomanders. Expain to them that a pomander is a mixture of fragrant substances used to make a room (or drawer) smell nice.
- Show the children how to tie a ribbon around their fruit (orange, apple, lemon or lime). Secure it at the bottom with a dab of glue.
- Next, show them how to push cloves into their fruit, using a toothpick to help if necessary.
- Then help each child to roll his/her fruit in a bowl of cinnamon before tying it in fabric, netting or tissue paper.

Planned independent activities
- In the writing corner, provide the children with a range of writing materials, including a writing frame for a letter to Santa (photocopiable page 161) and different shapes of paper.
- Ask the children to make their own Christmas star. They may use the star templates (printed from page 7 of the Notebook file) to cut out two stars from card, then cut along the dotted line to interlock the stars. The children can decorate their stars as desired.
- Show the children some pictures of Father Christmas from around the world (go to pages 3 and 5 of the Notebook file, showing Austrian and Italian versions). Suggest that the children make their own picture using paints and paper, or alternatively let them use a computer art package to create their own Father Christmas.

Plenary
- Go to page 8 and look at the world map together. Ask the children to help you to locate the UK and the countries discussed in this lesson.
- Invite the children to use the On-screen Keyboard to type the names of the different countries. Show them how to drag and drop the labels on the appropriate places on the map.

PSED Lesson 4

Chinese New Year

Learning objectives
- Development matters (Sense of Community): Have an awareness of, and an interest in, cultural and religious differences.
- ELG: Understand that people have different needs, views, cultures and beliefs that need to be treated with respect.
- ELG: Understand that they can expect others to treat their needs, views, cultures and beliefs with respect.

Resources
'Christmas and New Year' Notebook file; clean empty yoghurt pots; paints; ribbon or string; red felt; paper; sticky tape; brightly coloured strips of fabric; drums and gongs; digital video camera.

Links to other ELGs
CLL
Enjoy listening to and using spoken and written language, and readily turn to it in their play and learning.
- Create fortune cookies by cutting out brown card circles and writing messages on thin strips of paper. Add messages to the strips of paper such as Gung Hay Fat Choy. Stick the edges of the circle together, leaving space to insert the message strips.

Whiteboard tools
If a microphone is available, use Windows® Sound Recorder to record the children saying Happy New Year in Chinese. To upload video clips, open SMART Video player from the SMART Board tools menu. Select File, then Open, and browse to where you have saved the video file on your computer.

- Pen tray
- Select tool
- Delete button
- SMART video player

Introduction
Open page 9 of the Notebook file. Look at the pictures of celebrations of New Year in the UK and in Asia. Discuss the differences and similarities of the celebrations. With the children's help, sort them into two groups – UK and Asia.

Adult-focused whole-class activity
- Display page 10 of the Notebook file and teach the children how to say *Happy New Year* in Chinese – *Gung Hay Fat Choy*. If a microphone is available, use Windows® Sound Recorder to record the children saying this.

Adult-focused group activities
- Help the children to create their own Chinese dragon to celebrate Chinese New Year.
- Make the dragon as long or as short as you like by using more or less yoghurt pots. Paint all the pots a bright colour on the outside, with one (the mouth) to be painted black inside. Paint spots onto the pots.
- Pierce holes through the sides of the yoghurt pots and use ribbon or string to lace the cartons together.
- Add features to the head and glue it to the rest of the dragon, with the black mouth facing outwards. Cut a tongue out of red felt and glue it inside the mouth to finish the look.
- Show the children how to make a Chinese lantern by folding a piece of paper in half horizontally and decorating the paper. The children then need to cut into the paper from the fold, almost to the edge. Open out the paper and join the two long sides together with sticky tape. Suspend with string to make a lantern.

Planned independent activity
- Provide the children with long strips of brightly coloured material, ribbons, drums and gongs. Invite them to create their own celebratory dragon dance.
- Help the children to film their performances using a digital video camera.

Plenary
- Upload the videos of the children's dances and insert them on page 11 of the Notebook file.
- Go to pages 12 and 13, showing the year and the animal that is the symbol of that year. Discuss the different names of the Chinese years.
- Ask the children if they can guess what the names are before you use the Eraser from the Pen tray to rub out the red boxes underneath the images to reveal the answers.
- Open page 14 of the Notebook file. Invite the children to use a Pen from the Pen tray to write their names under the symbol for the year in which they were born. To create sufficient space on the page, either move the year symbols that are not needed to the side of the Notebook page, or delete them altogether by pressing the Delete button ✖ (or select the Delete option from the dropdown menu).

PSED Lesson 5

Birthdays

Learning objectives
- Development matters (Sense of Community): Have an awareness of, and show an interest in, cultural and religious differences.
- ELG: Understand that people have different needs, views, cultures and beliefs that need to be treated with respect.
- ELG: Understand that they can expect others to treat their needs, views, cultures and beliefs with respect.

Resources
'Birthdays' Notebook file; paper and drawing materials; Plasticine or play dough; candles; ribbons; party plates.

Links to other ELGs
PD
Handle tools, objects, construction and malleable materials safely and with increasing control.
- Provide the children with a variety of different papers and adhesives. Challenge them to wrap up different presents, ensuring that no parts are visible.

Introduction
Display page 2 of the Notebook file. Use the pictures as prompts for talking about why and how we celebrate birthdays. Ask: *What do we do? What do we wear? What do we eat?* Write down a few ideas on the page.

Adult-focused whole-class activity
- Ask the children which month they celebrate their birthday in.
- Go to pages 3 to 8 (there are two months on each page). Invite the children to take turns to press on the image of the birthday cake at the foot of the page, drag it into their birthday month and then write their name next to it.
- Discuss with the children how they celebrate their birthdays.

Adult-focused group activity
- Provide each child with a piece of paper and ask them to draw a large birthday present outline on it (or provide a simple template for them to draw around).
- Add lines for writing and ask the children to write about a present they would like to give to a friend or loved one. Ask: *Why did you choose this for them?*
- Work with the children to sound out the words needed and discuss their ideas.

Planned independent activity
- Show the children how to find the props needed for a birthday celebration on page 9 of the Notebook file. Let them work with a partner to create their own scenarios on the whiteboard.
- Show the children how to explore the Gallery to find extra party images if they wish to add more details to the page.

Child-initiated activity
- Provide Plasticine or play dough as well as other props such as candles, ribbons and party plates. Note whether the children use the materials during free play to continue their work on the party theme.

Plenary
- Use page 10 of the Notebook file to encourage the children to discuss the things they might see, hear, feel or taste at a birthday celebration.
- Write their suggestions into the relevant sections or allow them to draw or insert images as appropriate.
- Illustrate these with additional items from the Gallery as necessary.

Whiteboard tools
Use the Gallery to select props for acting out a birthday celebration.

- Pen tray
- Select tool
- Gallery

PSED Lesson 6

Easter

Learning objectives
- Development matters (Sense of Community): Have an awareness of, and show an interest in, cultural and religious differences.
- ELG: Understand that people have different needs, views, cultures and beliefs that need to be treated with respect.
- ELG: Understand that they can expect others to treat their needs, views, cultures and beliefs with respect.

Resources
'Easter' Notebook file; photocopiable page 162 'The Easter story'; Easter egg cut-outs; materials to decorate the Easter eggs; paints; cotton wool; paper.

Links to other ELGs
CD
Explore colour, texture, shape, form and space in two or three dimensions.
- Use images from the Gallery to create a scene for each season on the whiteboard.

Whiteboard tools
Use the On-screen Keyboard, accessed through the Pen tray or the SMART Board tools menu, to label the different sounds on page 4. The Spotlight tool can be used to look at the multiple-choice pictures in the Plenary.

- Pen tray
- Select tool
- On-screen Keyboard
- Spotlight tool
- Shapes tool
- Gallery

Introduction
Ask the children what they know about the Easter story.

Share the Easter story on page 2 with the children. Point out the important words.

Now ask the children if they celebrate Easter. If they do, ask them how they celebrate. Write down their suggestions on page 3 of the Notebook file. Discuss how we now celebrate Easter with eggs which represent new life and Jesus rising from the dead.

Adult-focused whole-class activity
- Display page 4 of the Notebook file. Ask the children to press on the star buttons to listen carefully to the spring sounds.
- Invite them to try to identify what the sounds are. Use the On-screen Keyboard to type the names onto the Notebook page and label the sounds.

Adult-focused group activity
- Work with the children to write shared text for the Easter story (photocopiable page 162). Encourage them to look carefully at the pictures and help them to understand what is happening and where it fits in with the story.

Planned independent activities
- Provide the children with a selection of collage and art materials for decorating Easter eggs. Encourage them to do this in repeating patterns.
- Invite them to paint their own Easter bunnies using cotton wool for a tail and the ears.
- Go to page 5. Encourage the children to use this page to create their own spring scene using a Pen from the Pen tray and the Shapes tool along with backgrounds and images from the Gallery.

Plenary
- Go to page 6 of the Notebook file. Tell the children that one of the images on the screen does not relate to the Easter theme.
- Enable the Spotlight tool and focus on one image at a time, asking the children which one they think is the odd one out. Can they explain their reasons?
- Invite a volunteer to press on the odd one out – if they are right they will hear a cheer (wrong answers produce an *oops* sound).
- Repeat the activity on pages 7 and 8.

PSED Lesson 7

Washing and dressing

Learning objectives
- Development matters (Self-care): Seek to do things for themselves, knowing that an adult is close by, ready to support and help if needed.
- ELG: Dress and undress independently and manage their own personal hygiene.

Resources
'Dressing toys' Notebook file; photocopiable pages 163 'Dressing teddy (1)' and 164 'Dressing teddy (2)'; pre-cut bears from photocopiable page 163; Blu-Tack; dressing-up box; real teddy bear.

Links to other ELGs
PD
Recognise the importance of keeping healthy, and those things which contribute to this.
- Show the children a variety of objects used for personal hygiene every day such as a hairbrush and sponge. Discuss how and why we use these objects. Practise hand-washing in basins.
KUW
Look closely at similarities, differences, patterns and change.
- Draw timelines of the clothes the children wear throughout the year.
KUW
Use programmable toys to support their learning.
- Make clothes for programmable toys and program them to move in a specified direction, such as towards the cloakrooms.

Whiteboard tools
- Pen tray
- Select tool

Introduction
Discuss what we do each morning when we get up: we get washed and we dress ourselves. Discuss the order in which we do things and what we might wear for different occasions.

Display page 2 of the Notebook file. Talk about how the person is dressed and why he is dressed this way. Remove the clothing, one item at a time, and then invite volunteers to dress the figure again in the correct order.

Repeat the activity on page 3.

Adult-focused whole-class activity
- Go to page 4 of the Notebook file. Discuss the clothes that can be seen on the page.
- Ask: *Is there a particular order in which we put on clothes?* Invite a volunteer to explain which item of clothing should be put on the clown first.
- After discussion, invite individuals to drag and drop the clothes on the figure in the correct order.
- Repeat the activity on pages 5 and 6. Each time, talk about the clothes the figure is wearing. Ask: *Why are they wearing these special clothes?*

Adult-focused group activity
- Provide each child with copies of photocopiable pages 163 and 164. Help the children to colour and cut out the bear and the items of clothing.
- Suggest that they dress the bear, fixing the clothes into place with small pieces of Blu-Tack.
- Provide ready cut-out clothes and bears for younger or less confident learners.
- Challenge older or more confident learners to design and cut out some extra clothes for teddy.

Planned independent activities
- Invite the children to practise putting on their coats and doing them up independently.
- Give the children a real teddy to dress and undress. Ask them to get him ready for bed.

Child-initiated activity
- Provide a box of dressing-up clothes for some free play.

Plenary
- Remind the children of when and why we wash our hands.
- Have a look at some of the people or toys dressed by the children. Are the clothes on in the right order?
- Discuss getting ready for bed and the order in which we might do things – for example, cleaning teeth, having a bath, putting on pyjamas and so on. Use a teddy or doll to model.
- Go to page 7 of the Notebook file and ask the children to help you move the pictures into the right order. Use a Pen from the Pen tray to write down the correct sequence of events on the page.

PSED Lesson 8

How do I feel?

Learning objectives
- Development matters (Self-confidence and Self-esteem): Express needs and feelings in appropriate ways.
- ELG: Have a developing awareness of their own needs, views and feelings, and be sensitive to the needs, views and feelings of others.

Resources
'Feelings and rules' Notebook file; photocopiable page 165 'How do you feel?'.

Links to other ELGs
CD
Use their imagination in art and design, music, dance, imaginative and role play and stories.
- Together, talk about different characters and emotions. Provide a dressing-up box and an area for the children to play in. Encourage them to develop scenarios together that involve exploring a range of emotions.

Whiteboard tools
Use the Fill Colour tool to change the colour of the boxes on pages 3 to 6 to reveal the emotions portrayed. Use Windows® Sound Recorder (accessed through Start>Programs>Accessories>Entertainment) to record the sounds made by the children in the Plenary.

- Pen tray
- Select tool
- Fill Colour tool

Introduction
Talk with the children about how we feel at certain times, such as when we fall over, when it is our birthday, and so on.

Go to page 2 of the Notebook file. Ask the children which emotions they think they can identify. Use the Eraser from the Pen tray to reveal the answers.

Adult-focused whole-class activity
- Use pages 3 to 6 of the Notebook file to show a series of photographs of a child with different facial expressions.
- Ask the children if they can identify each of the feelings portrayed. Reveal the answers by using the Fill Colour tool to change the colour of the red box underneath each photograph to white.
- Now sit in a circle and ask the children to take turns to make sad, angry, happy or scared faces. Invite the rest of the class to guess what feeling they are showing.
- Discuss how our bodies may look when we are making these faces.
- Encourage older or more confident learners to talk about how they feel inside as well.

Adult-focused group activity
- Work with small groups of children at a time.
- Provide each child with a copy of photocopiable page 165. Ask them to draw a face on the person on the sheet to show that they are angry.
- Alternatively, allow the children to each choose their own emotion to draw. Can the others in the group guess what their drawing shows?
- Make a display of the children's drawings.

Planned independent activity
- Show the children how to use a blank Notebook page to draw faces to show different emotions.
- Save and print the children's drawings to add to the display.

Plenary
- Share some of the children's drawings and completed photocopiable sheets.
- Discuss the sounds that we make to show different emotions. If a microphone is available, use Windows® Sound Recorder to record children laughing, crying, screaming and so on (a sound for each emotion covered in the lesson).
- Play back the recording at another circle time and challenge the children to remember which emotions they can hear.

PSED Lesson 9

Golden rules

Learning objectives
- Development matters (Making Relationships): Value and contribute to own well-being and self-control.
- ELG: Understand that there need to be agreed values and codes of behaviour for groups of people, including adults and children, to work together harmoniously.

Resources
'Feelings and rules' Notebook file; teddy bear; digital camera; video recorder.

Links to other ELGs
CLL
Write their own name and other things such as labels and captions.
- Invite the children to help you to write the captions and labels for the photographic display.

Introduction
This lesson is a good way to introduce children who have just started school to concepts such as putting their hand up or taking turns to speak.

With the children in a circle, talk about what they perceive as right and wrong in terms of how the class should work and play well together. Allow each child to have a turn at speaking. Explain that the person holding the teddy (or other object) is the person allowed to speak. Let them pass the teddy on to the next child if they do not have a contribution to make.

Jot down the children's ideas on page 7 of the Notebook file.

Adult-focused whole-class activity
- Explain to the children that they are going to think of things that will help them to work and play well together.
- Show the children page 8 of the Notebook file. Invite individuals to help you to sort the pictures into the 'right' and 'wrong' boxes. Drag and drop the pictures into the appropriate boxes.
- As the children sort, talk about why they have put particular pictures in the boxes. Ask: *Why does this action help us to work and play well together?*

Adult-focused group activity
- Work with groups of children to use child-friendly video recorders or digital cameras to take photographs of children behaving in the right way.
- Go for a walk around your school or setting. Help the children to take photographs or film of children doing the right thing, such as putting their hands up, listening to the teacher, walking down the corridor and so on. Remember to obtain parental permissions before photographing or filming children.

Plenary
- With the whole class, go through page 8 of the Notebook file and discuss the decisions made by the children. Ask: *Could we use any of these as our 'Golden rules' in this class?*
- Agree and write down the class Golden rules on page 9.
- Upload some of the digital photographs taken during the group activity or transfer some of the video clips that correspond to the rules chosen and insert them on the Notebook page.
- Make a display of the rest of the photographs to illustrate three or four simple ways to work and play well together.

Whiteboard tools
Upload digital photographs by selecting Insert, then Picture File, and browsing to where you have saved the images. To upload video clips, open SMART Video player from the SMART Board tools menu. Select File, then Open, and browse to where you have saved the video file on your computer.

- Pen tray
- Select tool
- SMART video player

PD Lesson 10

Firework night

Learning objectives
- Development matters (Movement and Space): Move freely with pleasure and confidence.
- ELG: Move with confidence, imagination and in safety.

Resources
'Firework night' Notebook file; ribbons or coloured cloth for dance; choice of music to represent fireworks; digital video camera.

Links to other ELGs
CD
Express and communicate their ideas, thoughts and feelings by using a widening range of materials.
- Play the children a piece of classical music. Provide a range of materials such as paints, crayons and collage materials and let the children create what the music makes them feel.

KUW
Find out about and identify the use of everyday technology to support their learning.
- Use a painting program such as Dazzle to create a firework picture. Make a display of the children's creations.

Whiteboard tools
To embed the video as a hyperlink on page 6, open SMART Video player from the SMART Board tools menu. Select File, then Open, and browse to where you have saved the video file on your computer. Your video will play in the SMART Video player window. Take a screen shot of a frame with the Image Capture tool in the toolbar of this window.

- Select tool
- Pen tray
- SMART video player

Introduction
Display page 2 of the Notebook file. Show the children the rocket-type fireworks and play the sounds by pressing on the stars.

Next, go to page 3 and compare the sounds and images of different kinds of fireworks. Repeat this for page 4.

Using page 5 of the Notebook file, draw the shapes that the different fireworks make. Ask the children to look at the patterns made by the different fireworks. Explain that they are going to use their bodies to become fireworks. Listen to the sounds and explain that there are explosions as well as crackles and fizzes.

Adult-focused whole-class activity
- Move the class to a suitable space in which to perform their dances.
- Warm up as a class with some stretches and aerobic movement to music.
- Explain that you would like the children to use their bodies to move like fireworks and also to make sounds to go with the different movements.
- Ask for ideas of fireworks and the way these might move.
- Demonstrate how a rocket begins on the ground as a small shape and explodes into the sky with a leap and a whooshing sound. Invite the children to copy your moves, adding their own variations if they wish!
- Next, ask the children to show you how they could be Catherine wheels and the sounds these might make.
- Split the class in half with one half as rockets and the other as Catherine wheels, using ribbons.
- Ask the rockets to perform first and invite the Catherine wheels to comment constructively on the moves.
- Now let the Catherine wheels move, with the rockets making a peer assessment.

Plenary
- Once the children have practised their moves sufficiently, invite them to perform their moves together.
- Use the video camera to record the children's dance to music. Show them their performance before the next lesson and ask if they could improve their performance, and how. The video recording can be added to page 6 of the Notebook file.
- Ask: *What did you like or dislike about your performance?* Write down the children's comments on page 6.

PD Lesson 11

What happens to our bodies as we exercise?

Learning objectives
- Development matters (Health and Bodily Awareness): Observe the effects of activity on their bodies.
- ELG: Recognise the changes that happen to their bodies when they are active.

Resources
'Exercise' Notebook file; stopwatch; skipping ropes; props for a role-play medical centre.

Links to other ELGs
KUW
Ask questions about why things happen and how things work.
- Use books and/or an appropriate website or CD-ROM to find out more about how the body works.

Introduction
Talk with the children about how doing exercise makes them feel. Ask them to predict what might happen to their breathing as they exercise. Ask: *What else might happen to our bodies?*

Use pages 2 to 5 of the Notebook file to show the children a simplified version of the human body, pointing out the position of the heart and lungs. Do the children know what these organs are for? Talk briefly about what these organs do in our bodies.

Move on to page 6. Ask a volunteer to drag and drop the heart, lungs, labels and arrows into the correct position on the body. Pull the screen on the left-hand side of the page over the diagram to reveal the answer.

Adult-focused whole-class activity
- If possible, take the children onto the playground or sports field and show them how to put their hand over their heart to feel it beating. Ask them to listen to their breathing.
- Ask the children to predict what they think will happen if half the class does some exercise and the other half doesn't. Which group's hearts do they think will beat faster? What will happen to each group's breathing?

Adult-focused group activity
- Ask half the class to sit quietly with another adult for one minute. Time the other half of the class for one minute as they run, jump, skip and so on.
- Next, feel the heart beat of both groups and listen to their breathing. Were the children's predictions correct?
- Swap over and repeat the activity.
- Ask: *What else happened when you exercised?* Lead the children to the answer that they got hot, sweated, felt thirsty, and so on.

Child-initiated activity
- Set up your role-play area as a medical centre, providing stethoscopes, stopwatches and so on. Encourage the children to use it during free play.
- Make a note of how they play. Do they measure pulse and heart beats based on the planned work that they took part in?

Plenary
- Back in the classroom, use page 7 of the Notebook file to make a mind map of what happened to the children's bodies as they exercised.
- Invite individual children to come to the whiteboard and use a Pen from the Pen tray to take turns to illustrate the mind map.
- Print this out and display it.

Whiteboard tools
Use a Pen from the Pen tray for the mind map in the Plenary.

- Pen tray
- Select tool

PD Lesson 12

Curly caterpillar letters

Learning objectives
- Development matters (Using Equipment and Materials): Demonstrate increasing skill and control in the use of mark-making implements.
- ELG: Handle tools, objects, construction and malleable materials safely and with increasing control.

Resources
'Build your own' file; photocopiable pages 166 'Curly caterpillar (1)' and 167 'Curly caterpillar (2)'; individual whiteboards and pens; paper; chalk boards and chalk; sand trays; play dough or similar.

Links to other ELGs
CLL
Use a pencil and hold it effectively to form recognisable letters, most of which are correctly formed.
- Provide children with large paintbrushes and water and suggest that they practise writing letters and names on the playground. Provide chalks for the same purpose.

KUW
Find out about and identify the use of everyday technology and use information and communication technology to support their learning.
- Use a program such as Magic Pencil to support early writing skills and the transition to joined-up writing.

Whiteboard tools
Use a Highlighter pen to trace over the letters on the Notebook page.

- Pen tray
- Select tool
- Highlighter pen
- Gallery

Introduction
Open the 'Build your own' file, which contains a blank Notebook page and a ready-made Gallery collection of resources saved under My Content. Use the Gallery collection of lower case letters, from the OAL folder under My Content, to model the formation of, for example, the curly caterpillar letters *c, a, d, g, o*.

Ask volunteers to trace the letters on the whiteboard using a Highlighter pen. Use different colours and thickness of pens to write the letters. Convert hanwritten letters to text by selecting the Recognise option from the dropdown menu to allow the children to see the letter formation more clearly. Ask them to write in the air, copying your movement as you write on the board.

On a new Notebook page, write large letters using a Highlighter pen and allow the children to trace over them in a different colour.

Adult-focused group activities
- With a small group of children, practise letter formation on the whiteboard. Ensure that they form the letters correctly, referring to the handwriting letters found in the Gallery.
- Save these pages to show in the Plenary.
- Provide each child with a copy of photocopiable page 166 'Curly caterpillar (1)'. Work closely with the children to ensure that they form and orientate the letters correctly.
- Provide patterns for younger or less confident learners to help them to practise the *c* movement.
- Let older or more confident learners practise the other curly caterpillar letters on photocopiable page 167. Invite them to extend the work to forming simple words, if applicable. Remind them that all these letters start with a 'curly caterpillar' movement.

Planned independent activities
- Provide plenty of opportunities for the children to practise their letter formation. Ideas include:
  - writing letters on dry wipe boards
  - painting letters on large paper
  - writing letters on chalk boards
  - forming letter shapes with malleable materials
  - writing letters in sand.

Plenary
- Display some of the Notebook pages with the children's writing.
- Suggest that the children write in the air as they look at the letters on the whiteboard. Once more, stress the correct orientation of the letters.

CD Lesson 13

Going on a bear hunt

Learning objectives
- Development matters (Being Creative): Capture experiences and responses with music, dance, paint and other materials and words.
- ELG: Use their imagination in art and design, music, dance, imaginative and role play and stories.
- ELG: Respond in a variety of ways to what they see, hear, smell, touch and feel.

Resources
We're Going on a Bear Hunt by Michael Rosen (Walker Books); 'Bear hunt' Notebook file; rucksack, stick, hats, scarf.

Links to other ELGs
CLL
Use language to imagine and recreate experiences and roles.
- Make a story sack linked to the story, filling the sack with a toy bear, a toy dog, people puppets, some grass, some rocks and so on. Encourage the children to use the sack, in pairs, to retell the story.

Introduction
Read the story *We're Going on a Bear Hunt* by Michael Rosen.
Encourage the children to join in with the words and make up appropriate actions to sections such as: *What a beautiful day... we're not scared; long wavy grass; swishy, swashy* and so on.

Adult-focused whole-class activity
- Open the 'Bear hunt' Notebook file and enjoy the story together again (on pages 2 to 9).
- Invite individuals to take turns to select the sound words to listen to the noises on each page. Tell them that they can also press on the text at the top of each page to hear the words read aloud.
- Encourage the children to make the actions as you move through the story and the Notebook pages.

Adult-focused group activities
- Go outside into a suitable area. Arrange for the children to work with talk partners. Ask them to retell the story with their partner. Can they sequence the events in the correct order?
- Encourage the children to include sounds and actions as they retell the story together.
- Now work with larger groups of children at a time. Help them to decide on who will be each character. (Mum, dad, children, dog and the bear.)
- Find localities that represent some of the physical features in the book, such as long wavy grass.
- Provide suitable props and divide these amongst the children. Support the children with their decisions and team work and encourage them to initiate their own ideas.
- Suggest that the children practise acting out the story, ready to perform it to the rest of the class.

Plenary
- Arrange for each group to perform their story to the rest of the class.
- Encourage the audience to evaluate their work. What did they like? What could they improve?

Whiteboard tools
- Pen tray
- Select tool

CD Lesson 14

Making sounds

Learning objectives
- Development matters (Creating Music and Dance): Show an interest in the way musical instruments sound.
- ELG: Recognise and explore how sounds can be changed; recognise repeated sounds and sound patterns.

Resources
We're Going on a Bear Hunt by Michael Rosen (Walker Books); 'Bear hunt' Notebook file; microphone; percussion instruments (drum, jingle bells, guiro, maracas, triangle, tambourine, woodblock, rainmaker).

Links to other ELGs
PD
Use a range of small and large equipment.
- Experiment with making sounds using everyday objects from around your setting. Do any of them make sounds that would be suitable to include in the story retelling?

Whiteboard tools
Use Windows® Sound Recorder (accessed through Start>Programs>Accessories>Entertainment) to record the children's percussion and voices. Focus on the pictures with the Spotlight tool.

- Pen tray
- Select tool
- Spotlight tool

Introduction
Use pages 2 to 9 of the Notebook file to tell the story of the 'We're going on a bear hunt'. Remind the children of the story as you go through each page, experimenting with the words and actions. Press on the text at the top of each page to hear the words spoken aloud, while pressing on the sound words will enable the children to hear the different sounds being made as the family progresses on their journey.

Adult-focused whole-class activities
- Go through the pages a second time, this time exploring the sounds in more detail.
- Ask the children to close their eyes. Can they identify the feature by listening to the sound?
- Discuss which sounds work best, and why. How do you think the sounds were made? (For example, running a tap for the water sound.)
- Go to page 10. Discuss all the physical features in the story: long wavy grass; deep cold river; thick oozing mud; big dark forest; swirling whirling snowstorm; and narrow gloomy cave. (The pictures and labels are available on page 10.)
- Provide some percussion instruments (drum, jingle bells, guiro, maracas, triangle, tambourine, woodblock and rainmaker) and encourage the children to explore the sounds that they make.
- Ask the children: *Do any of your sounds go with the places in the story?* Use the Spotlight tool to focus on individual scenes from the story.

Adult-focused group activities
- Next, divide the children into six groups and assign a physical feature to each group.
- Encourage them to use talk partners to discuss which instruments they could use, and why. Help them to consider the sounds that the instruments make and whether these sounds are effective in representing the different places.
- Allow the children to experiment with percussion instruments and body sounds to make suitable sounds for their assigned feature.
- Invite the children to perform their sounds for other groups.

Child-initiated activity
- Make the instruments available for the children to revisit at a time of their own choosing.

Plenary
- Read the story, inviting the children to perform their sounds at the appropriate time.
- If a microphone is available, use Windows® Sound Recorder to record the children's sounds.
- Play the sounds back. Encourage the children to evaluate their work. Which worked best, and why?

CD Lesson 15

Creating a role play

Learning objectives
- Development matters (Being Creative): Capture experiences and responses with music, dance, paint and other materials or words.
- ELG: Explore colour, texture, shape, form and space in two or three dimensions.
- ELG: Respond in a variety of ways to what they see, hear, smell, touch and feel.
- ELG: Express and communicate their ideas, thoughts and feelings by using a widening range of materials, suitable tools, imaginative and role play.

Resources
We're Going on a Bear Hunt by Michael Rosen (Walker Books); 'Bear hunt' Notebook file; green collage material; blue strips for weaving (ribbon, wool, plastic, fabric); large mesh; roll of paper; soil; paint; large sheets of black paper; white paper circles; a range of art and modelling materials.

Links to other ELGs
KUW
Observe, find out about and identify features in the place they live and the natural world.
- Suggest that the children make postcards to send from each of the places on the bear hunt.

Whiteboard tools
Use a Pen from the Pen tray to list ideas. Use the On-screen Keyboard, accessed through the Pen tray or the SMART Board tools menu, to type labels.

- Pen tray
- Select tool
- On-screen Keyboard

Introduction
Look at the 'Bear hunt' Notebook file again together. Read through pages 2 to 9 and enjoy the story and the actions together. Talk about the physical features in the story (long wavy grass, deep cold river, thick oozing mud, big dark forest, swirling whirling snow storm and narrow gloomy cave) and ask the children to imagine what these places would feel like.

Adult-focused whole-class activity
- Discuss how you might all make a bear hunt role play in the classroom. Encourage the children to think of ideas to include. List these on page 12 of the Notebook file.
- Explain that you would like the children to help you to make some labels for the role play.
- Go to page 13. Invite volunteers to help you use the On-screen Keyboard to type labels for the physical features shown on the page. (Alternatively, you could type the labels using a word-processing program such as Microsoft Word or Textease.)
- Explore different fonts and colours and invite the children to use a font and colour that reflects the word that they are typing.
- Print out the labels and laminate them for the role play.
- Encourage older or more confident learners to have a try at writing the labels on the whiteboard, unaided.

Adult-focused group activities
- Discuss ideas for role play and show the children the materials that they can choose from to make the different physical features.
- Divide the children into five groups and assign each group a physical feature. Ask them to create the physical features using the materials provided.
- Ideas include:
  - Long wavy grass: create a collage of different green materials in vertical directions.
  - Deep cold river: weave some blue materials (ribbon, wool, plastic, fabric) into a large mesh.
  - Big dark forest: make large-scale paintings of trees with collage leaves.
  - Thick oozing mud: mix together mud and paint and invite the children to make muddy footprints.
  - Swirling, whirling snowstorm: suggest that the children make white and yellow swirls on black paper. Cut out snowflakes from white paper.

Child-initiated activity
- Allow access to a range of art, craft and reclaimed modelling materials. Note whether the children create any features associated with the story.

Plenary
- Invite the children to evaluate their work. What art and craft techniques worked best, and why?
- Match the labels to the physical features.
- Ask the children to order them in the sequence of the story. Ask for suggestions of ways to display them in the role play.

153

CD Lesson 16

Using our imagination

Learning objectives
- Development matters (Being Creative): Explore and experience using a range of senses and movement.
- ELG: Use their imagination in art and design, music, dance, imaginative and role play and stories.
- ELG: Respond in a variety of ways to what they see, hear, smell, touch and feel.
- ELG: Express and communicate their ideas, thoughts and feelings by using a widening range of materials, suitable tools, imaginative and role play.

Resources
We're Going on a Bear Hunt by Michael Rosen (Walker Books); prepared letter from the bear (A3 size); dark blankets; strips of brown crêpe paper; large construction equipment; sand tray; outline pictures of bears; small-world figures.

Links to other ELGs
PD
Handle tools, objects, construction and malleable materials safely and with increasing control.
- Invite the children to make play dough caves for small toy bears.

Whiteboard tools
Use a Pen from the Pen tray to write the children's letter to the bear. Use a Highlighter pen to emphasise capital letters and full stops. Use images from the Gallery to illustrate the children's letter.

- Pen tray
- Select tool
- On-screen Keyboard
- Highlighter pen
- Gallery

Introduction
Before you start this activity, set up your role-play area as a bear cave. Drape a screen or table with dark blankets and add overhanging branches or strips of brown crêpe paper for a simple effect.

Say to the children that you wonder if the bear has been back to your role-play cave lately. Ask a child and their partner to go and find out if there is any sign that he has been for a visit. (You will have previously placed a letter from him in there!)

When the children find the letter, ask them to bring it to you quickly so that you can read it out to the class.

Read out the letter and discuss it. The letter should persuade the children that the bear is a friendly bear who only wanted to play and didn't want to hurt anyone. Say in the letter that the bear has now run away because he is upset.

Scan the bear's letter onto the whiteboard and display it. Highlight the important points.

Adult-focused whole-class activity
- Ask the children to discuss the problem with their talk partners. Encourage them to come up with a solution to find the bear and make him come home.
- Use the On-screen Keyboard to list the children's ideas on a blank Notebook page.

Adult-focused group activities
- Invite the children to write a group letter to the bear using the whiteboard tools on a new Notebook page.
- Discuss how to set out the letter and include mention of any simple punctuation that the children encounter.
- Select some lined paper from the Gallery and a Pen from the Pen tray to create a template for the letter.
- Encourage the children to think of all the ideas and act as their scribe to put the ideas down on the page.
- Suggest that they illustrate their letter with images from the Gallery.
- Print out the children's letter, place it in an envelope and post it to the bear by putting it in the bear cave.

Planned independent activities
- Provide the children with different outline pictures of bears. Let them choose one, colour it in and write a simple description. For example: *The bear is wearing a blue hat.*
- Provide large construction equipment and challenge the children to make a cave big enough for a teddy bear to fit into.
- Encourage younger or less confident learners to retell the story using play figures in the sand or tactile tray.

Plenary
- Ask each group to read their letter to the class, displaying it on the whiteboard.
- Discuss capital letters, full stops and finger spaces. Highlight the capital letters and full stops in different colours.
- At a later session, reply to the letters that the children leave in the cave and read them out to the class.

Lesson 17

Making a map

Learning objectives
- Development matters (Exploring Media and Materials): Work creatively on a large or small scale.
- ELG: Explore colour, texture, shape, form and space in two or three dimensions.

Resources
We're Going on a Bear Hunt by Michael Rosen (Walker Books); 'Bear hunt' Notebook file; large construction equipment; card; play dough; LEGO; sand tray; small-world figures; chalk and chalk boards; digital camera.

Links to other ELGs
KUW
Find out about and identify the uses of everyday technology and use information and communication technology to support their learning.
- Provide access to a simple drawing program and suggest that the children further develop their map-making skills by creating a bear hunt map on the computer.

Whiteboard tools
Use the Shapes tool and On-screen Keyboard, accessed through the Pen tray or the SMART Board tools menu, to create suitable labels to accompany the pictures.

- Pen tray
- Select tool
- Delete button
- Highlighter pen
- Lines tool
- Shapes tool
- On-screen Keyboard

Introduction
Show the children the 'Bear hunt' Notebook file and enjoy the story on pages 2 to 9 again. Read the words together, encouraging the children to join in with the actions. Discuss the physical features in the story.

Now go to page 14 and explain that the picture is like a map. Find the beginning of the story and mark in the route using a Highlighter pen. Alternatively, talk about the order of the story and delete the orange box (by selecting it and pressing the Delete button or by choosing the Delete option from the dropdown menu) to reveal the route of the journey.

Adult-focused whole-class activity
- Go to page 15 and model how to make your own map on the whiteboard.
- Ask the children to help you to remember the sequence of the story. Show them how to select, drag and resize the pictures.
- Draw the route with the Lines tool or a Pen from the Pen tray. (Alternatively, use the green arrows already provided on the page).
- Use the Shapes tool and the On-screen Keyboard to make suitable labels.

Adult-focused group activity
- Work with a group of children to make their own map of the bear hunt, using pages 16 to 20 of the Notebook file. (There are enough pages for five groups.)
- Help the children to use the On-screen Keyboard to type labels.
- Invite them to retell the story when the map is completed.
- Save the Notebook pages for the Plenary.

Planned independent activities
- Suggest that the children use large construction units to make a map of the bear hunt story (indoors or in the outside area). Provide them with card to make labels. Take a digital photograph of the map once it is completed.
- Invite the children to make bear hunt maps in the sand tray using small-world figures.
- Provide chalks and chalk boards for the children to use to draw maps.
- Provide younger or less confident learners with play dough for making some of the physical features from the story, such as the cave, the river and the forest.
- Challenge older or more confident learners to construct strong caves with LEGO. Ask them to evaluate their caves. How did they arrange the bricks to make a strong pattern?

Plenary
- Invite each group to retell the bear hunt story using their map (from pages 16 to 20) as an aid.
- Encourage the children to evaluate each other's work.

CD Lesson 18

Mondrian

Learning objectives
- Development matters (Exploring Media and Materials): Work creatively on a large or small scale.
- ELG: Explore colour, texture, shape, form and space in two or three dimensions.

Resources
Examples of Mondrian's work online (for example, *Composition with Large Blue Plane, Red, Black, Yellow, and Gray; Composition A: Composition with Black, Red, Gray, Yellow, and Blue; Composition with Red, Blue and Yellow; Broadway Boogie Woogie,* or *New York City*); a Mondrian poster (optional); blue, red, yellow and black paint; A3 paper; cut-out squares and rectangles in primary colours; A5 paper; multi-link cubes or Clixi; sand tray; different-coloured chalks; shape tiles.

Links to other ELGs
PSRN
Use vocabulary such as *circle* or *bigger* to describe the shape and size of solids and flat shapes.
- Encourage the children to describe shapes in simple models, pictures and patterns.

Whiteboard tools
Use the Shapes, Fill Colour and Lines tools to produce paintings in the style of Mondrian.

- Pen tray
- Select tool
- Shapes tool
- Fill Colour tool
- Lines tool

Introduction
Introduce the abstract artist, Mondrian. Look at a poster of his work, if you have one available. Display pictures of his work on the whiteboard. Discuss the pictures. Ask: *What shapes can you see? What colours has he used? What does it make you think of? How does it make you feel?*

Next, discuss primary colours and what colours they make when you mix them together.

Adult-focused whole-class activity
- Open a blank Notebook page. Demonstrate how to use the Shapes and Lines tools to add different-coloured shapes and lines to the page. Select, drag, resize and rotate the shapes and lines and create a picture in a similar style to Mondrian.
- Move the shapes and lines to create a different composition using the same elements.

Adult-focused group activity
- Display examples of Mondrian paintings on the whiteboard.
- Provide the children with sheets of A3 paper together with red, yellow, blue and black paint. Explain that they are going to recreate a Mondrian-style painting.
- Encourage the children to paint the straight black lines first, and then fill in the squares and rectangles with the primary colours.
- Support younger or less confident learners by providing them with cut-out squares and rectangles in blue, red and yellow. Help them to produce a collage from the shapes and create a Mondrian-type picture.

Planned independent activities
- Arrange for the children to work in pairs to create a Mondrian-style picture on the whiteboard. Print out some good examples and display them.
- Challenge the children to find square and rectangular shape tiles in the sand tray. Ask: *Can you make a pattern with them?*
- Invite the children to make cubes and cuboids using multi-link cubes or Clixi.
- Suggest that the children make peg board patterns using primary colours.
- Use chalks to create Mondrian-style pictures in your outdoor area.

Child-initiated activity
- Provide large shape tiles in your outdoor area. Note whether the children use them to make patterns.

Plenary
- Display the children's paintings in a classroom gallery.
- Encourage peer assessment by inviting the children to evaluate their work with their talk partners. Which is their favourite? Why do they like it? What could they improve?
- Write down some of the main points on a new Notebook page.

CD Lesson 19

Repeating patterns

Learning objectives
- Development matters (Exploring Media and Materials): Explore colour and begin to differentiate between colours.
- ELG: Explore colour, texture, shape, form and space in two or three dimensions.

Resources
'Patterns' Notebook file; photocopiable page 168 'Repeating patterns'; potato templates for printing (square, circle, triangle, rectangle); red, yellow, blue and green paint; large flat paint containers; strips of paper; multi-link cubes; beads; peg boards; shape tiles.

Links to other ELGs
PSRN
Use everyday words to describe position.
- Invite the children to describe their patterns. Ask questions such as: *Where is the circle? Is the square next to the triangle?*

Introduction
Display page 2 of the Notebook file. Encourage the children to name the shapes and recognise the repeating pattern. Ask: *What would come next? How can you tell? How many different shapes have been used?*
  Add the next couple of shapes, by pressing and dragging shapes to create a new copy. Make a deliberate mistake and see if the children spot your error. Ask them how you could fix it. Use the Undo button to clear the last action that you made and try again!

Adult-focused whole-class activity
- Go to page 3 of the Notebook file. Invite individuals to press and drag the shapes to make their own repeating pattern.
- Once they have done this, clear the page by repeatedly pressing the Undo button, so that the next child can have a turn.
- Limit the patterns to two-shape patterns for younger or less confident learners.
- Challenge older or more confident learners to use three or four shapes to make their patterns.

Adult-focused group activities
- Provide the children with shape potato templates for printing, together with a range of different-coloured paints (red, yellow, blue, green) in large flat containers.
- Look carefully at the shapes together and encourage the children to name and describe them.
- Invite them to select shapes and colours and print a pattern on a long strip of paper.
- Provide each child with a copy of photocopiable page 168 and challenge them to complete the repeating patterns of colours and shapes.

Planned independent activities
- Suggest that the children make repeating patterns using peg boards, multi-link cubes, beads and shape tiles.
- Encourage the children to work in pairs, using the Shapes and Fill Colour tools on the whiteboard to make repeating patterns.

Plenary
- Look at page 4 of the Notebook file. Can the children identify the missing shapes in the pattern?
- Invite volunteers to press and drag the correct shape into the relevant blank space in the row.

Whiteboard tools
Use the Shapes and Fill Colour tools to make new patterns.

- Pen tray
- Select tool
- Shapes tool
- Fill Colour tool
- Undo button

CD Lesson 20

Symmetrical patterns

Learning objectives
- Development matters (Being Creative): Begin to use representation as a form of communication.
- ELG: Respond in a variety of ways to what they see, hear, smell, touch and feel.

Resources
'Patterns' Notebook file; photocopiable page 169 'Symmetrical patterns'; A3 paper; red, blue, green, yellow and brown paint; selection of butterfly books; peg boards; beads; shape tiles.

Links to other ELGs
KUW
Use information and communication technology to support their learning.
- Challenge the children to make symmetrical patterns using the computer program Dazzle.

Whiteboard tools
Select the thinnest line thickness for the Pen tool to draw the other half of the shapes. Use the Lines tool to draw items accurately.

- Pen tray
- Select tool
- Lines tool
- Undo button

Introduction
Find out what the children understand by the term *symmetry*. Talk about simple symmetrical patterns and look for some examples from around your setting.

Go to page 5 of the Notebook file. Explain to the children that only half of the picture has been drawn. Ask: *What do you think can be done about this? Do any of you think that you could help by drawing the missing half of the picture?*

Adult-focused whole-class activity
- Do the children recognise what the picture on page 5 is meant to be? Encourage them to draw the whole shape with their fingers in the air. Ask: *What sort of shape is it? Is it straight or curvy?*
- Demonstrate how to draw the other half of the hot air balloon. Count the squares on the grid, ensuring that the completed drawing is symmetrical.
- Ask a volunteer to select the type of tool they think you will need to complete the picture. Try out the children's suggestions, undoing the last action if their suggestions don't look quite right. Finally, use the thinnest setting of the Pen tool to draw the shape.
- Encourage the children to select the correct colour and fill the balloon shape with it.

Adult-focused group activity
- Display the house picture on page 6 of the Notebook file. Show the children the Lines tool and demonstrate how to use it to complete the house picture. (The Lines tool is the best tool to use in this case, as it produces straight lines automatically.)
- Make some deliberate mistakes and encourage the older or more confident learners to make corrections.
- Once completed, clear the page by repeatedly pressing the Undo button (or select Edit>Clear Page), and invite the children to have a go.

Planned independent activities
- Look at some pictures of butterflies in books or on the internet. Discuss the fact that butterflies are symmetrical.
- Provide the children with sheets of A3 paper folded in half. Ask them to paint one half of a butterfly, then fold over the paper while the paint is still wet. They can then open up their paper and look at the symmetrical pattern that has been formed.
- Provide copies of photocopiable page 169. Challenge the children to complete the other half of the four drawings on the sheet.
- Suggest that younger or less confident learners focus on one of the shapes only. Help them to complete the shape by providing a mirror to place along the line of symmetry so that they can see the shape that they need to provide.

Child-initiated activities
- Provide a selection of butterfly books for the children to choose to look at when they wish.
- You could also provide peg boards, beads and shape tiles for the children to experiment with.

Plenary
- Go to page 7 of the Notebook file and ask for volunteers to help you to complete the picture.
- Repeat the activity on page 8.

Rangoli pattern

- Follow the lines carefully to create your own rangoli pattern.
- You may use pencils, crayons, sand, paper or paint to make your pattern.

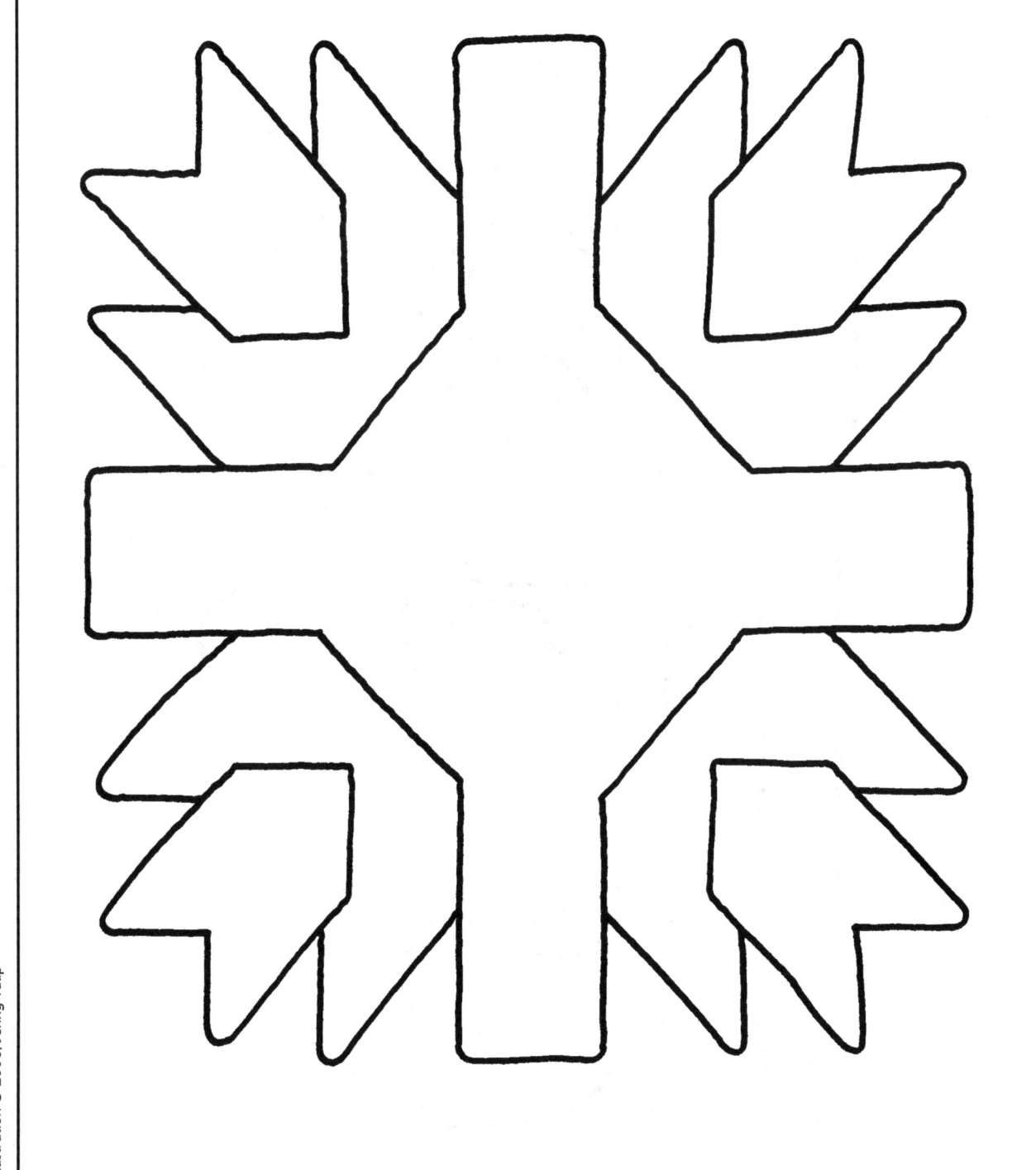

Dreidel

■ Cut out and fold to make a dreidel.

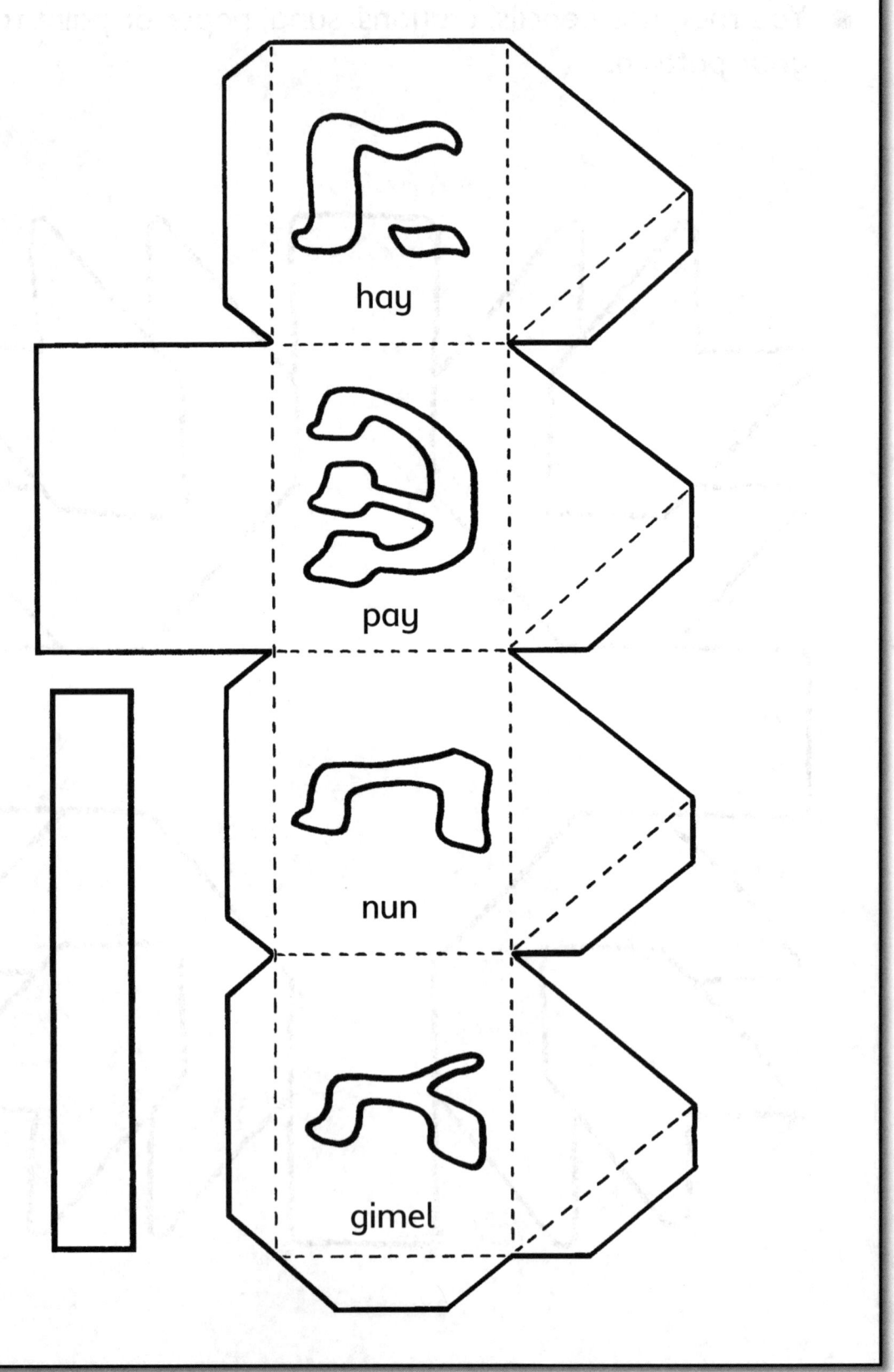

hay

pay

nun

gimel

Dear Santa

- Write your own letter to Santa.
- Remember to write your name, age, and what you would like for Christmas.

PSED LESSON 6   Name _____

The Easter story

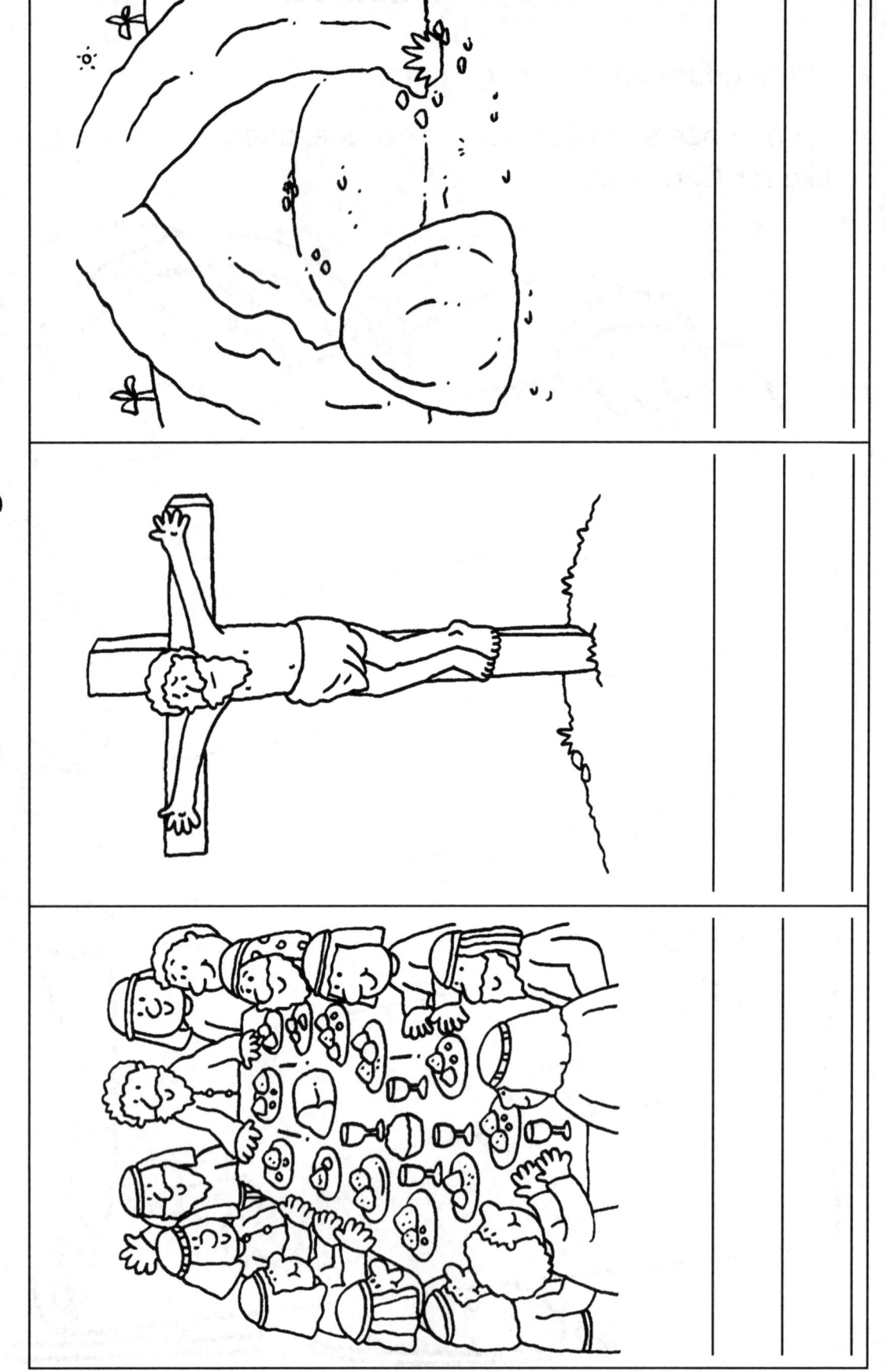

PSED LESSON 7

Dressing Teddy (1)

- Cut out Teddy.

PSED LESSON 7

Dressing Teddy (2)

- Cut out the clothes. Use them to dress Teddy.

PSED LESSON 8   Name _____

How do you feel?

- Show how this person is feeling.

PD ◼ LESSON 12   Name _____

Curly caterpillar (1)

166 ◼ **PHOTOCOPIABLE**
100 SMART Board™ LESSONS • YEAR R

PD LESSON 12 Name _____

Curly caterpillar (2)

c a d g

Repeating patterns

- Colour in the shapes to make a repeating pattern.

- Complete the repeating pattern.

Symmetrical patterns

■ Complete the symmetrical patterns.

Whiteboard diary

Teacher's name: _____

Date	Subject/Objective	How was the whiteboard used?	Evaluation

Whiteboard resources library

Teacher's name: _____

Name of resource and file location	Description of resource	How resource was used	Date resource was used

SMART BOARD™

Using your SMART Board™ interactive whiteboard

This brief guide to using your SMART Board interactive whiteboard and Notebook software is based on the training manual *SMART Board Interactive Whiteboard Masters Learner Workbook* © SMART Technologies Inc.

Your finger is your mouse
You can control applications on your computer from the interactive whiteboard. A press with your finger on a SMART Board interactive whiteboard is the same as a click with your mouse. To open an application on your computer through the interactive whiteboard, double-press the icon with your finger in the same way that you would use a mouse to double-click on your desktop computer.

The SMART Pen tray
The SMART Pen tray consists of four colour-coded slots for Pens (black, red, green and blue) and one slot for the Eraser. Each slot has a sensor to identify when the Pens or the Eraser have been picked up. You can write with the Pens, or with your finger, as long as the pen slot is empty. Likewise, if you remove the Eraser from the slot you can use either it or your hand to erase your digital ink.

The Pen tray has at least two buttons. One button is used to launch the On-screen Keyboard and the second button is used to make your next touch on the interactive whiteboard a right-click. Some interactive whiteboards have a third button, which is used to access the Help Centre quickly.

The On-screen Keyboard
The On-screen Keyboard allows you to type or edit text in any application without leaving the interactive whiteboard. It can be accessed either by pressing the appropriate button in the Pen tray, or through the SMART Board tools menu (see page 173).

A dropdown menu allows you to select which keyboard you would like to use. The default Classic setting is a standard 'qwerty' keyboard. Select the Simple setting to arrange the keyboard in alphabetical order, as a useful facility for supporting younger or less confident learners. A Number pad is also available through the On-screen Keyboard.

The Fonts toolbar appears while you are typing or after you double-press a text object. Use it to format properties such as font size and colour.

On-screen Keyboard

SMART BOARD™

Floating tools toolbar

Aware tools

SlideShow toolbar

The Transparency layer

When you remove a Pen from the Pen tray, a border appears around your desktop and the Floating tools toolbar launches. The border indicates that the 'transparency layer' is in place and you can write on the desktop just as you would write on a transparent sheet, annotating websites, or any images you display. The transparency layer remains in place until all the Pens and the Eraser have been returned to the Pen tray. Your first touch of the board thereafter will remove the border and any notes or drawings you have made.

Ink Aware applications

When software is Ink Aware, you can write and draw directly into the active file. For example, if you write or draw something while using Microsoft Word, you can save your Word file and your notes will be visible the next time you open it. Ink Aware software includes the Microsoft applications Word, Excel, PowerPoint; graphic applications such as Microsoft Paint and Imaging; and other applications such as Adobe Acrobat. Ensure that the SMART Aware toolbar is activated by selecting View, then toolbars, and checking that the SMART Aware toolbar option is ticked.

When you are using Microsoft Word or Excel, you will now notice three new buttons that will be either integrated into your current toolbar (as shown on the left), or separated as a floating toolbar. Press the first button to insert your drawing or writing as an image directly into your document or spreadsheet. The second button converts writing to typed text and insert it directly into your document or spreadsheet. Press the third button to save a screen capture in Notebook software.

When you are using Microsoft PowerPoint on an interactive whiteboard, the SlideShow toolbar appears automatically. Use the left- and right-hand buttons on the SlideShow toolbar to navigate your presentation. Press the centre button to launch the Command menu for additional options, including access to the SMART Floating tools (see page 175), and the facility to save notes directly into your presentation.

SMART Board tools

The SMART Board tools include functions that help you to operate the interactive whiteboard more effectively. Press the SMART Board icon at the bottom right of your screen to access the menu.

- SMART Recorder: Use this facility to make a video file of anything you do on the interactive whiteboard. You can then play the recording on any computer with SMART Video player or Windows® Media Player.
- Floating tools: The features you use most are included in the Floating toolbar. It can also be customised to incorporate any tools. Press the More button at the bottom-right of the toolbar and select Customise Floating Tools from the menu. Select a tool from the Available Tools menu and press Add to include it.
- Start Centre: This convenient toolbar gives you access to the most commonly used SMART Board interactive whiteboard tools.
- Control Panel: Use the Control Panel to configure a variety of software and hardware options for your SMART Board and software.

See page 175 for a visual guide to the SMART Board tools.

NOTEBOOK™ SOFTWARE

Using SMART Notebook™ software

Notebook software is SMART's whiteboard software. It can be used as a paper notebook to capture notes and drawings, and also enables you to insert multimedia elements like images and interactive resources.

Side tabs
There are three tabs on the right-hand side of the Notebook interface:

Page Sorter: The Page Sorter tab allows you to see a thumbnail image of each page in your Notebook file. The active page is indicated by a dropdown menu and a blue border around the thumbnail image. Select the dropdown menu for options including Delete page, Insert blank page, Clone page and Rename page. To change the page order, select a thumbnail and drag it to a new location within the order.

Gallery: The Gallery contains thousands of resources to help you quickly develop and deliver lessons in rich detail. Objects from the Gallery can be useful visual prompts; for example, searching for 'people' in an English lesson will bring up images that could help build pupils' ideas for verbs and so on. Objects you have created yourself can also be saved into the Gallery for future use, by dragging them into the My Content folder.

The Search facility in the Gallery usually recognises words in their singular, rather than plural, form. Type 'interactive' or 'flash' into the Gallery to bring up a bank of interactive resources for use across a variety of subjects including mathematics, science, music and design and technology.

Attachments: The Attachments tab allows you to link to supporting documents and webpages directly from your Notebook file. To insert a file, press the Insert button at the bottom of the tab and browse to the file location, or enter the internet address.

Objects in Notebook software
Anything you select inside the work area of a Notebook page is an object. This includes text, drawing or writing, shapes created with the drawing tools, or content from the Gallery, your computer, or the internet.

Manipulating objects: To resize an object, select it and drag the white handle (i). Use the green handle (ii) to rotate an object. To adjust the properties of a selected object, use the dropdown menu.
- Locking: This sub-menu includes options to 'Lock in place', which means that the object cannot be moved or altered in any way. Alternatively you can choose to 'Allow Move' or 'Allow Move and Rotate', which mean that your object cannot be resized.
- Grouping: Select two or more objects by pressing and dragging your finger diagonally so that the objects are surrounded by a selection box. Press the dropdown menu and choose Grouping > Group. If you want to separate the objects, choose Grouping > Ungroup.
- Order: Change the order in which objects are layered by selecting 'Bring forward' or 'Send backward' using this option.
- Infinite Cloner: Select 'Infinite Cloner' to reproduce an object an unlimited number of times.
- Properties: Use this option to change the colour, line properties and transparency of an object.
- Handwriting recognition: If you have written something with a Pen tool, you can convert it to text by selecting it and choosing the Recognise option from the dropdown menu.

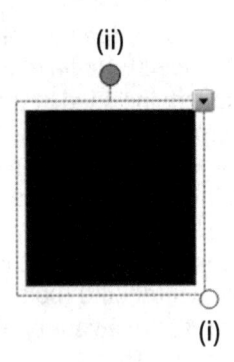

TOOLS GLOSSARY

Tools glossary

Notebook tools
Hints and tips
- Move the toolbar to the bottom of the screen to make it more accessible for children.

- Gradually reveal information to your class with the Screen Shade.

- Press the Full screen button to view everything on an extended Notebook page.

- Use the Capture tool to take a screenshot of work in progress, or completed work, to another page and print this out.

- Type directly into a shape created with the Shapes tool by double-pressing it and using the On-screen Keyboard.

Icon	Tool	Icon	Tool
	Pen tray		Lines tool
	Next page		Shapes tool
	Previous page	A	Text tool
	Blank Page button		Fill Colour tool
	Open		Transparency tool
	Save		Line properties
	Paste		Move toolbar to the top
	Undo button		
	Redo button		Capture tool
	Delete button		Area Capture tool
	Screen Shade		Area Capture 2
	Full screen		Area Capture 3
	Select tool		Area Capture (freehand) tool
	Pen tool		
	Highlighter pen		Page Sorter
	Creative pen		Gallery
	Eraser tool		Attachments

SMART Board tools
Hints and tips
- Use the SMART recorder to capture workings and methods, and play them back to the class for discussion in the Plenary.

- Adjust the shape and transparency of the Spotlight tool when focusing on elements of an image.

- Customise the Floating tools to incorporate any tools that you regularly use. Press the More button at the bottom right of the toolbar and select Customise Floating Tools from the menu.

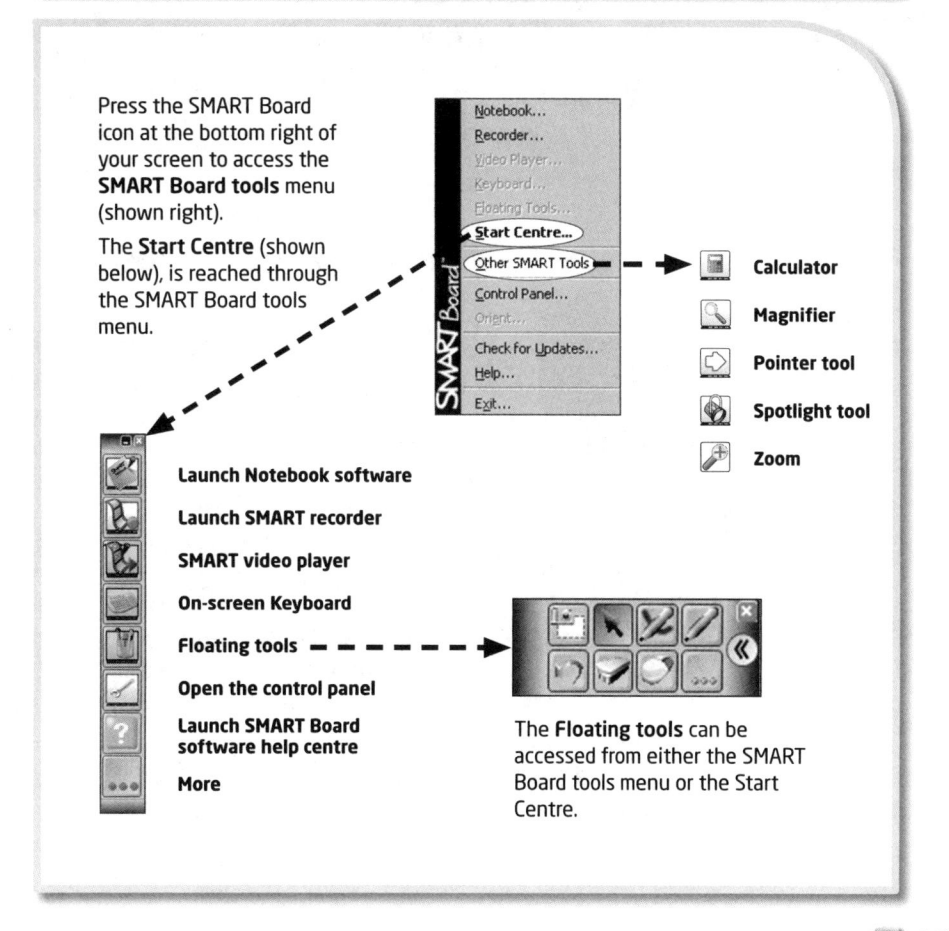

Press the SMART Board icon at the bottom right of your screen to access the **SMART Board tools** menu (shown right).

The **Start Centre** (shown below), is reached through the SMART Board tools menu.

Menu items: Notebook..., Recorder..., Video Player..., Keyboard..., Floating Tools..., **Start Centre...**, Other SMART Tools, Control Panel..., Orient..., Check for Updates..., Help..., Exit...

Other SMART Tools →
- Calculator
- Magnifier
- Pointer tool
- Spotlight tool
- Zoom

Start Centre:
- Launch Notebook software
- Launch SMART recorder
- SMART video player
- On-screen Keyboard
- Floating tools
- Open the control panel
- Launch SMART Board software help centre
- More

The **Floating tools** can be accessed from either the SMART Board tools menu or the Start Centre.

175

100 SMART Board™ LESSONS • YEAR R

SCHOLASTIC

Also available in this series:

100 SMART Board LESSONS YEAR R
ISBN 978-0439-94536-3

100 SMART Board LESSONS YEAR 1
ISBN 978-0439-94537-0

100 SMART Board LESSONS YEAR 2
ISBN 978-0439-94538-7

100 SMART Board LESSONS YEAR 3
ISBN 978-0439-94539-4

100 SMART Board LESSONS YEAR 4
ISBN 978-0439-94540-0

100 SMART Board LESSONS YEAR 5
ISBN 978-0439-94541-7

100 SMART Board LESSONS YEAR 6
ISBN 978-0439-94542-4

New for 2007-2008

100 MATHS FRAMEWORK LESSONS YEAR 1
ISBN 978-0439-94546-2

100 LITERACY FRAMEWORK LESSONS YEAR 3
ISBN 978-0439-94523-3

100 SCIENCE LESSONS YEAR 6
ISBN 978-0439-94508-0

To find out more, call: 0845 603 9091
or visit our website www.scholastic.co.uk